Central Europe

PHRASEBOOK & DICTIONARY

Acknowledgments

Associate Publisher Mina Patria
Managing Editor Bruce Evans
Editors Kate Mathews, Mardi O'Connor
Series Designer Mark Adams
Managing Layout Designer Chris Girdler
Layout Designer Carol Jackson
Production Support Larissa Frost

Thanks

Sasha Baske... i-
cott, James H... ens,
Wayne Murph... nislava
Vladisavljevic

Published b...
ABN 36 005...

4th Edition –
ISBN 978 1 74...
Text © Lonel...
Cover Imag... ...ber,
Franconia, Ba...

Printed in Ch...

Contact lonel...

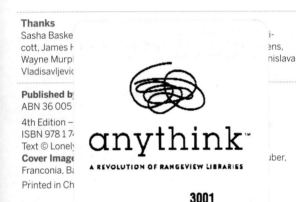

anythink™

A REVOLUTION OF RANGEVIEW LIBRARIES

3001

MIX
Paper from
responsible sources
FSC™ C021741

acknowledgments

This book is based on existing editions of Lonely Planet's phrasebooks as well as new content. It was developed with the help of the following people:

- Richard Nebeský for the Czech chapter
- Gunter Muehl for the German chapter
- Christina Mayer for the Hungarian chapter
- Piotr Czajkowski for the Polish chapter
- Katarina Nodrovicziova for the Slovak chapter
- Urška Pajer for the Slovene chapter

Thank you to Elmar Duenschede (German) and Hunor Csutoros (Hungarian) for additional language expertise.

contents

Central Europe

Baltic Sea

Lithuania

Gdańsk

Kaliningrad
(Russia)

Belarus

POLAND

Poznań

⊛ **Warsaw**

Łódź

Wrocław

Ukraine

Kraków

Ostrava

REPUBLIC

Brno

SLOVAKIA

Prešov
Košice

Vienna
⊛

Nitra

⊛ **Bratislava**

Miskolc

Moldova

Győr

Debrecen

⊛ **Budapest**

Graz

HUNGARY

Maribor

Szeged

Celje

Pécs

Romania

Croatia

Serbia

Bosnia and
Hercegovina

Polish

Slovak

Slovene

*Note: Language areas are approximate only.
For more details see the relevant introduction.*

EUROPE

language map

7

central europe – at a glance

One of the rewarding things about travelling through Central Europe is the rich variety of cuisine, customs, architecture and history. The flipside of course is that you'll encounter a number of very different languages. Most languages spoken in Central Europe belong to what's known as the Indo-European language family, believed to have originally developed from one language spoken thousands of years ago.

German belongs to the Germanic branch of the Indo European language family and is quite closely related to English. You should find that many basic words in German are similar to English words. The Slavic languages originated north of the Carpathians and are now divided into Eastern, Western and Southern subgroups. Czech, Slovak and Polish all belong to the Western subgroup of the Slavic language family, while Slovene belongs to the Southern subgroup. Fortunately (for travellers at least), all these Central European Slavic languages are written in the Latin alphabet. Hungarian is something of a linguistic oddity within Europe. Though classified as a member of the Finno-Ugric language group, making it a distant relative of Finnish, it has no other significant similarities to any other language in Europe – or the world for that matter.

did you know?

- The European Union (EU) was established by the Maastricht Treaty in 1992. It developed from the European Economic Community, founded by the Treaty of Rome in 1957. Since the 2007 enlargement, it has 27 member states and 23 official languages.
- The EU flag is a circle of 12 gold stars on a blue background – the number 12 representing wholeness.
- The EU anthem is the 'Ode to Joy' from Beethoven's Ninth Symphony.
- Europe Day, 9 May, commemorates the 1950 declaration by French Foreign Minister Robert Schuman which marked the creation of the European Union.
- The euro has been in circulation since E-Day, 1 January 2002. The euro's symbol (€) was inspired by the Greek letter epsilon (ε) – Greece being the cradle of European civilisation and ε being the first letter of the word 'Europe'.
- The Eurovision Song Contest, held each May, has been running since 1956. For the larger part of the competition's history, the performers were only allowed to sing in their country's national language, but that's no longer the case.

Czech

czech alphabet

A a uh	Á á a	B b bair	C c tsair	Č č chair
D d dair	Ď ď dyair	E e e	É é *dloh*·hair air	Ě ě e s *hach*·kem
F f ef	G g gair	H h ha	Ch ch cha	I i ee
Í í *dloh*·hair ee	J j yair	K k ka	L l el	M m em
N n en	Ň ň en'	O o o	P p pair	Q q kair
R r er	Ř ř erzh	S s es	Š š esh	T t tair
Ť ť tyair	U u u	Ú ú *dloh*·hair u	Ů ů u s *krohzh*·kem	V v vair
W w *dvo*·yi·tair vair	X x iks	Y y *ip*·si·lon	Ý ý *dloh*·hee *ip*·si·lon	Z z zet
Ž ž zhet				

 czech

ČEŠTINA

introduction

Czech (*čeština* chesh·tyi·nuh), the language which gave us words such as *dollar*, *pistol* and *robot*, has a turbulent history. The Czech Republic may now be one of the most stable and well-off Eastern European countries, but over the centuries the land and the language have been regularly swallowed and regurgitated by their neighbours. In 1993 the Velvet Divorce ended the patched-together affair that was Czechoslovakia, and allowed Czech to go its own way after being tied to Slovak for over 70 years.

Both Czech and Slovak belong to the western branch of the Slavic language family, pushed westward with the Slavic people by the onslaught of the Huns, Avars, Bulgars and Magyars in the 5th and 6th centuries. Czech is also related to Polish, though not as closely as to Slovak – adults in Slovakia and the Czech Republic can generally understand one another, although younger people who have not been exposed to much of the other language may have more difficulty.

The earliest written literature dates from the 13th century upswing in Czech political power, which continued for several centuries. In the 17th century, however, the Thirty Years War nearly caused literature in Czech to become extinct. Fortunately, the national revival of the late 18th century brought it to the forefront again, at least until the 20th century, when first Nazi and then Communist rule pressed it into a subordinate position once more.

Many English speakers flinch when they see written Czech, especially words like *prst* prst (finger) and *krk* krk (neck) with no apparent vowels, and the seemingly unpronounceable clusters of consonants in phrases like *čtrnáct dní* chtr·natst dnyee (fortnight). Don't despair! With a little practice and the coloured pronunciation guides in this chapter you'll be enjoying the buttery mouthfeel of Czech words in no time. Czech also has one big advantage in the pronunciation stakes – each Czech letter is always pronounced exactly the same way, so once you've got the hang of the Czech alphabet you'll be able to read any word put before you with aplomb. Thank religious writer and martyr Jan Hus for this – he reformed the spelling system in the 15th and 16th centuries and introduced the *háček* ha·chek (ˇ) and the various other accents you'll see above Czech letters.

So, whether you're visiting the countryside or marvelling at Golden Prague, launch into this Czech chapter and your trip will be transformed into a truly memorable one.

pronunciation

vowel sounds

The Czech vowel system is relatively easy to master and most sounds have equivalents in English.

symbol	english equivalent	czech example	transliteration
a	father	*já*	ya
ai	aisle	*krajka*	*krai*-kuh
air	hair	*veliké*	ve-lee-**kair**
aw	law	*balcón*	*bal*-kawn
e	bet	*pes*	pes
ee	see	*prosím*	*pro*-seem
ey	hey	*dej*	dey
i	bit	*kolik*	*ko*-lik
o	pot	*noha*	*no*-huh
oh	oh	*koupit*	*koh*-pit
oo	zoo	*ústa*	*oo*-stuh
oy	toy	*výstroj*	*vee*-stroy
ow	how	*autobus*	*ow*-to-bus
u	put	*muž*	muzh
uh	run	*nad*	n d

word stress

Word stress in Czech is easy – it's always on the first syllable of the word. Stress is marked with italics in the pronunciation guides in this chapter as a reminder.

consonant sounds

The consonants in Czech are mostly the same as in English, with the exception of the kh sound, the r sound (which is rolled as it is in Spanish) and the rzh sound.

symbol	english equivalent	czech example	transliteration
b	bed	bláto	bla·to
ch	cheat	odpočinek	ot·po·chi·nek
d	dog	nedávný	ne·dav·nee
f	fat	vyfotit	vi·fo·tit
g	go	vegetarián	ve·ge·tuh·ri·an
h	hat	zahrady	zuh·hruh·di
k	kit	navěky	na·vye·ki
kh	loch	kuchyně	ku·khi·nye
l	lot	loni	lo·nyi
m	man	menší	men·shee
n	not	nízký	nyeez·kee
p	pet	dopis	do·pis
r	run (rolled)	rok	rok
rzh	rolled r followed by zh	řeka	rzhe·kuh
s	sun	slovo	slo·vo
sh	shot	pošta	posh·tuh
t	top	fronta	fron·tuh
ts	hats	co	tso
v	very	otvor	ot·vor
y	yes	již	yizh
z	zero	zmiz	zmiz
zh	pleasure	už	uzh
'	a slight y sound	promiňte	pro·min'·te

basics

language difficulties

Do you speak English?
Mluvíte anglicky?
mlu·vee·te uhn·glits·ki

Do you understand?
Rozumíte?
ro·zu·mee·te

I understand.
Rozumím.
ro·zu·meem

I don't understand.
Nerozumím.
ne·ro·zu·meem

What does (*knedlík*) mean?
Co znamená (knedlík)?
tso znuh·me·na (kned·leek)

How do you ...? *Jak se ...?* yuhk se ...
  pronounce this *toto vyslovuje* toh·to vis·lo·vu·ye
  write (*krtek*) *píše (krtek)* pee·she (kr·tek)

Could you please ...? *Prosím, můžete ...?* pro·seem moo·zhe·te ...
  repeat that *to opakovat* to o·puh·ko·vuht
  speak more slowly *mluvit pomaleji* mlu·vit po·muh·le·yi
  write it down *to napsat* to nuhp·suht

essentials

Yes.	*Ano.*	uh·no
No.	*Ne.*	ne
Please.	*Prosím.*	pro·seem
Thank you	*(Mnohokrát)*	(mno·ho·krat)
(very much).	*Děkuji.*	dye·ku·yi
You're welcome.	*Prosím.*	pro·seem
Excuse me.	*Promiňte.*	pro·min'·te
Sorry.	*Promiňte.*	pro·min'·te

numbers

0	nula	nu·luh	16	šestnáct	shest·natst
1	jeden m	ye·den	17	sedmnáct	se·dm·natst
	jedna f	yed·na	18	osmnáct	o·sm·natst
	jedno n	yed·no	19	devatenáct	de·vuh·te·natst
2	dva/dvě m/f&n	dvuh/dvye	20	dvacet	dvuh·tset
3	tři	trzhi	21	dvacet jedna	dvuh·tset yed·nuh
4	čtyři	chti·rzhi		jednadvacet	yed·nuh·dvuh·tset
5	pět	pyet	22	dvacet dva	dvuh·tset dvuh
6	šest	shest		dvaadvacet	dvuh·uh·dvuh·tset
7	sedm	se·dm	30	třicet	trzhi·tset
8	osm	o·sm	40	čtyřicet	chti·rzhi·tset
9	devět	de·vyet	50	padesát	puh·de·sat
10	deset	de·set	60	šedesát	she·de·sat
11	jedenáct	ye·de·natst	70	sedmdesát	se·dm·de·sat
12	dvanáct	dvuh·natst	80	osmdesát	o·sm·de·sat
13	třináct	trzhi·natst	90	devadesát	de·vuh·de·sat
14	čtrnáct	chtr·natst	100	sto	sto
15	patnáct	puht·natst	1000	tisíc	tyi·seets

time & dates

What time is it?	Kolik je hodin?	ko·lik ye ho·dyin
It's one o'clock.	Je jedna hodina.	ye yed·nuh ho·dyi·nuh
It's (10) o'clock.	Je (deset) hodin.	ye (de·set) ho·dyin
Quarter past (10).	Čvrt na (jedenáct).	chtvrt nuh (ye·de·natst)
	(lit: quarter of eleven)	
Half past (10).	Půl (jedenácté).	pool (ye·de·nats·tair)
	(lit: half eleven)	
Quarter to (eleven).	Tříčtvrtě na (jedenáct).	trzhi·chtvr·tye nuh (ye·de·natst)
At what time?	V kolik hodin?	f ko·lik ho·dyin
At ...	V ...	f ...
am (midnight–8am)	ráno	ra·no
am (8am–noon)	dopoledne	do·po·led·ne
pm (noon–7pm)	odpoledne	ot·po·led·ne
pm (7pm–midnight)	večer	ve·cher

Monday	*pondělí*	pon·dye·lee
Tuesday	*úterý*	oo·te·ree
Wednesday	*středa*	strzhe·duh
Thursday	*čtvrtek*	chtvr·tek
Friday	*pátek*	pa·tek
Saturday	*sobota*	so·bo·tuh
Sunday	*neděle*	ne·dye·le

January	*leden*	le·den
February	*únor*	oo·nor
March	*březen*	brzhe·zen
April	*duben*	du·ben
May	*květen*	kvye·ten
June	*červen*	cher·ven
July	*červenec*	cher·ve·nets
August	*srpen*	sr·pen
September	*září*	za·rzhee
October	*říjen*	rzhee·yen
November	*listopad*	li·sto·puht
December	*prosinec*	pro·si·nets

What date is it today?
   Kolikátého je dnes?   ko·li·ka·tair·ho ye dnes

It's (18 October).
   Je (osmnáctého října).   ye (o·sm·nats·tair·ho rzheey·nuh)

last night	*včera v noci*	fche·ruh v no·tsi
last week/month	*minulý týden/měsíc*	mi·nu·lee tee·den/mye·seets
last year	*vloni*	vlo·nyi

next ...	*příští ...*	przheesh·tyee ...
week	*týden*	tee·den
month	*měsíc*	mye·seets
year	*rok*	rok

tomorrow/yesterday ...	*zítra/včera ...*	zee·truh/fche·ruh ...
morning (early/late)	*ráno/dopoledne*	ra·no/do·po·led·ne
afternoon	*odpoledne*	ot·po·led·ne
evening	*večer*	ve·cher

weather

What's the weather like?	*Jaké je počasí?*	*yuh*-kair ye *po*-chuh-see

It's ...

cloudy	*Je zataženo.*	ye *zuh*-tuh-zhe-no
cold	*Je chladno.*	ye *khluhd*-no
hot	*Je horko.*	ye *hor*-ko
raining	*Prší.*	*pr*-shee
snowing	*Sněží.*	*snye*-zhee
sunny	*Je slunečno.*	ye *slu*-nech-no
warm	*Je teplo.*	ye *tep*-lo
windy	*Je větrno.*	ye *vye*-tr-no

spring	*jaro* n	*yuh*-ro
summer	*léto* n	*lair*-to
autumn	*podzim* m	*pod*-zim
winter	*zima* f	*zi*-muh

border crossing

I'm here ...	*Jsem zde ...*	ysem zde ...
in transit	*v tranzitu*	f *truhn*-zi-tu
on business	*na služební cestě*	nuh *slu*-zheb-nyee *tses*-tye
on holiday	*na dovolené*	nuh *do*-vo-le-nair

I'm here for ...	*Jsem zde na ...*	ysem zde nuh ...
(10) days	*(deset) dní*	*(de*-set) dnyee
(three) weeks	*(tři) týdny*	*(trzhi) teed*-ni
(two) months	*(dva) měsíce*	*(dvuh) mye*-see-tse

I'm going to (Valtice).
Jedu do (Valtic). ye*-du do (*vuhl*-tyits)

I'm staying at the (Hotel Špalíček).
Jsem ubytovaný/á v ysem *u*-bi-to-vuh-nee/a v
(Hotelu Špalíček). m/f (*ho*-te-lu *shpuh*-lee-chek)

I have nothing to declare.
Nemám nic k proclení. *ne*-mam nyits k *prots*-le-nyee

I have something to declare.
Mám něco k proclení. mam *nye*-tso k *prots*-le-nyee

That's not mine.
To není moje. to *ne*-nyee *mo*-ye

transport

tickets & luggage

Where can I buy a ticket?
Kde koupím jízdenku? — gde *koh*·peem *yeez*·den·ku

Do I need to book a seat?
Potřebuji místenku? — pot·rzhe·bu·yi *mees*·ten·ku

One ... ticket **to (Telč), please.**	*... do (Telče),* *prosím.*	*... do (tel*·che) *pro*·seem
one-way	*Jednosměrnou* *jízdenku*	*yed*·no·smyer·noh *yeez*·den·ku
return	*Zpáteční jízdenku*	*zpa*·tech·nyee *yeez*·den·ku

I'd like to ... **my ticket, please.** m/f	*Chtěl/Chtěla bych ...* *mojí jízdenku, prosím.* m/f	khtyel/*khtye*·luh bikh ... mo·yee *yeez*·den·ku *pro*·seem
cancel	*zrušit*	*zru*·shit
change	*změnit*	*zmye*·nyit
collect	*vyzvednout*	*vi*·zved·noht
confirm	*potvrdit*	*pot*·vr·dyit

I'd like a ... **seat, please.**	*Chtěl/Chtěla* *bych ...* m/f	khtyel/*khtye*·luh bikh ...
nonsmoking	*nekuřácké místo*	ne·ku·rzhats·kair *mees*·to
smoking	*kuřácké místo*	ku·rzhats·kair *mees*·to

How much is it?
Kolik to stojí? — *ko*·lik to *sto*·yee

Is there a toilet?
Je tam toaleta? — ye tuhm *to*·uh·le·tuh

Is there air conditioning?
Je tam klimatizace? — ye tuhm *kli*·muh·ti·zuh·tse

How long does the trip take?
Jak dlouho trvá cesta? — yuhk *dloh*·ho *tr*·va *tses*·tuh

Is it a direct route?
Je to přímá cesta? — ye to *przhee*·ma *tses*·tuh

Where can I find a luggage locker?
Kde mohu najít
zavazadlová schránka? — gde *mo*·hu *nuh*·yeet
zuh·vuh·zuhd·lo·va *skhran*·kuh

My luggage	Moje zavazadlo	mo·ye zuh·vuh·zuhd·lo
has been ...	bylo ...	bi·lo ...
damaged	poškozeno	posh·ko·ze·no
lost	ztraceno	ztruh·tse·no
stolen	ukradeno	u·kruh·de·no

getting around

Where does flight (OK25) arrive?
Kam přiletí let (OK25)?   kuhm przhi·le·tyee let (*aw·*ka *dvuh·*tset pyet)

Where does flight (OK25) depart?
Kde odlítá let (OK25)?   gde od·lee·ta let (*aw·*ka *dvuh·*tset pyet)

Where's (the) ...?	Kde je ...?	gde ye ...
arrivals hall	příletová hala	przhee·le·to·va huh·luh
departures hall	odletová hala	od·le·to·va huh·luh
duty-free shop	prodejna	pro·dey·nuh
	bezcelního zboží	bez·tsel·nyee·ho zbo·zhee
gate (12)	východ k letadlu	vee·khod k le·tuhd·lu
	(dvanáct)	(dvuh·natst)

Is this the ...	Jede tento/tato ...	ye·de ten·to/tuh·to ...
to (Mělník)?	do (Mělníka)? m/f	do (myel·nyee·kuh)
bus	autobus m	ow·to·bus
train	vlak m	vluhk
tram	tramvaj f	truhm·vai
trolleybus	trolejbus m	tro·ley·bus

When's the	V kolik jede	f ko·lik ye·de
... bus?	... autobus?	... ow·to·bus
first	první	prv·nyee
last	poslední	po·sled·nyee
next	příští	przhee·shtyee

At what time does the bus/train leave?
V kolik hodin odjíždí   f ko·lik ho·dyin od·yeezh·dyee
autobus/vlak?   ow·to·bus/vluhk

How long will it be delayed?
Jak dlouho bude mít zpoždění?   yuhk dloh·ho bu·de meet zpozh·dye·nyee

What's the next station/stop?
Která je příští stanice/zastávka?   kte·ra ye przheesh·tyee stuh·nyi·tse/zuhs·taf·kuh

Does it stop at (Cheb)?
Zastaví to v (Chebu)? — zuhs·tuh·vee to f (khe·bu)

Please tell me when we get to (Přerov).
Prosím vás řekněte mi — pro·seem vas rzhek·nye·te mi
kdy budeme v (Přerově). — kdi bu·de·me f (przhe·ro·vye)

How long do we stop here?
Jak dlouho zde budeme stát? — yuhk dloh·ho zde bu·de·me stat

Is this seat available?
Je toto místo volné? — ye to·to mees·to vol·nair

That's my seat.
To je mé místo. — to ye mair mees·to

I'd like a taxi …	*Potřebuji taxíka …*	po·trzhe·bu·yi tuhk·see·kuh …
at (9am)	*v (devět hodin*	f (de·vyet ho·dyin
	dopoledne)	do·po·led·ne)
now	*teď*	teď
tomorrow	*zítra*	zee·truh

Is this taxi available?
Je tento taxík volný? — ye ten·to tuhk·seek vol·nee

How much is it to …?
Kolik stojí jízdenka do …? — ko·lik sto·yee yeez·den·kuh do …

Please put the meter on.
Prosím zapněte taxametr. — pro·seem zuhp·nye·te tuhk·suh·me·tr

Please take me to (this address).
Prosím odvezte mě na (tuto adresu). — pro·seem od·ves·te mye na (tu·to uh·dre·su)

Please …	*Prosím …*	pro·seem …
slow down	*zpomalte*	spo·muhl·te
stop here	*zastavte zde*	zuhs·tuhf·te zde
wait here	*počkejte zde*	poch·key·te zde

car, motorbike & bicycle hire

I'd like to hire	*Chtěl/Chtěla bych*	khtyel/khtye·luh bikh
a …	*si půjčit …* m/f	si pooy·chit …
bicycle	*kolo*	ko·lo
car	*auto*	ow·to
motorbike	*motorku*	mo·tor·ku

with ...	s ...	s ...
a driver	*řidičem*	*rzhi*·dyi·chem
air conditioning	*klimatizací*	*kli*·muh·ti·zuh·tsee
antifreeze	*nemrznoucí směsí*	ne·mrz·noh·tsee *smye*·see
snow chains	*sněhovými řetězy*	snye·ho·vee·mi *rzhe*·tye·zi

How much for	*Kolik stojí*	ko·lik *sto*·yee
... hire?	*půjčení na ...?*	pooy·che·nyee nuh ...
hourly	*hodinu*	ho·dyi·nu
daily	*den*	den
weekly	*týden*	tee·den

air	*vzduch* m	vz·dukh
oil	*olej* m	o·ley
petrol	*benzin* m	ben·zin
tyre	*pneumatika* f	pne·u·muh·ti·kuh

I need a mechanic.	*Potřebuji mechanika.*	pot·rzhe·bu·yi me·khuh·ni·kuh
I've run out of petrol.	*Došel mi benzin.*	do·shel mi ben·zin
I have a flat tyre.	*Mám defekt.*	mam de·fekt

directions

Where's the ...?	*Kde je ...?*	gde ye ...
bank	*banka*	buhn·kuh
city centre	*centrum*	tsen·trum
hotel	*hotel*	ho·tel
market	*trh*	trh
police station	*policejní stanice*	po·li·tsey·nyee stuh·nyi·tse
post office	*pošta*	posh·tuh
public toilet	*veřejný záchod*	ve·rzhey·nee za·khod
tourist office	*turistická informační kancelář*	tu·ris·tits·ka in·for·muhch·nyee kuhn·tse·larzh

Is this the road to (Cheb)?
Vede tato silnice do (Chebu)?   ve·de tuh·to sil·ni·tse do (khe·bu)

Can you show me (on the map)?
Můžete mi to ukázat (na mapě)?   moo·zhe·te mi to u·ka·zuht (nuh muh·pye)

What's the address?
Jaká je adresa?   yah·ka ye uh·dre·suh

How far is it?
Jak je to daleko?   yuhk ye to *duh*·le·ko

How do I get there?
Jak se tam dostanu?   yuhk se tuhm *dos*·tuh·nu

Turn ...	*Odbočte ...*	*od*·boch·te ...
at the corner	*za roh*	zuh rawh
at the traffic lights	*u semaforu*	u *se*·muh·fo·ru
left/right	*do leva/prava*	do *le*·vuh/*pruh*·vuh

It's ...	*Je to ...*	ye to ...
behind ...	*za ...*	zuh ...
far away	*daleko*	*duh*·le·ko
here	*zde*	zde
in front of ...	*před ...*	przhed ...
left	*na levo*	nuh *le*·vo
near	*blízko*	*bleez*·ko
next to ...	*vedle ...*	*ved*·le ...
on the corner	*na rohu*	nuh *ro*·hu
opposite ...	*naproti ...*	*nuh*·pro·tyi ...
right	*na pravo*	nuh *pruh*·vo
straight ahead	*přímo*	*przhee*·mo
there	*tam*	tuhm

by bus	*autobusem*	*ow*·to·bu·sem
by taxi	*taxikem*	*tuhk*·si·kem
by train	*vlakem*	*vluh*·kem
on foot	*pěšky*	*pyesh*·ki

north	*sever*	*se*·ver
south	*jih*	yih
east	*východ*	*vee*·khod
west	*západ*	*za*·puhd

Vchod/Východ	vkhod/*vee*-khod	**Entrance/Exit**
Otevřeno/Zavřeno	o-te-vrzhe-no/*zuh*-vrzhe-no	**Open/Closed**
Volné pokoje	vol-nair po-ko-ye	**Rooms Available**
Obsazeno	op-suh-ze-no	**No Vacancies**
Informace	in-for-muh-tse	**Information**
Policejní stanice	po-li-tsey-nyee stuh-nyi-tse	**Police Station**
Zakázáno	zuh-ka-za-no	**Prohibited**
Záchody	za-kho-di	**Toilets**
Páni	pa-nyi	**Men**
Ženy	zhe-ni	**Women**
Horké/Studené	hor-kair/stu-de-nair	**Hot/Cold**

accommodation

finding accommodation

Where's a ...?	*Kde je ...?*	gde ye ...
camping ground	*tábořiště*	ta-bo-rzhish-tye
guesthouse	*penzion*	pen-zi-on
hotel	*hotel*	ho-tel
youth hostel	*mládežnická*	mla-dezh-nyits-ka
	ubytovna	u-bi-tov-nuh

Can you recommend	*Můžete mi doporučit*	moo-zhe-te mi do-po-ru-chit
somewhere ...?	*něco ...?*	nye-tso ...
cheap	*levného*	lev-nair-ho
good	*dobrého*	dob-rair-ho
nearby	*nejbližšího*	ney-blizh-shee-ho

I'd like to book a room, please.
Chtěl/Chtěla bych   khtyel/*khtye*-luh bikh
rezervovat pokoj, prosím. m/f   re-zer-vo-vuht po-koy pro-seem

I have a reservation.
Mám rezervaci.   mam re-zer-vuh-tsi

My name is ...
Mé jméno je ...   mair ymair-no ye ...

Do you have a double room?
Máte pokoj s manželskou postelí?   ma-te po-koy s muhn-zhels-koh pos-te-lee

Do you have a ... room?	*Máte ... pokoj?*	*ma·te ... po·koy*
single	*jednolůžkový*	*yed·no·loozh·ko·vee*
twin	*dvoulůžkový*	*dvoh·loozh·ko·vee*
How much is it per ...?	*Kolik to stojí ...?*	*ko·lik to sto·yee ...*
night	*na noc*	nuh nots
person	*za osobu*	zuh o·so·bu
Can I pay ...?	*Mohu zaplatit ...?*	*mo·hu zuh·pluh·tyit ...*
by credit card	*kreditní kartou*	*kre·dit·nyee kuhr·toh*
with a travellers cheque	*cestovním šekem*	*tses·tov·nyeem she·kem*

For (three) nights/weeks.
Na (tři) noci/týdny.   nuh (trzhi) no·tsi/*teed*·ni

From (2 July) to (6 July).
Od (druhého července)   od (*dru*·hair·ho *cher*·ven·tse)
do (šestého července).   do (*shes*·tair·ho *cher*·ven·tse)

Can I see it?
Mohu se na něj podívat?   *mo*·hu se na nyey *po*·dyee·vuht

Am I allowed to camp here?
Mohu zde stanovat?   *mo*·hu zde *stuh*·no·vuht

Where can I find a camping ground?
Kde mohu najít stanový tábor?   gde *mo*·hu *nuh*·yeet *stuh*·no·vee *ta*·bor

requests & queries

When's breakfast served?
V kolik se podává snídaně?   f *ko*·lik se *po*·da·va *snyee*·duh·nye

Where's breakfast served?
Kde se podává snídaně?   gde se *po*·da·va *snyee*·duh·nye

Please wake me at (seven).
Prosím probuďte mě v (sedm).   *pro*·seem *pro*·bud'·te mye f (*se*·dm)

Could I have my key, please?
Můžete mi dát můj klíč, prosím?   *moo*·zhe·te mi dat mooy kleech *pro*·seem

Can I get another (blanket)?
Mohu dostat další (deku)?   *mo*·hu *dos*·tuht *duhl*·shee (*de*·ku)

Do you have a/an ...?	Máte ...?	ma·te ...
elevator	výtah	vee·tah
safe	trezor	tre·zor

The room is too ...	Je moc ...	ye mots ...
expensive	drahý	druh·hee
noisy	hlučný	hluch·nee
small	malý	muh·lee

The ... doesn't work.	... nefunguje.	... ne·fun·gu·ye
air conditioning	Klimatizace	kli·muh·ti·zuh·tse
fan	Větrák	vye·trak
toilet	Toaleta	to·uh·le·tuh

This ... isn't clean.	Tento ... neni čistý.	ten·to ... ne·nyi chis·tee
pillow	polštář	pol·shtarzh
towel	ručník	ruch·nyeek

checking out

What time is checkout?
  V kolik hodin máme vyklidit pokoj?   f ko·lik ho·dyin ma·me vi·kli·dyit po·koy

Can I leave my luggage here?
  Mohu si zde nechat zavazadla?   mo·hu si zde ne·khuht zuh·vuh·zuhd·luh

Could I have my ..., please?	Můžete mi vratit ..., prosím?	moo·zhe·te mi vra·tyit ... pro·seem
deposit	zálohu	za·lo·hu
passport	pas	puhs
valuables	cennosti	tse·nos·tyi

communications & banking

the internet

Where's the local Internet café?
  Kde je místní internetová kavárna?   gde ye meest·nyee in·ter·ne·to·va kuh·var·nuh

How much is it per hour?
  Kolik to stojí na hodinu?   ko·lik to sto·yee nuh ho·dyi·nu

I'd like to ...	*Chtěl/Chtěla bych ...* m/f	khtyel/*khtye*·luh bikh ...
check my email	*zkontrolovat*	*skon*·tro·lo·vuht
	můj email	mooy *ee*·meyl
get Internet access	*přístup na internet*	*przhees*·tup nuh *in*·ter·net
use a printer	*použít tiskárnu*	po·u·zheet *tyis*·kar·nu
use a scanner	*použít skener*	po·u·zheet *ske*·ner

mobile/cell phone

I'd like a ...	*Chtěl/Chtěla bych ...* m/f	ktyel/*khtye*·luh bikh ...
mobile/cell phone for hire	*si půjčit mobil*	si *pooy*·chit *mo*·bil
SIM card for your network	*SIM kartu pro vaší síť*	sim *kuhr*·tu pro *vuh*·shee seet'

| What are the rates? | *Jaké jsou tarify?* | yuh·kair ysoh *tuh*·ri·fi |

telephone

What's your phone number?
Jaké je vaše telefonní číslo? yuh·kair ye *vuh*·she te·le·fo·nyee *chees*·lo

The number is ...
Číslo je ... *chees*·lo ye ...

Where's the nearest public phone?
Kde je nejbližší veřejný telefon? gde ye *ney*·blizh·shee ve·rzhey·nee *te*·le·fon

I'd like to buy a phonecard.
Chtěl/Chtěla bych koupit ktyel/*khtye*·luh bikh *koh*·pit
telefonní kartu. m/f te·le·fo·nyee *kuhr*·tu

I want to ...	*Chtěl/Chtěla bych ...* m/f	ktyel/*khtye*·luh bikh ...
call (Singapore)	*telefonovat do (Singapůru)*	te·le·fo·no·vuht do *sin*·guh·poo·ru
make a local call	*si zavolat místně*	si *zuh*·vo·luht *meest*·nye
reverse the charges	*telefonovat na účet volaného*	te·le·fo·no·vuht na *oo*·chet *vo*·luh·nair·ho

How much does ... cost?	*Kolik stojí ...?*	ko·lik sto·yee ...
a (three)-minute	*(tří) minutový*	(trzhee) mi·nu·to·vee
call	*hovor*	ho·vor
each extra minute	*každá další*	kuhzh·da duhl·shee
	minuta	mi·nu·tuh

(Seven crowns) per minute.
(Sedm korun) za jednu minutu. (se·dm ko·run) zuh yed·nu mi·nu·tu

post office

I want to send a ...	*Chci poslat ...*	khtsi po·sluht ...
fax	*fax*	fuhks
letter	*dopis*	do·pis
parcel	*balík*	buh·leek
postcard	*pohled*	po·hled

I want to buy a/an ...	*Chci koupit ...*	khtsi koh·pit ...
envelope	*obálku*	o·bal·ku
stamp	*známku*	znam·ku

Please send it by	*Prosím vás pošlete*	pro·seem vas po·shle·te
... to (Australia).	*to ... do (Austrálie).*	to ... do (ow·stra·li·ye)
airmail	*letecky poštou*	le·tets·ki posh·toh
express mail	*expresní poštou*	eks·pres·nyee posh·toh
registered mail	*doporučenou poštou*	do·po·ru·che·noh posh·toh
surface mail	*obyčejnou poštou*	o·bi·chey·noh posh·toh

Is there any mail for me?
Mám zde nějakou poštu? mam zde nye·yuh·koh posh·tu

bank

I'd like to ...	*Chtěl/Chtěla bych ...* m/f	khtyel/khtye·luh bikh ...
Where can I ...?	*Kde mohu ...?*	gde mo·hu ...
arrange a transfer	*převést peníze*	przhe·vairst pe·nyee·ze
cash a cheque	*proměnit šek*	pro·mye·nyit shek
change a travellers	*proměnit*	pro·mye·nyit
cheque	*cestovní šek*	tses·tov·nyee shek
change money	*vyměnit peníze*	vi·mye·nyit pe·nyee·ze
get a cash advance	*zálohu v hotovosti*	za·lo·hu v ho·to·vos·tyi
withdraw money	*vybrat peníze*	vi·bruht pe·nyee·ze

Where's a/an ...?	Kde je ...?	gde ye ...
ATM	bankomat	buhn·ko·muht
foreign exchange office	směnárna	smye·nar·nuh

What's the ...?	Jaký je ...?	yuh·kee ye ...
charge for that	poplatek za to	po·pluh·tek zuh to
exchange rate	devizový kurz	de·vi·zo·vee kurz

It's ...	Je to ...	ye to ...
(12) crowns	(dvanáct) korun	(dvuh·natst) ko·run
(five) euros	(pět) eur	(pyet) e·ur
free	bez poplatku	bez po·pluht·ku

What time does the bank open?
Jaké jsou úřední hodiny?   yuh·kair ysoh oo·rzhed·nyee ho·dyi·ni

Has my money arrived yet?
Přišly už moje peníze?   przhi·shli uzh mo·ye pe·nyee·ze

sightseeing

getting in

What time does it open/close?
V kolik hodin otevírají/ zavírají?   f ko·lik ho·dyin o·te·vee·ruh·yee/ zuh·vee·ruh·yee

What's the admission charge?
Kolik stojí vstupné?   ko·lik sto·yee vstup·nair

Is there a discount for students/children?
Máte slevu pro studenty/děti?   ma·te sle·vu pro stu·den·ti/dye·tyi

I'd like a ...	Chtěl/Chtěla bych ... m/f	khtyel/khtye·luh bikh ...
catalogue	katalog	kuh·tuh·log
guide	průvodce	proo·vod·tse
local map	mapu okolí	ma·pu o·ko·lee

I'd like to see ...
Chtěl/Chtěla bych vidět ... m/f   khtyel/*khtye*·luh bikh *vi*·dyet ...

What's that?
Co je to?   tso ye to

Can I take a photo of this?
Mohu toto fotografovat?   *mo*·hu *to*·to *fo*·to·gruh·fo·vuht

Can I take a photo of you?
Mohu si vás vyfotit?   *mo*·hu si vas *vi*·fo·tyit

tours

When's the next ...?   *Kdy je příští ...?*   gdi ye *przheesh*·tyee ...
  day trip   *celodenní výlet*   tse·lo·de·nyee *vee*·let
  tour   *okružní jízda*   o·kruzh·nyee *yeez*·duh

Is ... included?   *Je zahrnuto/a ...?* n/f   ye zuh·hr·nu·to/a ...
  accommodation   *ubytování* n   u·bi·to·va·nyee
  the admission charge   *vstupné* n   fstup·nair
  food   *strava* f   struh·vuh
  transport   *doprava* f   do·pruh·vuh

How long is the tour?
Jak dlouho bude trvat   yuhk *dloh*·ho *bu*·de *tr*·vuht
tento zájezd?   ten·to za·yezd

What time should we be back?
V kolik hodin se máme vrátit?   f *ko*·lik *ho*·dyin se *ma*·me *vra*·tyit

sightseeing		
castle	*hrad* m	hruhd
cathedral	*katedrála* f	*kuh*·te·dra·luh
church	*kostel* m	kos·tel·
main square	*hlavní náměstí* n	*hluhv*·nyee *na*·myes·tyee
monastery	*klášter* m	*klash*·ter
monument	*památník* m	*puh*·mat·nyeek
museum	*muzeum* f	*mu*·ze·um
old city	*staré město* n	*stuh*·rair *myes*·to
palace	*palác* m	*puh*·lats
ruins	*zřiceniny* f pl	*zrzhee*·tse·nyi·ni
stadium	*stadion* m	*stuh*·di·yon
statue	*socha* f	*so*·khuh

shopping

enquiries

Where's a ...?	Kde je ...?	gde ye ...
bank	banka	buhn·kuh
bookshop	knihkupectví	knyikh·ku·pets·tvee
camera shop	foto potřeby	fo·to pot·rzhe·bi
department store	obchodní dům	op·khod·nyee doom
grocery store	smíšené zboží	smee·she·nair zbo·zhee
market	tržnice	tr·zhnyi·tse
newsagency	tabák	tuh·bak
supermarket	samoobsluha	suh·mo·op·slu·huh

Where can I buy (a padlock)?
Kde si mohu koupit (zámek)?   gde si mo·hu koh·pit (za·mek)

I'm looking for ....
Hledám ...   hle·dam ...

Can I look at it?
Mohu se na to podívat?   mo·hu se nuh to po·dyee·vuht

Do you have any others?
Máte ještě jiné?   ma·te yesh·tye yi·nair

Does it have a guarantee?
Je na to záruka?   ye nuh to za·ru·kuh

Can I have it sent abroad?
Můžete mi to poslat   moo·zhe·te mi to pos·luht
do zahraničí?   do zuh·hruh·nyi·chee

Can I have my ... repaired?
Můžete zde opravit ...?   moo·zhe·te zde o·pruh·vit ...

It's faulty.
Je to vadné.   ye to vuhd·nair

I'd like ..., please.	Chtěl/Chtěla bych ..., prosím. m/f	khtyel/khtye·la bikh ... pro·seem
a bag	tašku	tuhsh·ku
a refund	vrátit peníze	vra·tyit pe·nyee·ze
to return this	toto vrátit	to·to vra·tyit

paying

How much is it?
Kolik to stojí?
ko·lik to *sto*·yee

Can you write down the price?
Můžete mi napsat cenu?
moo·zhe·te mi *nuhp*·suht *tse*·nu

That's too expensive.
To je moc drahé.
to ye mots *druh*·hair

What's your lowest price?
Jaká je vaše konečná cena?
yuh·ka ye *vuh*·she ko·nech·na *tse*·nuh

I'll give you (200 crowns).
Dám vám (dvěstě korun).
dam vam (*dvye*·stye *ko*·run)

There's a mistake in the bill.
Na účtu je chyba.
nuh *ooch*·tu ye *khi*·buh

Do you accept ...?	*Mohu platit ...?*	*mo*·hu *pluh*·tyit ...
credit cards	*kreditními kartami*	kre·dit·nyee·mi *kuhr*·tuh·mi
debit cards	*platebními*	*pluh*·teb·nyee·mi
	kartami	*kuhr*·tuh·mi
travellers cheques	*cestovními šeky*	tses·tov·nyee·mi *she*·ki

I'd like ..., please.	*Můžete mi dát*	*moo*·zhe·te mi dat
	..., prosím?	... *pro*·seem
a receipt	*účet*	*oo*·chet
my change	*mé drobné*	mair *drob*·nair

clothes & shoes

Can I try it on?	*Mohu si to zkusit?*	*mo*·hu si to *sku*·sit
My size is (40).	*Mám číslo (čtyřicet).*	mam *chee*·slo (*chti*·rzhi·tset)
It doesn't fit.	*Nepadne mi to.*	*ne*·puhd·ne mi to
small	*malý*	*muh*·le
medium	*střední*	*strzhed*·nyee
large	*velký*	*vel*·keeh

books & music

I'd like a ...	Chtěl/Chtěla bych ... m/f	khtyel/khtye luh bikh ...
newspaper	noviny	no·vi·ni
(in English)	(v angličtině)	(f uhn·glich·tyi·nye)
pen	propisovací pero	pro·pi·so·vuh·tsee pe·ro

Is there an English-language bookshop?
Je tam knihkupectví   ye tuhm *knyih*·ku·pets·tvee
s anglickýma knihama?   s *uhn*·glits·kee·muh *knyi*·huh·muh

I'm looking for something by (Kabát).
Hledám něco od (Kabátu).   hle·dam *nye*·tso od (*kuh*·ba·tu)

Can I listen to this?
Mohu si to poslechnout?   mo·hu si to po·slekh·noht

photography

Can you ...?	Můžete ...?	moo·zhe·te ...
develop this film	vyvolat tento film	vi·vo·luht ten·to film
load my film	vložit můj film	vlo·zhit mooy film
transfer photos	uložit fotografie	u·lo·zhit fo·to·gruh·fi·ye
from my camera	z mého	z mair·ho
to CD	fotoaparátu	fo·to·uh·puh·ra·tu
	na CD	nuh tsair·dairch·ko

I need a/an ... film	Potřebuji ... film	pot·rzhe·bu·yi ... film
for this camera.	pro tento fotoaparát.	pro ten·to fo·to·uh·puh·rat
APS	APS	a·pair·es
B&W	černobílý	cher·no·bee·lee
colour	barevný	buh·rev·nee
slide	diapozitivní	di·uh·po·zi·tiv·nyee
(200) speed	film s citlivostí	film s tsit·li·vos·tyee
	(dvěstě)	(dvye·stye)

When will it be ready?   *Kdy to bude hotové?*   gdi to bu·de ho·to·vair

meeting people

greetings, goodbyes & introductions

Hello/Hi.	*Ahoj/Čau.*	*uh*·hoy/chow
Good night.	*Dobrou noc.*	*do*·broh nots
Goodbye.	*Na shledanou.*	nuh·skhle·duh·noh
Bye.	*Ahoj/Čau.*	*uh*·hoy/chow
See you later.	*Na viděnou.*	nuh *vi*·dye·noh
Mr/Mrs	*pan/paní*	puhn/*puh*·nyee
Miss	*slečna*	*slech*·nuh
How are you?	*Jak se máte/máš?* pol/inf	yuhk se *ma*·te/mash
Fine. And you?	*Dobře. A vy/ty?* pol/inf	*dob*·rzhe a vi/ti
What's your name?	*Jak se jmenujete/*	yuhk se *yme*·nu·ye·te/
	jmenuješ? pol/inf	*yme*·nu·yesh
My name is ...	*Jmenuji se ...*	*yme*·nu·yi se ...
I'm pleased to meet you.	*Těší mě.*	*tye*·shee mye
This is my ...	*To je můj/moje ...* m/f	to ye mooy/*mo*·ye ...
boyfriend	*přítel*	*przhee*·tel
brother	*bratr*	*bruh*·tr
daughter	*dcera*	*dtse*·ruh
father	*otec*	*o*·tets
friend	*přítel* m	*przhee*·tel
	přítelkyně f	*przhee*·tel·ki·nye
girlfriend	*přítelkyně*	*przhee*·tel·ki·nye
husband	*manžel*	*muhn*·zhel
mother	*matka*	*muht*·kuh
partner (intimate)	*partner/partnerka* m/f	*puhrt*·ner/*puhrt*·ner·kuh
sister	*sestra*	*ses*·truh
son	*syn*	sin
wife	*manželka*	*muhn*·zhel·kuh
Here's my ...	*Zde je moje ...*	zde ye *mo*·ye ...
What's your ...?	*Jaké/Jaká je*	yuh·*kair*/yuh·ka ye
	vaše ...? n/f	*vuh*·she ...
(email) address	*(email) adresa* f	(*ee*·meyl) *uh*·dre·suh
fax number	*faxové číslo* n	*fuhk*·so·vair *chees*·lo
phone number	*telefonní číslo* n	te·le·fo·nyee *chees*·lo

occupations

What's your occupation?
Jaké je vaše povolání? — yuh·kair ye *vuh*·she po·vo·la·nyee

I'm a/an ...	Jsem ...	ysem ...
artist	umělec/umělkyně m/f	u·mye·lets/u·myel·ki·nye
businessperson	obchodník m&f	ob·khod·nyeek
farmer	zemědělec m	ze·mye·dye·lets
	zemědělkyně f	ze·mye·dyel·ki·nye
manual worker	dělník m&f	dyel·nyeek
office worker	úředník m	oo·rzhed·nyeek
	úřednice f	oo·rzhed·nyi·tse
scientist	vědec/vědkyně m/f	vye·dets/vyed·ki·nye

background

Where are you from?	Odkud jste?	ot·kud yste
I'm from ...	Jsem z ...	ysem s ...
Australia	Austrálie	ow·stra·li·ye
Canada	Kanady	kuh·nuh·di
England	Anglie	uhn·gli·ye
New Zealand	Nového Zélandu	no·vair·ho zair·luhn·du
the USA	Ameriky	uh·meh·ri·ki

Are you married?	Jste ženatý/vdaná? m/f	yste zhe·nuh·tee/fduh·na
I'm married.	Jsem ženatý/vdaná. m/f	ysem zhe·nuh·tee/fduh·na
I'm single.	Jsem svobodný/á. m/f	ysem svo·bod·nee/a

age

How old ...?	Kolik ...?	ko·lik ...
are you	je vám let pol	ye vam let
	ti je let inf	ti ye let
is your daughter	let je vaší dceři	let ye vuh·shee dtse·rzhi
is your son	let je vašemu synovi	let ye vuh·she·mu si·no·vi
I'm ... years old.	Je mi ... let.	ye mi ... let
He's ... years old.	Je mu ... let.	ye mu ... let
She's ... years old.	Jí je ... let.	yee ye ... let

feelings

Are you ...?	Jste ...?	yste ...
I'm/I'm not ...	Jsem/Nejsem ...	ysem/ney·sem ...
happy	šťastný/šťastná m/f	shtyuhst·nee/shtyuhst·na
hungry	hladový/hladová m/f	hluh·do·vee/hluh·do·va
sad	smutný/smutná m/f	smut·nee/smut·na
thirsty	žíznivý/žíznivá m/f	zheez·nyi·vee/zheez·nyi·va

Are you ...?	Je vám ...?	ye vam ...
I'm/I'm not ...	Je/Neni mi ...	ye/ne·nyi mi ...
cold	zima	zi·muh
hot	horko	hor·ko

entertainment

going out

Where can I find ...?	Kde mohu najít ...?	gde mo·hu nuh·yeet ...
clubs	kluby	klu·bi
gay venues	homosexuální	ho·mo·sek·su·al·nyee
	zábavné podniky	za·buhv·nair pod·ni·ki
pubs	hospody	hos·po·di

I feel like going	Rád bych šel ... m	rad bikh shel ...
to a/the ...	Ráda bych šla ... f	ra·duh bikh shluh ...
concert	na koncert	nuh kon·tsert
movies	do kina	do ki·nuh
party	na mejdan/	nuh mey·duhn/
	večírek	ve·chee·rek
theatre	na hru	nuh hru
restaurant	do restaurace	do res·tow·ruh·tse

interests

Do you like to ...?		
go to concerts	Chodíte na koncerty?	kho·dyee·te nuh kon·tser·ti
dance	Tancujete?	tuhn·tsu·ye·te
listen to music	Posloucháte hudbu?	po·sloh·kha·te hud·bu

Do you like ...?	Máte rád/ráda ...? m/f	ma·te rad/ra·duh ...
I like ...	Mám rád/ráda ... m/f	mam rad/ra·duh ...
I don't like ...	Nemám rád/ráda ... m/f	ne·mam rad/ra·duh ...
art	umění	u·mye·nyee
cooking	vaření	vuh·rzhe·nyee
movies	filmy	fil·mi
reading	čtení	chte·nyee
sport	sport	sport
travelling	cestování	tses·to·va·nyee

food & drink

finding a place to eat

Can you recommend a ...?	Můžete doporučit ...?	moo·zhe·te do·po·ru·chit ...
café	kavárnu	kuh·var·nu
pub	hospodu	hos·po·du
restaurant	restauraci	res·tow·ruh·tsi
I'd like ..., please.	Chtěl/Chtěla bych ..., prosím. m/f	khtyel/khtye·luh bikh ... pro·seem
a table for (five)	stůl pro (pět)	stool pro (pyet)
the nonsmoking section	nekuřáckou místnost	ne·ku·rzhats·koh meest·nost
the smoking section	kuřáckou místnost	ku·rzhats·koh meest·nost

ordering food

breakfast	snídaně f	snee·duh·nye
lunch	oběd m	o·byed
dinner	večeře f	ve·che·rzhe
snack	občerstvení n	ob·cherst·ve·nyee
What would you recommend?	Co byste doporučil/ doporučila? m/f	tso bis·te do·po·ru·chil/ do·po·ru·chi·luh

I'd like (the) ..., please.	Chtěl/Chtěla bych ..., prosím. m/f	khtyel/khtye·luh bikh ... pro·seem
bill	účet	oo·chet
drink list	nápojový lístek	na·po·yo·vee lees·tek
menu	jídelníček	yee·del·nyee·chek
that dish	ten pokrm	ten po·krm

drinks

(cup of) coffee ...	(šálek) kávy ...	(sha·lek) ka·vi ...
(cup of) tea ...	(šálek) čaje ...	(sha·lek) chuh·ye ...
with milk	s mlékem	s mlair·kem
without sugar	bez cukru	bez tsu·kru
(orange) juice	(pomerančový) džus m	(po·me·ruhn·cho·vee) dzhus
soft drink	nealkoholický nápoj m	ne·uhl·ko·ho·lits·kee na·poy
(hot) water	(horká) voda f	(hor·ka) vo·duh
... mineral water	... minerální voda	... mi·ne·ral·nyee vo·duh
sparkling	perlivá	per·li·va
still	neperlivá	ne·per·li·va

in the bar

I'll have a ...	Dám si ...	dam si ...
I'll buy you a drink.	Zvu vás/tě na sklenku. pol/inf	zvu vas/tye nuh sklen·ku
What would you like?	Co byste si přál/přála? m/f	tso bis·te si przhal/przha·la
Cheers!	Na zdraví!	nuh zdruh·vee
brandy	brandy f	bruhn·di
champagne	šampaňské n	shuhm·puhn'·skair
cocktail	koktejl m	kok·teyl
a shot of (whisky)	panák (whisky)	puh·nak (vis·ki)
a bottle/jug of beer	láhev/džbán piva	la·hef/dzhban pi·vuh
a bottle/glass of ... wine	láhev/skleničku ... vína	la·hef/skle·nyich·ku ... vee·nuh
red	červeného	cher·ve·nair·ho
sparkling	šumivého	shu·mi·vair·ho
white	bílého	bee·lair·ho

self-catering

What's the local speciality?
Co je místní specialita? — tso ye *meest*·nyee spe·tsi·uh·li·tuh

What's that?
Co to je? — tso to ye

How much is (500 grams of cheese)?
Kolik stojí (padesát deka sýra)? — ko·lik sto·yee (*puh*·de·sat de·kuh see·ruh)

I'd like ...	*Chtěl/Chtěla bych ...* m/f	khtyel/*khtye*·luh bikh ...
200 grams	*dvacet deka*	*dvuh*·tset de·kuh
(two) kilos	*(dvě) kila*	(dvye) *ki*·luh
(three) pieces	*(tři) kusy*	(trzhi) *ku*·si
(six) slices	*(šest) krajíců*	(shest) *kruh*·yee·tsoo

Less.	*Méně.*	*mair*·nye
Enough.	*Stačí.*	*stuh*·chee
More.	*Trochu více.*	*tro*·khu vee·tse

special diets & allergies

Is there a vegetarian restaurant near here?
Je zde blízko vegetariánská restaurace? — ye zde *blees*·ko ve·ge·tuh·ri·ans·ka res·tow·ruh·tse

Do you have vegetarian food?
Máte vegetariánská jídla? — ma·te ve·ge·tuh·ri·ans·ka *yeed*·luh

Could you prepare a meal without ...?
Mohl/Mohla by jste připravit jídlo bez ...? m/f — mo·hl/*mo*·hluh bi yste *przhi*·pruh·vit *yeed*·lo bez ...

butter	*máslo* n	*mas*·lo
eggs	*vejce* n pl	*vey*·tse
meat stock	*bujón* m	*bu*·yawn

I'm allergic to ...	*Mám alergii na ...*	mam *uh*·ler·gi·yi nuh ...
dairy produce	*mléčné výrobky*	*mlair*·chnair *vee*·rob·ki
gluten	*lepek*	*le*·pek
MSG	*glutaman sodný*	*glu*·tuh·muhn *sod*·nee
nuts	*ořechy*	*o*·rzhe·khi
seafood	*plody moře*	*plo*·di mo·rzhe

menu decoder

boršč m	*borshch*	*beetroot soup*
bramboračka f	*bruhm·bo·ruhch·kuh*	*thick soup of potatoes & mushrooms*
bramborák m	*bruhm·bo·rak*	*potato cake*
čevapčiči n pl	*che·vuhp·chi·chi*	*fried or grilled minced veal, pork & mutton made into cone-like shapes*
dršťky f pl	*drsht·ki*	*sliced tripe*
dušená roštěnka f	*du·she·na rosh·tyen·kuh*	*braised beef slices in sauce*
fazolová polévka f	*fuh·zo·lo·va po·lairf·kuh*	*bean soup*
guláš m	*gu·lash*	*thick, spicy stew, usually made with beef & potatoes*
gulášová polévka f	*gu·la·sho·va po·lairf·kuh*	*beef goulash soup*
houskové knedlíky m pl	*hohs·ko·vair kned·lee·ki*	*bread dumplings*
hovězí guláš n	*ho·vye·zee gu·lash*	*beef stew, sometimes served with dumplings*
hrachová polévka f	*hra·kho·va po·lairf·kuh*	*thick pea soup with bacon*
hranolky f pl	*hruh·nol·ki*	*French fries*
jablečný závin m	*yuh·blech·nee za·vin*	*apple strudel*
jelito n	*ye·li·to*	*black pudding*
karbanátek m	*kuhr·buh·na·tek*	*hamburger with breadcrumbs, egg, diced bread roll & onions*
klobása f	*klo·ba·suh*	*thick sausage*
koprová polévka f	*kop·ro·va po·lairf·kuh*	*dill & sour cream soup*

krokety f pl	*kro·ke·ti*	*deep-fried mashed potato balls*
kuřecí polévka s nudlemi f	*ku·rzhe·tsee po·lairf·kuh s nud·le·mi*	*chicken noodle soup*
kuře na paprice n	*ku·rzhe nuh puh·pri·tse*	*chicken boiled in spicy paprika cream sauce*
lečo n	*le·cho*	*stewed onions, capsicums, tomatoes, eggs & sausage*
míchaná vejce f pl	*mee·khuh·na vey·tse*	*scrambled eggs*
nudlová polévka f	*nud·lo·va po·lairf·kuh*	*noodle soup made from chicken broth with vegetables*
oplatka f	*o·pluht·kuh*	*large paper-thin waffle*
ovocné knedlíky m pl	*o·vots·nair kned·lee·ki*	*fruit dumplings*
palačinka f	*puh·luh·chin·kuh*	*crepe • pancake*
plněná paprika f	*pl·nye·na puh·pri·kuh*	*capsicum stuffed with minced meat & rice, in tomato sauce*
Pražská šunka f	*pruzh·ska shun·kuh*	*Prague ham – ham pickled in brine & spices & smoked over a fire*
přírodní řízek m	*przhee·rod·nyee rzhee·zek*	*pork or veal schnitzel without breadcrumbs*
rizoto n	*ri·zo·to*	*a mixture of pork, onions, peas & rice*
ruské vejce n pl	*rus·kair vey·tse*	*hard-boiled eggs & ham, topped with mayonnaise & caviar*
rybí polévka f	*ri·bee po·lairf·kuh*	*fish soup usually made with carp & some carrots, potatoes & peas*
smažený květák s bramborem m	*smuh·zhe·nee kvye·tak s bruhm·bo·rem*	*cauliflower florets fried in breadcrumbs & served with boiled potatoes & tartar sauce*
svíčková na smetaně f	*sveech·ko·va nuh sme·ta·nye*	*roast beef & dumplings in carrot cream sauce, topped with lemon, cranberries & whipped cream*
tvarohový koláč m	*tvuh·ro·ho·vee ko·lach*	*pastry with cottage cheese & raisins*

emergencies

basics

Help!	Pomoc!	*po*-mots
Stop!	Zastav!	*zuhs*-tuhf
Go away!	Běžte pryč!	*byezh*-te prich
Thief!	Zloděj!	*zlo*-dyey
Fire!	Hoří!	*ho*-rzhee
Watch out!	Pozor!	*po*-zor

Call ...!	Zavolejte ...!	*zuh*-vo-ley-te ...
a doctor	lékaře	*lair*-kuh-rzhe
an ambulance	sanitku	*suh*-nit-ku
the police	policii	*po*-li-tsi-yi

It's an emergency.
To je naléhavý případ. — to ye nuh-lair-huh-vee przhee-puhd

Could you help me, please?
Můžete prosím pomoci? — moo-zhe-te pro-seem po-mo-tsi

Can I use the phone?
Mohu si zatelefonovat? — mo-hu si zuh-te-le-fo-no-vuht

I'm lost.
Zabloudil/Zabloudila jsem. m/f — zuh-bloh-dyil/zuh-bloh-dyi-luh ysem

Where are the toilets?
Kde jsou toalety? — gde ysoh to-uh-le-ti

police

Where's the police station?
Kde je policejní stanice? — gde ye po-li-tsey-nyee stuh-nyi-tse

I want to report an offence.
Chci nahlásit trestný čin. — khtsi nuh-hla-sit trest-nee chin

I have insurance.
Jsem pojištěný/pojištěná. m/f — ysem po-yish-tye-nee/po-yish-tye-na

I've been ...	... mě.	... mye
assaulted	Přepadli	*przhe*-puhd-li
raped	Znásilnili	*zna*-sil-nyi-li
robbed	Okradli	*o*-kruhd-li

I've lost my ...	Ztratil/Ztratila jsem ... m/f	ztruh·tyil/ztruh·tyi·luh ysem ...
My ... was/were stolen.	Ukradli mě ...	u·kruhd·li mye ...
backpack	batoh	buh·tawh
credit card	kreditní kartu	kre·dit·nyee kuhr·tu
bag	zavazadlo	zuh·vuh·zuhd·lo
handbag	kabelku	kuh·bel·ku
jewellery	šperky	shper·ki
money	peníze	pe·nyee·ze
passport	pas	puhs
travellers cheques	cestovní šeky	tses·tov·nyee she·ki
wallet	peněženku	pe·nye·zhen·ku
I want to contact my ...	Potřebuji se obrátit na ...	pot·rzhe·bu·yi se o·bra·tyit nuh ...
consulate	můj konzulát	mooy kon·zu·lat
embassy	mé velvyslanectví	mair vel·vi·sluh·nets·tvee

health

medical needs

Where's the nearest ...?	Kde je nejbližší ...?	gde ye ney·blizh·shee ...
dentist	zubař	zu·buhrzh
doctor	lékař	lair·kuhrzh
hospital	nemocnice	ne·mots·nyi·tse
(night) pharmacist	(non-stop) lékárník	(non·stop) lair·kar·nyeek

I need a doctor (who speaks English).
Potřebuji (anglickomluvícího) doktora.   pot·rzhe·bu·yi (uhn·glits·kom·lu·vee·tsee·ho) dok·to·ruh

Could I see a female doctor?
Mohla bych být vyšetřená lékařkou?   mo·hluh bikh beet vi·shet·rzhe·na lair·kuhrzh·koh

I've run out of my medication.
Došly mi léky.   dosh·li mi lair·ki

symptoms, conditions & allergies

I'm sick.	Jsem nemocný/ nemocná. m/f	ysem ne·mots·nee/ ne·mots·na
It hurts here.	Tady to bolí.	tuh·di to bo·lee
I have (a) …	Mám …	mam …

asthma	astma n	uhst·muh
bronchitis	zánět průdušek m	za·nyet proo·du·shek
constipation	zácpa f	zats·puh
cough n	kašel m	kuh·shel
diarrhoea	průjem m	proo·yem
fever	horečka f	ho·rech·kuh
headache	bolesti hlavy f	bo·les·tyi hluh·vi
heart condition	srdeční porucha f	sr·dech·nye po·ru·khuh
nausea	nevolnost f	ne·vol·nost
pain n	bolest f	bo·lest
sore throat	bolest v krku f	bo·lest f kr·ku
toothache	bolení zubu n	bo·le·nye zu·bu

I'm allergic to …	Jsem alergický/ alergická na … m/f	ysem uh·ler·gits·kee/ uh·ler·gits·ka nuh …
antibiotics	antibiotika	uhn·ti·bi·o·ti·kuh
anti-inflammatories	protizánětlivé léky	pro·tyi·za·nyet·li·vair lair·ki
aspirin	aspirin	uhs·pi·rin
bees	včely	fche·li
codeine	kodein	ko·deyn
penicillin	penicilin	pe·ni·tsi·lin

antiseptic	antiseptický prostředek m	uhn·ti·sep·tits·kee prost·rzhe·dek
bandage	obvaz m	ob·vuhz
condoms	prezervativy m pl	pre·zer·vuh·ti·vi
contraceptives	antikoncepce f	uhn·ti·kon·tsep·tse
diarrhoea medicine	lék na průjem m	lairk nuh proo·yem
insect repellent	prostředek na hubení hmyzu m	pros·trzhe·dek nuh hu·be·nye hmi·zu
laxatives	projímadla m pl	pro·yee·muhd·la
painkillers	prášky proti bolesti m pl	prash·ki pro·tyi bo·les·tyi
rehydration salts	iontový nápoj m	yon·to·vee na·poy
sleeping tablets	prášky na spaní m pl	prash·ki nuh spuh·nyee

english–czech dictionary

Czech nouns in this dictionary have their gender indicated by ⓜ (masculine), ⓕ (feminine) or ⓝ (neuter). If it's a plural noun, you'll also see see pl. Adjectives are given in the masculine form only. Words are also marked as a (adjective), v (verb), sg (singular), pl (plural), inf (informal) or pol (polite) where necessary.

A

accident *nehoda* ⓕ ne-ho-duh
accommodation *ubytování* ⓝ
    u-bi-to-va-nyee
adaptor *adaptor* ⓜ uh-duhp-tor
address *adresa* ⓕ uh-dre-suh
after *po* po
air-conditioned *klimatizovaný* kli-muh-ti-zo-vuh-nee
airplane *letadlo* ⓝ le-tuhd-lo
airport *letiště* ⓝ le-tyish-tye
alcohol *alkohol* ⓜ uhl-ko-hol
all *všichni* vshikh-nyi
allergy *alergie* ⓕ uh-ler-gi-ye
ambulance *ambulance* ⓕ uhm-bu-luhn-tse
and *a* uh
ankle *kotník* ⓜ kot-nyeek
arm *paže* ⓕ puh-zhe
ashtray *popelník* ⓜ po-pel-nyeek
ATM *bankomat* ⓜ buhn-ko-muht

B

baby *nemluvně* ⓝ nem-luv-nye
back (body) *záda* ⓕ za-duh
backpack *batoh* ⓜ buh-tawh
bad *špatný* shpuht-nee
bag *taška* ⓕ tuhsh-kuh
baggage claim *výdej zavazadel* ⓜ
    vee-dey zuh-vuh-zuh-del
bank *banka* ⓕ buhn-kuh
bar *bar* ⓜ buhr
bathroom *koupelna* ⓕ koh-pel-nuh
battery *baterie* ⓕ buh-te-ri-ye
beautiful *krásný* kras-nee
bed *postel* ⓕ pos-tel
beer *pivo* ⓝ pi-vo
before *před* przhed
behind *za* zuh
bicycle *kolo* ⓝ ko-lo
big *velký* vel-kee
bill *účet* ⓜ oo-chet
black *černý* cher-nee

blanket *deka* ⓕ de-kuh
blood group *krevní skupina* ⓕ
    krev-nyee sku-pi-nuh
blue *modrý* mod-ree
book (make a reservation) v *objednat* ob-yed-nuht
bottle *láhev* ⓕ la-hef
bottle opener *otvírák na láhve* ⓜ
    ot-vee-rak nuh lah-ve
boy *chlapec* ⓜ khluh-pets
brakes (car) *brzdy* ⓕ pl brz-di
breakfast *snídaně* ⓕ snee-duh-nye
broken (faulty) *zlomený* zlo-me-nee
bus *autobus* ⓜ ow-to-bus
business *obchod* ⓜ op-khod
buy *koupit* koh-pit

C

café *kavárna* ⓕ kuh-var-nuh
camera *fotoaparát* ⓜ fo-to-uh-puh-rat
camp site *autokempink* ⓜ ow-to-kem-pink
cancel *zrušit* zru-shit
can opener *otvírák na konzervy* ⓜ
    ot-vee-rak nuh kon-zer-vi
car *auto* ⓝ ow-to
cash *hotovost* ⓕ ho-to-vost
cash (a cheque) v *inkasovat šek* in-kuh-so-vuht shek
cell phone *mobil* ⓜ mo-bil
centre *střed* ⓜ strzhed
change (money) v *vyměnit* vi-mye-nyit
cheap *levný* lev-nee
check (bill) *účet* ⓜ oo-chet
check-in *recepce* ⓕ re-tsep-tse
chest *hruď* ⓕ hrud'
child *dítě* ⓝ dyee-tye
cigarette *cigareta* ⓕ tsi-guh-re-tuh
city *město* ⓝ myes-to
clean a *čistý* chis-tee
closed *zavřený* zuh-vrzhe-nee
coffee *káva* ⓕ ka-vuh
coins *mince* ⓕ min-tse
cold a *chladný* khluhd-nee
collect call *hovor na účet volaného* ⓜ
    ho-vor nuh oo-chet vo-luh-nair-ho

come *přijít* ⓟ *przhi-yeet*
computer *počítač* ⓜ *po-chee-tuhch*
condom *prezervativ* ⓜ *pre-zer-vuh-tif*
contact lenses *kontaktní čočky* ⓕ pl
  kon-tuhkt-nyee choch-ki
cook v *vařit* *vuh-rzhit*
cost *cena* ⓕ *tse-nuh*
credit card *kreditní karta* ⓕ
  kre-dit-nyee kuhr-tuh
cup *šálek* ⓜ *sha-lek*
currency exchange *směnárna* ⓕ *smye-nar-nuh*
customs (immigration) *celnice* ⓕ *tsel-ni-tse*
Czech a *český* *ches-kee*
Czech (language) *čeština* ⓕ *chesh-tyi-nuh*
Czech Republic *Česká republika* ⓕ
  ches-ka re-pu-bli-kuh

D

dangerous *nebezpečný* *ne-bez-pech-nee*
date (time) *schůzka* ⓕ *skhooz-kuh*
day *den* ⓜ *den*
delay *zpoždění* ⓝ *zpozh-dye-nyee*
dentist *zubař/zubařka* ⓜ/ⓕ *zu-buhrzh/zu-buhrzh-kuh*
depart *odjet* *od-yet*
diaper *plénka* ⓕ *plairn-kuh*
dictionary *slovník* ⓜ *slov-nyeek*
dinner *večeře* ⓕ *ve-che-rzhe*
direct *přímý* *przhee-mee*
dirty *špinavý* *shpi-nuh-vee*
disabled *invalidní* *in-vuh-lid-nyee*
discount *sleva* ⓕ *sle-vuh*
doctor *doktor/doktorka* ⓜ/ⓕ *dok-tor/dok-tor-kuh*
double bed *manželská postel* ⓕ *muhn-zhels-ka pos-tel*
double room *dvoulůžkový pokoj* ⓜ
  dvoh-loozh-ko-vee po-koy
drink *nápoj* ⓜ *na-poy*
drive v *řídit* *rzhee-dyit*
drivers licence *řidičský průkaz* ⓜ
  rzhi-dyich-skee proo-kuhz
drugs (illicit) *drogy* ⓕ pl *dro-gi*
dummy (pacifier) *dudlík* ⓜ *dud-leek*

E

ear *ucho* ⓝ *u-kho*
east *východ* ⓜ *vee-khod*
eat *jíst* *yeest*
economy class *turistická třída* ⓕ *tu-ris-tits-ka trzhee-duh*
electricity *elektřina* ⓕ *e-lek-trzhi-nuh*
elevator *výtah* ⓜ *vee-tuh*
email *email* ⓜ *ee-meyl*

embassy *velvyslanectví* ⓝ *vel-vi-sluh-nets-tvee*
emergency *pohotovost* ⓕ *po-ho-to-vost*
English (language) *angličtina* ⓕ *uhn-glich-tyi-nuh*
entrance *vstup* ⓜ *vstup*
evening *večer* ⓜ *ve-cher*
exchange rate *směnný kurz* ⓜ *smye-nee kurz*
exit *východ* ⓜ *vee-khod*
expensive *drahý* *druh-hee*
express mail *expresní zásilka* ⓕ *eks-pres-nyee za-sil-kuh*
eye *oko* ⓝ *o-ko*

F

far *daleko* *duh-le-ko*
fast *rychlý* *rikh-lee*
father *otec* ⓜ *o-tets*
film (camera) *film* ⓜ *film*
finger *prst* ⓜ *prst*
first-aid kit *lékárnička* ⓕ *lair-kar-nyich-kuh*
first class *první třída* ⓕ *prv-nyee trzhee-duh*
fish *ryba* ⓕ *ri-buh*
food *jídlo* ⓝ *yeed-lo*
foot *chodidlo* ⓝ *kho-dyid-lo*
fork *vidlička* ⓕ *vid-lich-kuh*
free (of charge) *bezplatný* *bez-pluht-nee*
friend *přítel/přítelkyně* ⓜ/ⓕ
  przhee-tel/przhe-tel-ki-nye
fruit *ovoce* ⓝ *o-vo-tse*
full *plný* *pl-nee*
funny *legrační* *le-gruhch-nyee*

G

gift *dar* ⓜ *duhr*
girl *dívka* ⓕ *dyeef-kuh*
glass (drinking) *sklenička* ⓕ *skle-nyich-kuh*
glasses *brýle* ⓕ pl *bree-le*
go *jít* *yeet*
good *dobrý* *do-bree*
green *zelený* *ze-le-nee*
guide *průvodce* ⓜ *proo-vod-tse*

H

half *polovina* ⓕ *po-lo-vi-nuh*
hand *ruka* ⓕ *ru-kuh*
handbag *kabelka* ⓕ *kuh-bel-kuh*
happy *šťastný* *shtyast-nee*
have *mít* *meet*
he *on* *on*
head *hlava* ⓕ *hluh-vuh*
heart *srdce* ⓝ *srd-tse*

heat *horko* ⑩ hor-ko
heavy *těžký* tyuzh-kee
help v *pomoci* po-mo-tsi
here *tady* tuh-di
high *vysoký* vi-so-kee
highway *dálnice* ① dal-nyi-tse
hike v *trampovat* truhm-po-vuht
holiday *svátek* ⑩ sva-tek
homosexual *homosexuál* ⑩ ho-mo-sek-su-al
hospital *nemocnice* ① ne-mots-nyi-tse
hot *horký* hor-kee
hotel *hotel* ⑩ ho-tel
hungry *hladový* hluh-do-vee
husband *manžel* ⑩ muhn-zhel

I

I *já* ya
identification (card) *osobní doklad* ①
o-sob-nyee dok-luhd
ill *nemocný* ne-mots-nee
important *důležitý* doo-le-zhi-tee
included *včetně* fchet-nye
injury *zranění* ⑪ zruh-nye-nyee
insurance *pojištění* ⑪ po-yish-tye-nyee
Internet *internet* ⑩ in-ter-net
interpreter *tlumočník/tlumočnice* ⑩/①
tlu-moch-nyeek/tlu-moch-nyi-tse

J

jewellery *šperky* ⑪ pl shper-ki
job *zaměstnání* ⑪ zuh-myest-na-nyee

K

key *klíč* ⑩ kleech
kilogram *kilogram* ⑩ ki-lo-gruhm
kitchen *kuchyň* ① ku-khin'
knife *nůž* ⑩ noozh

L

laundry (place) *prádelna* ① pra-del-nuh
lawyer *advokát/advokátka* ⑩/①
uhd-vo-kat/uhd-vo-kat-kuh
left (direction) *levý* le-vee
left-luggage office *úschovna zavazadel* ①
oos-khov-nuh zuh-vuh-zuh-del
leg *noha* ① no-huh

lesbian *lesbička* ① les-bich-kuh
less *menší* men-shee
letter (mail) *dopis* ⑩ do-pis
lift (elevator) *výtah* ⑩ vee-tah
light *světlo* ⑪ svyet-lo
like v *mít rád* meet rad
lock *zámek* ⑩ za-mek
long *dlouhý* dloh-hee
lost *ztracený* ztruh-tse-nee
lost-property office *ztráty a nálezy* ①
ztra-ti uh na-le-zi
love v *milovat* mi-lo-vuht
luggage *zavazadlo* ⑪ zuh-vuh-zuhd-lo
lunch *oběd* ⑩ o-byed

M

mail *pošta* ① posh-tuh
man *muž* ⑩ muzh
map (of country) *mapa* ① muh-puh
map (of town) *plán* ⑩ plan
market *trh* ⑩ trh
matches *zápalky* ① pl za-puhl-ki
meat *maso* ⑪ muh-so
medicine *lék* ⑩ lairk
menu *jídelní lístek* ① yee-del-nyee lees-tek
message *zpráva* ① zpra-vuh
milk *mléko* ⑪ mlair-ko
minute *minuta* ① mi-nu-tuh
mobile phone *mobil* ⑩ mo-bil
money *peníze* ⑩ pe-nyee-ze
month *měsíc* ⑩ mye-seets
morning *ráno* ⑪ ra-no
mother *matka* ① muht-kuh
motorcycle *motorka* ① mo-tor-kuh
motorway *dálnice* ① dal-nyi-tse
mouth *ústa* ⑪ oos-tuh
music *hudba* ① hud-buh

N

name *jméno* ⑪ ymair-no
napkin *ubrousek* ⑩ u-broh-sek
nappy *plenka* ① plen-kuh
near *blízko* bleez-ko
neck *krk* ⑩ krk
new *nový* no-vee
news *zprávy* ⑪ pl zpra-vi
newspaper *noviny* ① pl no-vi-ni
night *noc* ① nots
no *ne* ne

noisy *hlučný* hluch·nee
nonsmoking *nekuřácký* ne·ku·rzhats·kee
north *sever* ⓜ se·ver
nose *nos* ⓜ nos
now *teď* 'teď'
number *číslo* ⓝ chees·lo

O

oil (engine) *olej* ⓜ o·ley
old *starý* stuh·ree
one-way ticket *jednoduchá jízdenka* ⓕ
    yed·no·du·kha yeez·den·kuh
open a *otevřený* o·tev·rzhe·nee
outside *venku* ven·ku

P

package *balík* ⓜ buh·leek
paper *papír* ⓜ puh·peer
park (car) v *parkovat* puhr·ko·vuht
passport *pas* ⓜ puhs
pay *platit* pluh·tyit
pen *propiska* ⓕ pro·pis·kuh
petrol *benzín* ⓜ ben·zeen
pharmacy *lékárna* ⓕ lair·kar·nuh
phonecard *telefonní karta* ⓕ
    te·le·fo·nyee kuhr·tuh
photo *fotka* ⓕ fot·kuh
plate *talíř* ⓜ tuh·leerzh
police *policie* ⓕ po·li·tsi·ye
postcard *pohled* ⓜ po·hled
post office *pošta* ⓕ posh·tuh
pregnant *těhotná* tye·hot·na
price *cena* ⓕ tse·nuh

Q

quiet *tichý* tyi·khee

R

rain *déšť* ⓜ dairsht'
razor *břitva* ⓕ brzhit·vuh
receipt *stvrzenka* ⓕ stvr·zen·kuh
red *červený* cher·ve·nee
refund *vracení peněz* ⓝ vruh·tse·nyee pe·nyez
registered mail *doporučená zásilka* ⓕ
    do·po·ru·che·na za·sil·kuh
rent v *pronajmout* pro·nai·moht

repair v *opravit* o·pruh·vit
reservation *rezervace* ⓕ re·zer·vuh·tse
restaurant *restaurace* ⓕ res·tow·ruh·tse
return v *vrátit se* vra·tyit se
return ticket *zpáteční jízdenka* ⓕ
    zpa·tech·nyee yeez·den·kuh
right (direction) *pravý* pruh·vee
road *silnice* ⓕ sil·nyi·tse
room *pokoj* ⓜ po·koy

S

safe a *bezpečný* bez·pech·nee
sanitary napkins *dámské vložky* ⓕ pl
    dams·kair vlozh·ki
seat *místo* ⓝ mees·to
send *poslat* pos·luht
service station *benzínová pumpa* ⓕ
    ben·zee·no·va pum·puh
sex *pohlaví* ⓝ po·hluh·vee
shampoo *šampon* ⓜ shuhm·pon
share (a dorm) *spolubývat* spo·lu·o·bee·vuht
shaving cream *pěna na holení* ⓕ
    pye·nuh nuh ho·le·nyee
she *ona* o·nuh
sheet (bed) *prostěradlo* ⓝ pros·tye·ruhd·lo
shirt *košile* ⓕ ko·shi·le
shoes *boty* ⓕ pl bo·ti
shop *obchod* ⓜ op·khod
short *krátký* krat·kee
shower *sprcha* ⓕ spr·khuh
single room *jednolůžkový pokoj* ⓝ
    yed·no·loozh·ko·vee po·koy
skin *kůže* ⓕ koo·zhe
skirt *sukně* ⓕ suk·nye
sleep v *spát* spat
slowly *pomalu* po·muh·lu
small *malý* muh·lee
smoke (cigarettes) v *kouřit* koh·rzhit
soap *mýdlo* ⓝ meed·lo
some *několik* nye·ko·lik
soon *brzy* br·zi
south *jih* ⓜ yih
souvenir shop *obchod se suvenýry* ⓜ
    op·khod se su·ve·nee·ri
speak *říci* rzhee·tsi
spoon *lžíce* ⓕ lzhee·tse
stamp *známka* ⓕ znam·kuh
station (train) *nádraží* ⓝ na·druh·zhee
stomach *žaludek* ⓜ zhuh·lu·dek

stop v *zastavit* zuhs-tuh-vit
stop (bus) *zastávka* ① zuhs-tuf-kuh
street *ulice* ① u-li-tse
student *student/studentka* ⓜ/① stu-dent/stu-dent-kuh
sun *slunce* ① slun-tse
sunscreen *opalovací krém* ⓜ o-puh-lo-vuh-tsee krairm
swim v *plavat* pluh-vuht

T

tampons *tampon* ⓜ tuhm-pon
taxi *taxík* ⓜ tuhk-seek
teaspoon *lžička* ① lzhich-kuh
teeth *zuby* ① pl zu-bi
telephone *telefon* ⓜ te-le-fon
television *televize* ① te-le-vi-ze
temperature (weather) *teplota* ① te-plo-tuh
tent *stan* ⓜ stuhn
that (one) *tamten* tuhm-ten
they *oni* o-nyi
thirsty *žíznivý* zheez-nyi-vee
this (one) *tenhle* ten-hle
throat *hrdlo* ⓝ hrd-lo
ticket *vstupenka* ① fstu-pen-kuh
time *čas* ⓜ chuhs
tired *unavený* u-nuh-ve-nee
tissues *kosmetické kapesníčky* ⓜ pl kos-me-tits-kair kuh-pes-neech-ki
today *dnes* dnes
toilet *toaleta* ① to-uh-le-tuh
tomorrow *zítra* zeet-ruh
tonight *dnes večer* dnes ve-cher
toothbrush *zubní kartáček* ⓜ zub-nyee kuhr-ta-chek
toothpaste *zubní pasta* ① zub-nyee puhs-tuh
torch (flashlight) *baterka* ① buh-ter-kuh
tour *okružní jízda* ① o-kruzh-nyee yeez-duh
tourist office *turistická informační kancelář* ① tu-ris-tits-ka in-for-muhch-nyee kuhn-tse-larzh
towel *ručník* ⓜ ruch-nyeek
train *vlak* ⓜ vluhk
translate *přeložit* przhe-lo-zhit
travel agency *cestovní kancelář* ① tses-tov-nyee kuhn-tse-larzh
travellers cheque *cestovní šek* ① tses-tov-nyee shek
trousers *kalhoty* ① pl kuhl-ho-ti
twin beds *dvoupostel* ① dvoh-pos-tel
tyre *pneumatika* ① pne-u-muh-ti-kuh

U

underwear *spodní prádlo* ⓝ spod-nyee prad-lo
urgent *naléhavý* nuh-lair-huh-vee

V

vacant *volný* vol-nee
vacation (from school) *prázdniny* ① prazd-nyi-ni
vacation (from work) *dovolená* ① do-vo-le-na
vegetable *zelenina* ① ze-le-nyi-nuh
vegetarian a *vegetariánský* ve-ge-tuh-ri-yans-kee

W

waiter/waitress *číšník/číšnice* ⓜ/① cheesh-nyeek/cheesh-nyi-tse
wallet *peněženka* ① pe-nye-zhen-ka
walk v *jít* yeet
warm a *teplý* tep-lee
wash (something) *umýt* u-meet
watch *hodinky* ① pl ho-dyin-ki
water *voda* ① vo-duh
we *my* mi
weekend *víkend* ⓜ vee-kend
west *západ* ⓜ za-puhd
wheelchair *invalidní vozík* ⓜ in-vuh-lid-nyee vo-zeek
when *kdy* gdi
where *kde* gde
white *bílý* bee-lee
who *kdo* gdo
why *proč* proch
wife *manželka* ① muhn-zhel-kuh
window *okno* ⓝ ok-no
wine *víno* ⓝ vee-no
with *s* s
without *bez* bez
woman *žena* ① zhe-nuh
write *psát* p-sat

Y

yellow *žlutý* zhlu-tee
yes *ano* uh-no
yesterday *včera* fche-ruh
you sg inf *ty* ti
you sg pol&pl *vy* vi

German

german alphabet

Aa	Bb	Cc	Dd	Ee
a	be	tse	de	e
Ff	Gg	Hh	Ii	Jj
ef	ge	ha	i	yot
Kk	Ll	Mm	Nn	Oo
ka	el	em	en	o
Pp	Qq	Rr	Ss	Tt
pe	ku	er	es	te
Uu	Vv	Ww	Xx	Yy
u	fau	ve	iks	*ewp*·si·lon
Zz				
tset				

german

DEUTSCH

introduction

Romantic, flowing, literary ... not usually how German (*Deutsch* doytsh) is described, but maybe it's time to reconsider. After all, this is the language that's played a major role in the history of Europe and remains one of the most widely spoken languages on the continent. It's taught throughout the world and chances are you're already familiar with a number of German words that have entered English – *kindergarten*, *kitsch* and *hamburger*, for example, are all of German origin.

German is spoken by around 100 million people, and is the official language of Germany, Austria and Liechtenstein, as well as one of the official languages of Belgium, Switzerland and Luxembourg. German didn't spread across the rest of the world with the same force as English, Spanish or French. Germany only became a unified nation in 1871 and never established itself as a colonial power. After the reunification of East and West Germany, however, German has become more important in global politics and economics. Its role in science has long been recognised and German literature lays claim to some of the most famous written works ever printed. Just think of the enormous influence of Goethe, Nietzsche, Freud and Einstein.

German is usually divided into two forms – Low German (*Plattdeutsch* plat-doytsh) and High German (*Hochdeutsch* hokh-doytsh). Low German is an umbrella term used for the dialects spoken in Northern Germany. High German is considered the standard form and is understood throughout German-speaking communities, from the Swiss Alps to the cosy cafés of Vienna; it's also the form used in this phrasebook.

Both German and English belong to the West Germanic language family, along with a number of other languages including Dutch and Yiddish. The primary reason why German and English have grown apart is that the Normans, on invading England in 1066, brought with them a large number of non-Germanic words. As well as the recognisable words, the grammar of German will also make sense to an English speaker. Even with a slight grasp of German grammar, you'll still manage to get your point across. On the other hand, German tends to join words together (while English uses a number of separate words) to express a single notion. You shouldn't be intimidated by this though – after a while you'll be able to tell parts of words and recognising 'the Football World Cup qualifying match' hidden within *Fussballwelt-meisterschaftsqualifikationsspiel* won't be a problem at all!

pronunciation

vowel sounds

German vowels can be short or long, which influences the meaning of words. They're pronounced crisply and distinctly, so *Tee* (tea) is tey, not *tey*-ee.

symbol	english equivalent	german example	transliteration
a	run	*hat*	hat
aa	father	*habe*	*haa*-be
ai	aisle	*mein*	main
air	fair	*Bär*	bair
aw	saw	*Boot*	bawt
e	bet	*Männer*	*me*-ner
ee	see	*fliegen*	*flee*-gen
eu	nurse	*schön*	sheun
ew	ee pronounced with rounded lips	*zurück*	tsu-*rewk*
ey	as in 'bet', but longer	*leben*	*ley*-ben
i	hit	*mit*	mit
o	pot	*Koffer*	*ko*-fer
oo	zoo	*Schuhe*	*shoo*-e
ow	now	*Haus*	hows
oy	toy	*Leute, Häuser*	*loy*-te, *hoy*-zer
u	put	*unter*	*un*-ter

word stress

Almost all German words are pronounced with stress on the first syllable. While this is a handy rule of thumb, you can always rely on the coloured pronunciation guides, which show the stressed syllables in italics.

consonant sounds

All German consonant sounds exist in English except for the kh and r sounds. The kh sound is generally pronounced at the back of the throat, like the 'ch' in 'Bach' or the Scottish 'loch'. The r sound is pronounced at the back of the throat, almost like saying g, but with some friction, a bit like gargling.

symbol	english equivalent	german example	transliteration
b	bed	*Bett*	bet
ch	cheat	*Tschüss*	chews
d	dog	*dein*	dain
f	fat	*vier*	feer
g	go	*gehen*	*gey*·en
h	hat	*helfen*	*hel*·fen
k	kit	*kein*	kain
kh	loch	*ich*	ikh
l	lot	*laut*	lowt
m	man	*Mann*	man
n	not	*nein*	nain
ng	ring	*singen*	*zing*·en
p	pet	*Preis*	prais
r	run (throaty)	*Reise*	*rai*·ze
s	sun	*heiß*	hais
sh	shot	*schön*	sheun
t	top	*Tag*	taak
ts	hits	*Zeit*	tsait
v	very	*wohnen*	*vaw*·nen
y	yes	*ja*	yaa
z	zero	*sitzen*	*zi*·tsen
zh	pleasure	*Garage*	ga·*raa*·zhe

basics

language difficulties

Do you speak English?
Sprechen Sie Englisch?   shpre·khen zee *eng*·lish

Do you understand?
Verstehen Sie?   fer·*shtey*·en zee

I (don't) understand.
Ich verstehe (nicht).   ikh fer·*shtey*·e (nikht)

What does (Kugel) mean?
Was bedeutet (Kugel)?   vas be·*doy*·tet (*koo*·gel)

How do you ...?	*Wie ...?*	vee ...
pronounce this	*spricht man dieses Wort aus*	shprikht man *dee*·zes vort ows
write (Schweiz)	*schreibt man (Schweiz)*	shraipt man (shvaits)

Could you please ...?	*Könnten Sie ...?*	*keun*·ten zee ...
repeat that	*das bitte wiederholen*	das *bi*·te vee·der·*haw*·len
speak more slowly	*bitte langsamer sprechen*	*bi*·te *lang*·za·mer shpre·khen
write it down	*das bitte aufschreiben*	das *bi*·te *owf*·shrai·ben

essentials

Yes.	*Ja.*	yaa
No.	*Nein.*	nain
Please.	*Bitte.*	*bi*·te
Thank you.	*Danke.*	*dang*·ke
Thank you very much.	*Vielen Dank.*	*fee*·len dangk
You're welcome.	*Bitte.*	*bi*·te
Excuse me.	*Entschuldigung.*	ent·*shul*·di·gung
Sorry.	*Entschuldigung.*	ent·*shul*·di·gung

0	*null*	nul	16	*sechzehn*	zeks·tseyn
1	*eins*	ains	17	*siebzehn*	zeep·tseyn
2	*zwei*	tsvai	18	*achtzehn*	akht·tseyn
3	*drei*	drai	19	*neunzehn*	noyn·tseyn
4	*vier*	feer	20	*zwanzig*	tsvan·tsikh
5	*fünf*	fewnf	21	*einundzwanzig*	ain·unt·tsvan·tsikh
6	*sechs*	zeks	22	*zweiundzwanzig*	tsvai·unt·tsvan·tsikh
7	*sieben*	zee·ben	30	*dreißig*	drai·tsikh
8	*acht*	akht	40	*vierzig*	feer·tsikh
9	*neun*	noyn	50	*fünfzig*	fewnf·tsikh
10	*zehn*	tseyn	60	*sechzig*	zekh·tsikh
11	*elf*	elf	70	*siebzig*	zeep·tsikh
12	*zwölf*	zveulf	80	*achtzig*	akht·tsikh
13	*dreizehn*	drai·tseyn	90	*neunzig*	noyn·tsikh
14	*vierzehn*	feer·tseyn	100	*hundert*	hun·dert
15	*fünfzehn*	fewnf·tseyn	1000	*tausend*	tow·sent

time & dates

What time is it?	*Wie spät ist es?*	vee shpeyt ist es
It's one o'clock.	*Es ist ein Uhr.*	es ist ain oor
It's (10) o'clock.	*Es ist (zehn) Uhr.*	es ist (tseyn) oor
Quarter past (one).	*Viertel nach (eins).*	fir·tel naakh (ains)
Half past (one).	*Halb (zwei).* (lit: half two)	halp (tsvai)
Quarter to (one).	*Viertel vor (eins).*	fir·tel fawr (ains)
At what time ...?	*Um wie viel Uhr ...?*	um vee feel oor ...
At ...	*Um ...*	um ...

am	*vormittags*	fawr·mi·taaks
pm (midday–6pm)	*nachmittags*	naakh·mi·taaks
pm (6pm–midnight)	*abends*	aa·bents

Monday	*Montag*	mawn·taak
Tuesday	*Dienstag*	deens·taak
Wednesday	*Mittwoch*	mit·vokh
Thursday	*Donnerstag*	do·ners·taak
Friday	*Freitag*	frai·taak
Saturday	*Samstag*	zams·taak
Sunday	*Sonntag*	zon·taak

January	Januar	*yan*-u-aar
February	Februar	*tey*-bru-aar
March	März	merts
April	April	a-*pril*
May	Mai	mai
June	Juni	*yoo*-ni
July	Juli	*yoo*-li
August	August	ow-*gust*
September	September	zep-*tem*-ber
October	Oktober	ok-*taw*-ber
November	November	no-*vem*-ber
December	Dezember	de-*tsem*-ber

What date is it today?
> *Der Wievielte ist heute?*   dair *vee*-feel-te ist *hoy*-te

It's (18 October).
> *Heute ist (der achtzehnte Oktober).*   *hoy*-te ist dair (*akh*-tseyn-te ok-*taw*-ber)

| since (May) | seit (Mai) | zait (mai) |
| until (June) | bis (Juni) | bis (*yoo*-ni) |

yesterday	gestern	*ges*-tern
today	heute	*hoy*-te
tonight	heute Abend	*hoy*-te *aa*-bent
tomorrow	morgen	*mor*-gen

last ...		
night	vergangene Nacht	fer-*gang*-e-ne nakht
week	letzte Woche	*lets*-te *vo*-khe
month	letzten Monat	*lets*-ten *maw*-nat
year	letztes Jahr	*lets*-tes yaar

next ...		
week	nächste Woche	*neykhs*-te *vo*-khe
month	nächsten Monat	*neykhs*-ten *maw*-nat
year	nächstes Jahr	*neykhs*-tes yaar

yesterday/	gestern/	*ges*-tern/
tomorrow ...	morgen ...	*mor*-gen ...
morning	Morgen	*mor*-gen
afternoon	Nachmittag	*naakh*-mi-taak
evening	Abend	*aa*-bent

weather

What's the weather like?	*Wie ist das Wetter?*	vee ist das *ve*·ter
It's ...		
cloudy	*Es ist wolkig.*	es ist *vol*·kikh
cold	*Es ist kalt.*	es ist kalt
hot	*Es ist heiß.*	es ist hais
raining	*Es regnet.*	es *reyg*·net
snowing	*Es schneit.*	es shnait
sunny	*Es ist sonnig.*	es ist *zo*·nikh
warm	*Es ist warm.*	es ist varm
windy	*Es ist windig.*	es ist *vin*·dikh
spring	*Frühling* m	*frew*·ling
summer	*Sommer* m	*zo*·mer
autumn	*Herbst* m	herpst
winter	*Winter* m	*vin*·ter

border crossing

I'm here ...	*Ich bin hier ...*	ikh bin heer ...
in transit	*auf der Durchreise*	owf dair *durkh*·rai·ze
on business	*auf Geschäftsreise*	owf ge·*shefts*·rai·ze
on holiday	*im Urlaub*	im *oor*·lowp
I'm here for ...	*Ich bin hier für ...*	ikh bin heer fewr ...
(10) days	*(zehn) Tage*	(tseyn) *taa*·ge
(three) weeks	*(drei) Wochen*	(drai) *vo*·khen
(two) months	*(zwei) Monate*	(tsvai) *maw*·na·te

I'm going to (Salzburg).
Ich gehe nach (Salzburg).　　　　ikh *gey*·e nakh *zalts*·boorg

I'm staying at the (Hotel Park).
Ich wohne im (Hotel Park).　　　　ikh *vaw*·ne im (ho·*tel* park)

I have nothing to declare.
Ich habe nichts zu verzollen.　　　ikh *haa*·be nikhts tsoo fer·*tso*·len

I have something to declare.
Ich habe etwas zu verzollen.　　　ikh *haa*·be *et*·vas tsoo fer·*tso*·len

That's (not) mine.
Das ist (nicht) meins.　　　　　　das ist (nikht) mains

transport

tickets & luggage

Where can I buy a ticket?
Wo kann ich eine Fahrkarte kaufen? vaw kan ikh *ai*·ne *faar*·kar·te *kow*·fen

Do I need to book a seat?
Muss ich einen Platz mus ikh *ai*·nen plats
reservieren lassen? re·zer·*vee*·ren *la*·sen

One ...ticket to	*Einen ... nach*	*ai*·nen ... naakh
(Berlin), please.	*(Berlin), bitte.*	(ber·*leen*) *bi*·te
one-way	*einfache Fahrkarte*	*ain*·fa·khe *faar*·kar·te
return	*Rückfahrkarte*	*rewk*·faar·kar·te

I'd like to ...	*Ich möchte meine*	ikh *meukh*·te *mai*·ne
my ticket, please.	*Fahrkarte bitte ...*	*faar*·kar·te *bi*·te ...
cancel	*zurückgeben*	tsu·*rewk*·gey·ben
change	*ändern lassen*	*en*·dern *la*·sen
collect	*abholen*	*ab*·ho·len
confirm	*bestätigen lassen*	be·*shtey*·ti·gen *la*·sen

I'd like a ...	*Ich hätte gern*	ikh *he*·te gern
seat, please.	*einen ...*	*ai*·nen ...
nonsmoking	*Nichtraucherplatz*	*nikht*·row·kher·plats
smoking	*Raucherplatz*	*row*·kher·plats

How much is it?
Was kostet das? vas *kos*·tet das

Is there air conditioning?
Gibt es eine Klimaanlage? gipt es *ai*·ne *klee*·ma·an·*laa*·ge

Is there a toilet?
Gibt es eine Toilette? gipt es *ai*·ne to·a·*le*·te

How long does the trip take?
Wie lange dauert die Fahrt? vee *lang*·e *dow*·ert dee faart

Is it a direct route?
Ist es eine direkte Verbindung? ist es *ai*·ne di·*rek*·te fer·*bin*·dung

I'd like a luggage locker.
Ich hätte gern ein Gepäckschließfach. ikh *he*·te gern ain ge·*pek*·shlees·fakh

My luggage has been ...	Mein Gepäck ist ...	main ge·*pek* ist ...
damaged	beschädigt	be·*shey*·dikht
lost	verloren gegangen	fer·*law*·ren ge·*gang*·en
stolen	gestohlen worden	ge·*shtaw*·len *vor*·den

getting around

Where does flight (D4) arrive?
Wo ist die Ankunft des Fluges (D4)?   vaw ist dee *an*·kunft des *floo*·ges (de feer)

Where does flight (D4) depart?
Wo ist die der Abflug des Fluges (D4)?   vaw ist dair *ab*·flug des *floo*·ges (de feer)

Where's the ...?	Wo ist ...?	vaw ist ...
arrivalls hall	Ankunftshalle	an·kunfts·*ha*·le
departures hall	Abflughalle	ab·flug·*ha*·le

Is this the ...	Fährt ...	fairt ...
to (Hamburg)?	nach (Hamburg)?	nakh (*ham*·burg)
boat	das Boot	das bawt
bus	der Bus	dair bus
plane	das Flugzeug	das *flook*·tsoyk
train	der Zug	dair tsook

What time's the ... bus?	Wann fährt der ... Bus?	van fairt dair ... bus
first	erste	*ers*·te
last	letzte	*lets*·te
next	nächste	*neykhs*·te

At what time does it leave?
Wann fährt es ab?   van fairt es ap

At what time does it arrive?
Wann kommt es an?   van komt es an

How long will it be delayed?
Wie viel Verspätung wird es haben?   vee feel fer·*shpey*·tung virt es *haa*·ben

What station/stop is this?
Welcher Bahnhof/Halt ist das?   *vel*·kher *baan*·hawf/halt ist das

What's the next station/stop?
Welches ist der nächste Bahnhof/Halt?   *vel*·khes ist dair *neykhs*·te *baan*·hawf/halt

Does it stop at (Freiburg)?
Hält es in (Freiburg)?   helt *es* in (*frai*·boorg)

Please tell me when we get to (Kiel).
Könnten Sie mir bitte sagen,   *keun*·ten zee meer *bi*·te *zaa*·gen
wann wir in (Kiel) ankommen?   van veer in (keel) *an*·ko·men

How long do we stop here?
Wie lange halten wir hier?   vee *lan*·ge *hal*·ten veer heer

Is this seat available?
Ist dieser Platz frei?   ist *dee*·zer plats frai

That's my seat.
Dieses ist mein Platz.   *dee*·zes ist main plats

I'd like a taxi ...   *Ich hätte gern*   ikh *he*·te gern
     ein Taxi für ...   ain *tak*·si fewr ...
   at (9am)   *(neun Uhr vormittags)*   (noyn oor *fawr*·mi·taaks)
   now   *sofort*   zo·*fort*
   tomorrow   *morgen*   *mor*·gen

Is this taxi available?
Ist dieses Taxi frei?   ist *dee*·zes *tak*·si frai

How much is it to ...?
Was kostet es bis ...?   vas *kos*·tet es bis ...

Please put the meter on.
Schalten Sie bitte den Taxameter ein.   *shal*·ten zee *bi*·te deyn tak·sa·*mey*·ter ain

Please take me to (this address).
Bitte bringen Sie mich zu   *bi*·te *bring*·en zee mikh tsoo
(dieser Adresse).   (*dee*·zer a·*dre*·se)

Please ...   *Bitte ...*   *bi*·te ...
   slow down   *fahren Sie langsamer*   *faa*·ren zee *lang*·za·mer
   stop here   *halten Sie hier*   *hal*·ten zee heer
   wait here   *warten Sie hier*   *var*·ten zee heer

car, motorbike & bicycle hire

I'd like to hire a ...	Ich möchte ... mieten.	ikh meukh·te ... mee·ten
bicycle	ein Fahrrad	ain faar·raat
car	ein Auto	ain ow·to
motorbike	ein Motorrad	ain maw·tor·raat

with ...	mit ...	mit ...
a driver	Fahrer	faa·rer
air conditioning	Klimaanlage	klee·ma·an·laa·ge

How much for ... hire?	Wie viel kostet es pro ...?	vee feel kos·tet es praw ...
hourly	Stunde	shtun·de
daily	Tag	taak
weekly	Woche	vo·khe

air	Luft f	luft
oil	Öl n	eul
petrol	Benzin n	ben·tseen
tyres	Reifen m pl	rai·fen

I need a mechanic.
Ich brauche einen Mechaniker. ikh brow·khe ai·nen me·khaa·ni·ker

I've run out of petrol.
Ich habe kein Benzin mehr. ikh haa·be kain ben·tseen mair

I have a flat tyre.
Ich habe eine Reifenpanne. ikh haa·be ai·ne rai·fen·pa·ne

directions

Where's the ...?	Wo ist ...?	vaw ist ...
bank	die Bank	dee bangk
city centre	die Innenstadt	i·nen·shtat
hotel	das Hotel	das ho·tel
market	der Markt	dair markt
police station	das Polizeirevier	das po·li·tsai·re·veer
post office	das Postamt	das post·amt
public toilet	die öffentliche	dee eu·fent·li·khe
	Toilette	to·a·le·te
tourist office	das Fremden-	das frem·den·
	verkehrsbüro	fer·kairs·bew·raw

Is this the road to (Frankfurt)?
Fuhrt diese Straße fewrt dee·ze shtraa·se
nach (Frankfurt)? naakh (frank·foort)

Can you show me (on the map)?
Können Sie es mir keu·nen zee es meer
(auf der Karte) zeigen? (owf dair kar·te) tsai·gen

What's the address?
Wie ist die Adresse? vee ist dee a·dre·se

How far is it?
Wie weit ist es? vee vait ist es

How do I get there?
Wie kann ich da hinkommen? vee kan ikh daa hin·ko·men

Turn ...	*Biegen Sie ... ab.*	bee·gen zee ... ap
at the corner	*an der Ecke*	an dair e·ke
at the traffic lights	*bei der Ampel*	bai dair am·pel
left/right	*links/rechts*	lingks/rekhts

It's ...	*Es ist ...*	es ist ...
behind ...	*hinter ...*	hin·ter ...
far away	*weit weg*	vait vek
here	*hier*	heer
in front of ...	*vor ...*	fawr ...
left	*links*	lingks
near (to ...)	*nahe (zu ...)*	naa·e (zoo ...)
next to ...	*neben ...*	ney·ben ...
on the corner	*an der Ecke*	an dair e·ke
opposite ...	*gegenüber ...*	gey·gen·ew·ber ...
right	*rechts*	rekhts
straight ahead	*geradeaus*	ge·raa·de·ows
there	*dort*	dort

north	*Norden* m	nor·den
south	*Süden* m	zew·den
east	*Osten* m	os·ten
west	*Westen* m	ves·ten

by bus	*mit dem Bus*	mit deym bus
by taxi	*mit dem Taxi*	mit deym tak·si
by train	*mit dem Zug*	mit deym tsook
on foot	*zu Fuß*	tsoo foos

Eingang/Ausgang	*ain*-gang/*ows*-gang	**Entrance/Exit**
Offen/Geschlossen	*o*-fen/ge-*shlo*-sen	**Open/Closed**
Zimmer Frei	*tsi*-mer frai	**Rooms Available**
Ausgebucht	*ows*-ge-bukht	**No Vacancies**
Auskunft	*ows*-kunft	**Information**
Polizeirevier	po-li-*tsai*-re-veer	**Police Station**
Verboten	fer-*baw*-ten	**Prohibited**
Toiletten/WC	to-a-*le*-ten/vee-*tsee*	**Toilets**
Herren	*hair*-en	**Men**
Damen	*daa*-men	**Women**
Heiß/Kalt	hais/kalt	**Hot/Cold**

accommodation

finding accommodation

Where's a/an ...?	*Wo ist ...?*	vaw ist ...
camping ground	*ein Campingplatz*	ain *kem*-ping-plats
guesthouse	*eine Pension*	*ai*-ne paang-*zyawn*
hotel	*ein Hotel*	ain ho-*tel*
inn	*ein Gasthof*	ain *gast*-hawf
youth hostel	*eine Jugendherberge*	*ai*-ne *yoo*-gent-her-ber-ge

Can you recommend	*Können Sie etwas*	*keu*-nen zee *et*-vas
somewhere ...?	*... empfehlen?*	... emp-*fey*-len
cheap	*Billiges*	*bi*-li-ges
good	*Gutes*	*goo*-tes
luxurious	*Luxuriöses*	luk-su-ri-*eu*-ses
nearby	*in der Nähe*	in dair *ney*-e

I'd like to book a room, please.
Ich möchte bitte ein   ikh *meukh*-te *bi*-te ain
Zimmer reservieren.   *tsi*-mer re-zer-*vee*-ren

I have a reservation.
Ich habe eine Reservierung.   ikh *haa*-be *ai*-ne re-zer-*vee*-rung

My name's ...
Mein Name ist ...   main *naa*-me ist ...

Do you have a ... room? — *Haben Sie ein ...?* — haa·ben zee ain ...
- single — *Einzelzimmer* — ain·tsel·tsi·mer
- double — *Doppelzimmer mit einem Doppelbett* — do·pel·tsi·mer mit ai·nem do·pel·bet
- twin — *Doppelzimmer mit zwei Einzelbetten* — do·pel·tsi·mer mit tsvai ain·tsel·be·ten

Can I pay by ...? — *Nehmen Sie ...?* — ney·men zee ...
- credit card — *Kreditkarten* — kre·deet·kar·ten
- travellers cheque — *Reiseschecks* — rai·ze·sheks

How much is it per ...? — *Wie viel kostet es pro ...?* — vee feel kos·tet es praw ...
- night — *Nacht* — nakht
- person — *Person* — per·zawn

I'd like to stay for (two) nights.
Ich möchte für (zwei) Nächte bleiben. — ikh meukh·te fewr (tsvai) nekh·te blai·ben

From (July 2) to (July 6).
Vom (zweiten Juli) bis zum (sechsten Juli). — vom (tsvai·ten yoo·li) bis tsum (zeks·ten yoo·li)

Can I see it?
Kann ich es sehen? — kan ikh es zey·en

Am I allowed to camp here?
Kann ich hier zelten? — kan ikh heer tsel·ten

Is there a camp site nearby?
Gibt es in der Nähe einen Zeltplatz? — gipt es in dair ney·e ai·nen tselt·plats

requests & queries

When/Where is breakfast served?
Wann/Wo gibt es Frühstück? — van/vaw gipt es frew·shtewk

Please wake me at (seven).
Bitte wecken Sie mich um (sieben) Uhr. — bi·te ve·ken zee mikh um (zee·ben) oor

Could I have my key, please?
Könnte ich bitte meinen Schlüssel haben? — keun·te ikh bi·te mai·nen shlew·sel haa·ben

Can I get another (blanket)?
Kann ich noch (eine Decke) bekommen? — kan ikh nokh (ai·ne de·ke) be·ko·men

64

Is there a/an ...?	Haben Sie ...?	haa·ben zee ...
elevator	einen Aufzug	ai·nen owf·tsook
safe	einen Safe	ai·nen sayf

The room is too ...	Es ist zu ...	es ist tsoo ...
expensive	teuer	toy·er
noisy	laut	lowt
small	klein	klain

The ... doesn't work.	... funktioniert nicht.	... fungk·tsyo·neert nikht
air conditioning	Die Klimaanlage	dee klee·ma·an·laa·ge
fan	Der Ventilator	dair ven·ti·laa·tor
toilet	Die Toilette	dee to·a·le·te

This ... isn't clean.	Dieses ... ist nicht sauber.	dee·zes ... ist nikht zow·ber
pillow	Kopfkissen	kopf·ki·sen
sheet	Bettlaken	bet·laa·ken
towel	Handtuch	hant·tookh

checking out

What time is checkout?
Wann muss ich auschecken?   van mus ikh ows·che·ken

Can I leave my luggage here?
Kann ich meine Taschen hier lassen?   kan ikh mai·ne ta·shen heer la·sen

Could I have my ..., please?	Könnte ich bitte ... haben?	keun·te ikh bi·te ... haa·ben
deposit	meine Anzahlung	mai·ne an·tsaa·lung
passport	meinen Pass	mai·nen pas
valuables	meine Wertsachen	mai·ne vert·za·khen

communications & banking

the internet

Where's the local Internet café?
Wo ist hier ein Internet-Café?   vaw ist heer ain in·ter·net·ka·fey

How much is it per hour?
Was kostet es pro Stunde?   vas kos·tet es praw shtun·de

I'd like to ...	Ich möchte ...	ikh *meukh*·te ...
check my email	meine E-Mails checken	*mai*·ne ee·mayls *che*·ken
get internet access	Internetzugang haben	*in*·ter·net·tsoo·gang *haa*·ben
use a printer	einen Drucker benutzen	*ai*·nen *dru*·ker be·*nu*·tsen
use a scanner	einen Scanner benutzen	*ai*·nen *ske*·ner be·*nu*·tsen

mobile/cell phone

I'd like a ...	Ich hätte gern ...	ikh *he*·te gern ...
mobile/cell phone for hire	ein Miethandy	ain *meet*·hen·di
SIM card for your network	eine SIM-Karte für Ihr Netz	*ai*·ne *zim*·kar·te fewr eer nets

What are the rates?
Wie hoch sind die Gebühren? vee hawkh zint dee ge·*bew*·ren

telephone

What's your phone number?
Wie ist Ihre Telefonnummer? vee ist *ee*·re te·le·*fawn*·nu·mer

The number is ...
Die Nummer ist ... dee *nu*·mer ist ...

Where's the nearest public phone?
Wo ist das nächste öffentliche Telefon? vaw ist das *neykhs*·te *eu*·fent·li·khe te·le·*fawn*

I'd like to buy a phonecard.
Ich möchte eine Telefonkarte kaufen. ikh *meukh*·te *ai*·ne te·le·*fawn*·kar·te *kow*·fen

I want to ...	Ich möchte ...	ikh *meukh*·te ...
call (Singapore)	(nach Singapur) telefonieren	(naakh *zing*·a·poor) te·le·fo·*nee*·ren
make a local call	ein Ortsgespräch machen	ain awrts·ge·*shpreykh* *ma*·khen
reverse the charges	ein R-Gespräch führen	ain *air*·ge·shpreykh *few*·ren

How much does ... cost?	*Wie viel kostet ...?*	vee feel *kos*·tet ...
a (three)-minute	*ein (drei)-minutiges*	ain *(drai)*·mi·noo·ti·ges
call	*Gespräch*	ge·*shpreykh*
each extra	*jede zusätzliche*	*yey*·de tsoo·*zeyts*·li·khe
minute	*Minute*	mi·*noo*·te

It's (one euro) per (minute).
(Ein Euro) für (eine Minute). (ain *oy*·ro) fewr (*ai*·ne mi·*noo*·te)

post office

I want to send a ...	*Ich möchte ... senden.*	ikh *meukh*·te ... *zen*·den
fax	*ein Fax*	ain faks
letter	*einen Brief*	*ai*·nen breef
parcel	*ein Paket*	ain pa·*keyt*
postcard	*eine Postkarte*	*ai*·ne *post*·kar·te

I want to buy a/an ...	*Ich möchte ... kaufen.*	ikh *meukh*·te ... *kow*·fen
envelope	*einen Umschlag*	*ai*·nen *um*·shlaak
stamp	*eine Briefmarke*	*ai*·ne *breef*·mar·ke

Please send it	*Bitte schicken Sie das*	*bi*·te *shi*·ken zee das
(to Australia) by ...	*(nach Australien) per ...*	(nakh ows·*traa*·li·en) per ...
airmail	*Luftpost*	*luft*·post
express mail	*Expresspost*	eks·*pres*·post
registered mail	*Einschreiben*	*ain*·shrai·ben
surface mail	*Landbeförderung*	*lant*·be·feur·de·rung

| Is there any mail for me? | *Ist Post für mich da?* | ist post fewr mikh da |

bank

Where's a/an ...?	*Wo ist ...?*	vaw ist ...
ATM	*der Geldautomat*	dair *gelt*·ow·to·maat
foreign exchange office	*die Geldwechselstube*	dee *gelt*·vek·sel·shtoo·be

I'd like to ...	Ich möchte ...	ikh meukh-te ...
Where can I ...?	Wo kann ich ...?	vaw kan ikh ...
arrange a transfer	einen Transfer tätigen	ai-nen trans-fer tay-ti-gen
cash a cheque	einen Scheck einlösen	ai-nen shek ain-leu-zen
change a travellers cheque	einen Reisescheck einlösen	ai-nen rai-ze-shek ain-leu-zen
change money	Geld umtauschen	gelt um-tow-shen
get a cash advance	eine Barauszahlung	ai-ne baar-ows-tsaa-lung
withdraw money	Geld abheben	gelt ap-hey-ben

What's the ...?	Wie ...?	vee ...
charge for that	hoch sind die Gebühren dafür	hawkh zint dee ge-bew-ren da-fewr
exchange rate	ist der Wechselkurs	ist dair vek-sel-kurs

It's ...	Das ...	das ...
(12) euros	kostet (zwölf) euro	kos-tet (zveulf) oy-ro
free	ist umsonst	ist um-zonst

What time does the bank open?
Wann macht die Bank auf?
van makht dee bangk owf

Has my money arrived yet?
Ist mein Geld schon angekommen?
ist main gelt shawn an-ge-ko-men

sightseeing

getting in

What time does it open/close?
Wann macht es auf/zu?
van makht es owf/tsoo

What's the admission charge?
Was kostet der Eintritt?
vas kos-tet dair ain-trit

Is there a discount for children/students?
Gibt es eine Ermäßigung für Kinder/Studenten?
gipt es ai-ne er-mey-si-gung fewr kin-der/shtu-den-ten

I'd like a ...	Ich hätte gern ...	ikh *he*·te gern ...
catalogue	einen Katalog	*ai*·nen ka·ta·*lawg*
guide	einen Reiseführer	*ai*·nen *rai*·ze·few·rer
local map	eine Karte von hier	*ai*·ne *kar*·te fon heer

I'd like to see ...	Ich möchte ... sehen.	ikh *meukh*·te ... *zey*·en
What's that?	Was ist das?	vas ist das
Can I take a photo?	Kann ich fotografieren?	kan ikh fo·to·gra·*fee*·ren

tours

When's the	Wann ist der/die	van ist dair/dee
next ...?	nächste ...? m/f	*neykhs*·te ...
day trip	Tagesausflug m	*taa*·ges·ows·flook
tour	Tour f	toor

Is ... included?	Ist ... inbegriffen?	ist ... *in*·be·gri·fen
accommodation	die Unterkunft	dee *un*·ter·kunft
the admission charge	der Eintritt	dair *ain*·trit
food	das Essen	das *e*·sen
transport	die Beförderung	dee be·*feur*·de·rung

How long is the tour?
Wie lange dauert die Führung?   vee *lang*·e *dow*·ert dee *few*·rung

What time should we be back?
Wann sollen wir zurück sein?   van *zo*·len veer tsu·*rewk* zain

sightseeing		
castle	Burg f	burk
cathedral	Dom m	dawm
church	Kirche f	*kir*·khe
main square	Hauptplatz m	*howpt*·plats
monastery	Kloster n	*klaws*·ter
monument	Denkmal n	*dengk*·maal
museum	Museum n	mu·*zey*·um
old city	Altstadt f	*alt*·stat
palace	Schloss n	shlos
ruins	Ruinen f pl	ru·*ee*·nen
stadium	Stadion n	*shtaa*·di·on
statues	Statuen f pl	*shtaa*·tu·e

shopping

enquiries

Where's a ...?	Wo ist ...?	vaw ist ...
bank	*die Bank*	dee bangk
bookshop	*die Buchhandlung*	dee *bookh*·hand·lung
camera shop	*das Fotogeschäft*	das fo·to·ge·*sheft*
department store	*das Warenhaus*	das *vaa*·ren·hows
grocery store	*der Lebensmittelladen*	dair *ley*·bens·mi·tel·laa·den
market	*der Markt*	dair markt
newsagency	*der Zeitungshändler*	dair *tsai*·tungks·hen·dler
supermarket	*der Supermarkt*	dair *zoo*·per·markt

Where can I buy (a padlock)?
Wo kann ich (ein Vorhängeschloss) kaufen?
vaw kan ikh (ain *fawr*·heng·e·shlos) *kow*·fen

I'm looking for ...
Ich suche nach ...
ikh *zoo*·khe nakh ...

Can I look at it?
Können Sie es mir zeigen?
keu·nen zee es meer *tsai*·gen

Do you have any others?
Haben Sie noch andere?
haa·ben zee nokh *an*·de·re

Does it have a guarantee?
Gibt es darauf Garantie?
gipt es da·*rowf* ga·ran·*tee*

Can I have it sent overseas?
Kann ich es ins Ausland verschicken lassen?
kan ikh es ins *ows*·lant fer·*shi*·ken *la*·sen

Can I have my ... repaired?
Kann ich mein ... reparieren lassen?
kan ikh main ... re·pa·*ree*·ren *la*·sen

It's faulty.
Es ist fehlerhaft.
es ist *fey*·ler·haft

I'd like …, please.	Ich möchte bitte …	ikh *meukh*·te *bi*·te …
a bag	eine Tüte	*ai*·ne *tew*·te
a refund	mein Geld	main gelt
	zurückhaben	tsu·*rewk*·haa·ben
to return this	dieses zurückgeben	*dee*·zes tsu·*rewk*·gey·ben

paying

How much is it?
Wie viel kostet das? — vee feel *kos*·tet das

Can you write down the price?
Können Sie den Preis aufschreiben? — *keu*·nen zee deyn prais *owf*·shrai·ben

That's too expensive.
Das ist zu teuer. — das ist tsoo *toy*·er

Can you lower the price?
Können Sie mit dem Preis *keu*·nen zee mit dem prais
heruntergehen? — he·*run*·ter·gey·en

I'll give you (five) euros.
Ich gebe Ihnen (fünf) euro. — ikh *gey*·be *ee*·nen (fewnf) *oy*·ro

There's a mistake in the bill.
Da ist ein Fehler in der Rechnung. — daa ist ain *fey*·ler in dair *rekh*·nung

Do you accept …?	Nehmen Sie …?	*ney*·men zee …
credit cards	Kreditkarten	kre·*deet*·kar·ten
debit cards	Debitkarten	*dey*·bit·kar·ten
travellers cheques	Reiseschecks	*rai*·ze·sheks

I'd like …, please.	Ich möchte bitte …	ikh *meukh*·te *bi*·te …
a receipt	eine Quittung	*ai*·ne *kvi*·tung
my change	mein Wechselgeld	main *vek*·sel·gelt

clothes & shoes

Can I try it on?	Kann ich es anprobieren?	kan ikh es *an*·pro·bee·ren
My size is (40).	Ich habe Größe (vierzig).	ikh *haa*·be *greu*·se (*feer*·tsikh)
It doesn't fit.	Es passt nicht.	es past nikht

small	klein	klain
medium	mittelgroß	*mi*·tel·graws
large	groß	graws

books & music

I'd like a ...
Ich hätte gern ... ıkh *he*·te gern ...
- **newspaper** — *eine Zeitung* — *ai*·ne *tsai*·tung
- **(in English)** — *(auf Englisch)* — (owf *eng*·lish)
- **pen** — *einen Kugelschreiber* — *ai*·nen *koo*·gel·shrai·ber

Is there an English-language bookshop?
Gibt es einen Buchladen — gipt es *ai*·nen *bookh*·laa·den
für englische Bücher? — fewr *eng*·li·she *bew*·kher

I'm looking for something by (Herman Hesse).
Ich suche nach etwas von — ikh *zoo*·khe nakh *et*·vas fon
(Herman Hesse). — (*her*·man *he*·se)

Can I listen to this?
Kann ich mir das anhören? — kan ikh meer das *an*·heu·ren

photography

Can you ...?
Können Sie ...? *keu*·nen zee ...
- **burn a CD from** — *eine CD von meiner* — *ai*·ne tse de von *mai*·ner
- **my memory card** — *Speicherkarte brennen* — *shpai*·kher·kar·te *bre*·nen
- **develop this film** — *diesen Film entwickeln* — *dee*·zen film ent·*vi*·keln
- **load my film** — *mir den Film einlegen* — meer deyn film *ain*·ley·gen

I need a ... film
for this camera.
Ich brauche einen — ikh *brow*·khe *ai*·nen
... für diese Kamera. — ... fewr *dee*·ze ka·me·ra
- **APS** — *APS-Film* — aa·pey·*es*·film
- **B&W** — *Schwarzweißfilm* — shvarts·*vais*·film
- **colour** — *Farbfilm* — *farp*·film
- **slide** — *Diafilm* — *dee*·a·film
- **(200) speed** — *(zweihundert)-* — (*tsvai*·hun·dert)·
  ASA-Film — *aa*·za·film

When will it be ready? — *Wann ist er fertig?* — van ist air *fer*·tikh

meeting people

greetings, goodbyes & introductions

Hello. (Austria)	*Servus.*	*zer*·vus
Hello. (Germany)	*Guten Tag.*	*goo*·ten taak
Hello. (Switzerland)	*Grüezi.*	*grew*·e·tsi
Hi.	*Hallo.*	*ha*·lo
Good night.	*Gute Nacht.*	*goo*·te nakht
Goodbye.	*Auf Wiedersehen.*	owf *vee*·der·zey·en
Bye.	*Tschüss/Tschau.*	chews/chow
See you later.	*Bis später.*	bis *shpey*·ter

Mr	*Herr*	her
Mrs	*Frau*	frow
Miss	*Fräulein*	*froy*·lain

How are you?	*Wie geht es Ihnen?*	vee geyt es *ee*·nen
Fine. And you?	*Danke, gut. Und Ihnen?*	*dang*·ke goot unt *ee*·nen
What's your name?	*Wie ist Ihr Name?*	vee ist eer *naa*·me
My name is …	*Mein Name ist …*	main *naa*·me ist …
I'm pleased to meet you.	*Angenehm.*	*an*·ge·neym

This is my …	*Das ist mein/meine …* m/f	das ist main/*mai*·ne …
brother	*Bruder*	*broo*·der
daughter	*Tochter*	*tokh*·ter
father	*Vater*	*faa*·ter
friend	*Freund/Freundin* m/f	froynt/*froyn*·din
husband	*Mann*	man
mother	*Mutter*	*mu*·ter
partner (intimate)	*Partner/Partnerin* m/f	*part*·ner/*part*·ne·rin
sister	*Schwester*	*shves*·ter
son	*Sohn*	zawn
wife	*Frau*	frow

Here's my …	*Hier ist meine …*	heer ist *mai*·ne …
What's your…?	*Wie ist Ihre …?*	vee ist *ee*·re …
address	*Adresse*	a·*dre*·se
email address	*E-mail-Adresse*	ee·mayl·a·*dre*·se
fax number	*Faxnummer*	*faks*·nu·mer
phone number	*Telefonnummer*	te·le·*fawn*·nu·mer

occupations

What's your occupation?	Als was arbeiten Sie? pol	als vas ar·bai·ten zee
	Als was arbeitest du? inf	als vas ar·bai·test doo
I'm a/an ...	Ich bin ein/eine ... m/f	ikh bin ain/ai·ne ...
artist	Künstler/Künstlerin m/f	kewnst·ler/kewnst·le·rin
business person	Geschäftsmann m	ge·shefts·man
	Geschäftsfrau f	ge·shefts·frow
farmer	Bauer/Bäuerin m/f	bow·er/boy·e·rin
manual worker	Arbeiter/Arbeiterin m/f	ar·bai·ter/ar·bai·te·rin
office worker	Büroangestellte m&f	bew·raw·an·ge·shtel·te
scientist	Wissenschaftler m	vi·sen·shaft·ler
	Wissenschaftlerin f	vi·sen·shaft·le·rin
student	Student/Studentin m/f	shtu·dent/shtu·den·tin

background

Where are you from?	Woher kommen Sie? pol	vaw·hair ko·men zee
	Woher kommst du? inf	vaw·hair komst doo
I'm from ...	Ich komme aus ...	ikh ko·me ows ...
Australia	Australien	ows·traa·li·en
Canada	Kanada	ka·na·daa
England	England	eng·lant
New Zealand	Neuseeland	noy·zey·lant
the USA	den USA	deyn oo·es·aa
Are you married?	Sind Sie verheiratet? pol	zint zee fer·hai·ra·tet
	Bist du verheiratet? inf	bist doo fer·hai·ra·tet
I'm married.	Ich bin verheiratet.	ikh bin fer·hai·ra·tet
I'm single.	Ich bin ledig.	ikh bin ley·dikh

age

How old ...?	Wie alt ...?	vee alt ...
are you	sind Sie pol	zint zee
	bist du inf	bist doo
is your daughter	ist Ihre Tochter pol	ist ee·re tokh·ter
is your son	ist Ihr Sohn pol	ist eer zawn
I'm ... years old.	Ich bin ... Jahre alt.	ikh bin ... yaa·re alt
He/She is ... years old.	Er/Sie ist ... Jahre alt.	air/zee ist ... yaa·re alt

feelings

I'm (not) ...	*Ich bin (nicht) ...*	ikh bin (nikht) ...
Are you ...?	*Sind Sie ...?* pol	zint zee ...
	Bist du ...? inf	bist doo ...
happy	*glücklich*	*glewk*·likh
sad	*traurig*	*trow*·rikh
I'm (not) ...	*Ich habe (kein) ...*	ikh *haa*·be (kain) ...
Are you ...?	*Haben Sie ...?* pol	*haa*·ben zee ...
	Hast du ...? inf	hast doo ...
hungry	*Hunger*	*hung*·er
thirsty	*Durst*	durst
I'm (not) ...	*Mir ist (nicht) ...*	meer ist (nikht) ...
Are you ...?	*Ist Ihnen/dir ...?* pol/inf	ist *ee*·nen/deer ...
cold	*kalt*	kalt
hot	*heiß*	hais

entertainment

going out

Where can I find ...?	*Wo sind die ...?*	vaw zint dee ...
clubs	*Klubs*	klups
gay venues	*Schwulen- und Lesbenkneipen*	*shvoo*·len unt *les*·ben·knai·pen
pubs	*Kneipen*	*knai*·pen
I feel like going to a/the ...	*Ich hätte Lust, ... zu gehen.*	ikh *he*·te lust ... tsoo *gey*·en
concert	*zum Konzert*	tsoom kon·*tsert*
movies	*ins Kino*	ins *kee*·no
party	*zu eine Party*	tsoo *ai*·ne *par*·ti
restaurant	*in ein Restaurant*	in ain res·to·*rang*
theatre	*ins Theater*	ins te·*aa*·ter

interests

Do you like ...?	Magst du ...? inf	maakst doo ...
I (don't) like ...	Ich mag (keine/ keinen) ... m/f	ikh maak (kai·ne/ kai·nen) ...
art	Kunst f	kunst
sport	Sport m	shport

I (don't) like ...	Ich ... (nicht) gern.	ikh ... (nikht) gern
cooking	koche	ko·khe
reading	lese	ley·ze
travelling	reise	rai·ze

Do you like to dance?
Tanzt du gern? inf — tantst doo gern

Do you like music?
Hörst du gern Musik? inf — heurst doo gern mu·zeek

food & drink

finding a place to eat

Can you recommend a ...?	Können Sie ... empfehlen?	keu·nen zee ... emp·fey·len
bar	eine Kneipe	ai·ne knai·pe
café	ein Café	ain ka·fey
restaurant	ein Restaurant	ain res·to·rang

I'd like ..., please.	Ich hätte gern ..., bitte.	ikh he·te gern ... bi·te
a table for (five)	einen Tisch für (fünf) Personen	ai·nen tish fewr (fewnf) per·zaw·nen
the (non)smoking section	einen (Nicht-) rauchertisch	ai·nen (nikht·) row·kher·tish

ordering food

breakfast	Frühstück n	frew·shtewk
lunch	Mittagessen n	mi·taak·e·sen
dinner	Abendessen n	aa·bent·e·sen
snack	Snack m	snek

What would you recommend?
Was empfehlen Sie?   vas emp·*fey*·len zee

I'd like (the) ..., please.   *Bitte bringen Sie ...*   *bi*·te *bring*·en zee ...
  bill   *die Rechnung*   dee *rekh*·nung
  drink list   *die Getränkekarte*   dee ge·*treng*·ke·kar·te
  menu   *die Speisekarte*   dee *shpai*·ze·kar·te
  that dish   *dieses Gericht*   *dee*·zes ge·*rikht*

drinks

(cup of) coffee ...	*(eine Tasse) Kaffee ...*	(*ai*·ne *ta*·se) *ka*·fey ...
(cup of) tea ...	*(eine Tasse) Tee ...*	(*ai*·ne *ta*·se) tey ...
with milk	*mit Milch*	mit milkh
without sugar	*ohne Zucker*	*aw*·ne *tsu*·ker
(orange) juice	*(Orangen)Saft* m	(o·*rang*·zhen·)zaft
mineral water	*Mineralwasser* n	mi·ne·*raal*·va·ser
soft drink	*Softdrink* m	*soft*·dringk
(boiled) water	*(heißes) Wasser* n	(*hai*·ses) *va*·ser

in the bar

I'll have ...	*Ich hätte gern ...*	ikh *he*·te gern ...
I'll buy you a drink.	*Ich gebe dir einen aus.* inf	ikh *gey*·be deer *ai*·nen ows
What would you like?	*Was möchtest du?* inf	vas *meukh*·test doo
Cheers!	*Prost!*	prawst
brandy	*Weinbrand* m	*vain*·brant
cognac	*Kognak* m	*ko*·nyak
cocktail	*Cocktail* m	*kok*·tayl
a shot of (whisky)	*einen (Whisky)*	*ai*·nen (*vis*·ki)
a bottle of ...	*eine Flasche ...*	*ai*·ne *fla*·she ...
a glass of ...	*ein Glas ...*	ain glaas ...
red wine	*Rotwein*	*rawt*·vain
sparkling wine	*Sekt*	zekt
white wine	*Weißwein*	*vais*·vain
a ... of beer	*... Bier*	... beer
bottle	*eine Flasche*	*ai*·ne *fla*·she
glass	*ein Glas*	ain glaas

What's the local speciality?
Was ist eine örtliche Spezialität? vas ist *ai*·ne *eurt*·li·khe shpe·tsya·li·*teyt*

What's that?
Was ist das? vas ist das

How much is (a kilo of cheese)?
Was kostet (ein Kilo Käse)? vas *kos*·tet (ain *kee*·lo *key*·ze)

I'd like ...	*Ich möchte ...*	ikh *meukh*·te ...
(100) grams	*(hundert) Gramm*	(*hun*·dert) gram
(two) kilos	*(zwei) Kilo*	(tsvai) *kee*·lo
(three) pieces	*(drei) Stück*	(drai) shtewk
(six) slices	*(sechs) Scheiben*	(zeks) *shai*·ben

Less.	*Weniger.*	*vey*·ni·ger
Enough.	*Genug.*	ge·*nook*
More.	*Mehr.*	mair

special diets & allergies

Is there a vegetarian restaurant near here?
Gibt es ein vegetarisches gipt es ain vege·*tar*·ish·shes
Restaurant hier in der Nähe? res·to·*rang* heer in dair *ney*·e

Do you have vegetarian food?
Haben Sie vegetarisches Essen? haa·ben zee ve·ge·*taa*·ri·shes *e*·sen

Could you prepare	*Können Sie ein Gericht*	keu·nen zee ain ge·*rikht*
a meal without ...?	*ohne ... zubereiten?*	*aw*·ne ... tsoo·be·rai·ten
butter	*Butter*	*bu*·ter
eggs	*Eiern*	*ai*·ern
meat stock	*Fleischbrühe*	*flaish*·brew·e

I'm allergic to ...	*Ich bin allergisch*	ikh bin a·*lair*·gish
	gegen ...	*gey*·gen ...
dairy produce	*Milchprodukte*	*milkh*·pro·duk·te
gluten	*Gluten*	*gloo*·ten
MSG	*Natrium-glutamat*	*naa*·tri·um·glu·ta·maat
nuts	*Nüsse*	*new*·se
seafood	*Meeresfrüchte*	*mair*·res·frewkh·te

menu decoder

Bayrisch Kraut n	*bai*-rish krowt	shredded cabbage cooked with sliced apples, wine & sugar
Berliner m	ber-*lee*-ner	jam doughnut
Cervelatwurst f	ser-ve-*laat*-vurst	spicy pork & beef sausage
Erdäpfelgulasch n	ert-ep-fel-*goo*-lash	spicy sausage & potato stew
gekochter Schinken m	ge-*kokh*-ter *shing*-ken	cooked ham
Graupensuppe f	*grow*-pen-zu-pe	barley soup
Greyerzer m	*grai*-er-tser	a smooth, rich cheese
Grießklößchensuppe f	grees-kleus-khen-zu-pe	soup with semolina dumplings
Gröstl n	greustl	grated fried potatoes with meat
Grünkohl mit Pinkel m	*grewn*-kawl mit *ping*-kel	cabbage with sausages
Holsteiner Schnitzel n	*hol*-shtai-ner *shni*-tsel	veal schnitzel with fried egg & seafood
Husarenfleisch n	hu-*zaa*-ren-flaish	braised beef, veal & pork fillets with sweet peppers, onions & sour cream
Hutzelbrot n	*hu*-tsel-brawt	bread made of prunes & other dried fruit
Kaiserschmarren m	*kai*-zer-shmar-ren	pancakes with raisins, fruit compote or chocolate sauce
Kaisersemmeln f pl	*kai*-zer-ze-meln	Austrian bread rolls
Katenwurst f	*kaa*-ten-vurst	country-style smoked sausage
Königinsuppe f	*keu*-ni-gin-zu-pe	creamy chicken soup
Königstorte f	*keu*-niks-tor-te	rum-flavoured fruit cake
Krautsalat m	*krowt*-za-laat	coleslaw
Leipziger Allerlei n	*laip*-tsi-ger *a*-ler-lai	mixed vegetable stew
Linzer Torte f	*lin*-tser *tor*-te	latticed tart with jam topping

Nudelauflauf m	noo-del-owf-lowf	pasta casserole
Obatzter m	uw-bats-ter	Bavarian soft cheese mousse
Ochsenschwanzsuppe f	ok-sen-shvants-zu-pe	oxtail soup
Palatschinken m	pa-lat-shing-ken	pancakes filled with jam or cheese
Rollmops m	rol-mops	pickled herring fillet rolled around chopped onions or gherkins
Sauerbraten m	zow-er-braa-ten	marinated roasted beef served with a sour cream sauce
Sauerkraut n	zow-er-krowt	pickled cabbage
Schafskäse m	shaafs-key-ze	sheep's milk feta
Schmorbraten m	shmawr-braa-ten	beef pot roast
Schnitzel n	shni-tsel	pork, veal or chicken breast rolled in breadcrumbs & fried
Strammer Max m	shtra-mer maks	ham, sausage or pork sandwich, served with fried eggs & onions
Streichkäse m	shtraikh-key-ze	any kind of soft cheese spread
Streuselkuchen m	shtroy-zel-koo-khen	coffee cake topped with cinnamon
Strudel m	shtroo-del	loaf-shaped pastry with a sweet or savoury filling
Tascherl n	ta-sherl	pastry with meat, cheese or jam
Voressen n	fawr-e-sen	meat stew
Weinkraut n	vain-krowt	white cabbage, braised with apples & simmered in wine
Wiener Schnitzel n	vee-ner shni-tsel	crumbed veal schnitzel
Wiener Würstchen n	vee-ner vewrst-khen	frankfurter (sausage)
Zwetschgendatschi m	tsvetsh-gen-dat-shi	damson plum tart
Zwiebelsuppe f	tsvee-bel-zu-pe	onion soup
Zwiebelwurst f	tsvee-bel-vurst	liver & onion sausage

emergencies

basics

Help!	Hilfe!	*hil*-fe
Stop!	Halt!	halt
Go away!	Gehen Sie weg!	*gey*-en zee vek
Thief!	Dieb!	deeb
Fire!	Feuer!	*foy*-er
Watch out!	Vorsicht!	for-*zikht*
Call ...!	Rufen Sie ...!	*roo*-fen zee ...
a doctor	einen Arzt	*ai*-nen artst
an ambulance	einen Krankenwagen	*ai*-nen *krang*-ken-vaa-gen
the police	die Polizei	dee po-li-*tsai*

It's an emergency!
Es ist ein Notfall!   es ist ain *nawt*-fal

Could you help me, please?
Könnten Sie mir bitte helfen?   *keun*-ten zee meer *bi*-te *hel*-fen

I have to use the telephone.
Ich muss das Telefon benutzen.   ikh mus das te-le-*fawn* be-*nu*-tsen

I'm lost.
Ich habe mich verirrt.   ikh *haa*-be mikh fer-*irt*

Where are the toilets?
Wo ist die Toilette?   vo ist dee to-a-*le*-te

police

Where's the police station?
Wo ist das Polizeirevier?   vaw ist das po-li-*tsai*-re-veer

I want to report an offence.
Ich möchte eine Straftat melden.   ikh *meukh*-te *ai*-ne *shtraaf*-taat *mel*-den

I have insurance.
Ich bin versichert.   ikh bin fer-*zi*-khert

I've been ...	Ich bin ... worden.	ikh bin ... *vor*-den
assaulted	angegriffen	*an*-ge-gri-fen
raped	vergewaltigt	fer-ge-*val*-tikht
robbed	bestohlen	be-*shtaw*-len

I've lost my ...	Ich habe ... verloren.	ikh haa·be ... fer·law·ren
My ... were stolen.	Man hat mir ... gestohlen.	man hat meer ... ge·shtaw·len
backpack	meinen Rucksack	mai·nen ruk·zak
bags	meine Reisetaschen	mai·ne rai·ze·ta·shen
credit card	meine Kreditkarte	mai·ne kre·deet·karte
handbag	meine Handtasche	mai·ne hant·ta·she
jewellery	meinen Schmuck	mai·nen shmuk
money	mein Geld	main gelt
passport	meinen Pass	mai·nen pas
travellers cheques	meine Reiseschecks	mai·ne rai·ze·sheks
wallet	meine Brieftasche	mai·ne breef·ta·she

I want to contact my ...	Ich mochte mich mit ... in Verbindung setzen.	ikh meukh·te mikh mit ... in fer·bin·dung ze·tsen
consulate	meinem Konsulat	mai·nem kon·zu·laat
embassy	meiner Botschaft	mai·ner bawt·shaft

health

medical needs

Where's the nearest ...? m/f/n	Wo ist der/die/das nächste ...? m/f/n	vaw ist dair/dee/das neykhs·te ...
dentist	Zahnarzt m	tsaan·artst
doctor	Arzt m	artst
hospital	Krankenhaus n	krang·ken·hows
(night) pharmacist	(Nacht)Apotheke f	(nakht·)a·po·tey·ke

I need a doctor (who speaks English).
Ich brauche einen Arzt
(der Englisch spricht).
ikh brow·khe ai·nen artst
(dair eng·lish shprikht)

Could I see a female doctor?
Könnte ich von einer
Ärztin behandelt werden?
keun·te ikh fon ai·ner
erts·tin be·han·delt ver·den

I've run out of my medication.
Ich habe keine
Medikamente mehr.
ikh haa·be kai·ne
me·di·ka·men·te mair

symptoms, conditions & allergies

| I'm sick. | Ich bin krank. | ikh bin krangk |
| It hurts here. | Es tut hier weh. | es toot heer *vey* |

I have (a) ...	Ich habe ...	ikh *haa*·be ...
asthma	Asthma	*ast*·ma
bronchitis	Bronchitis	bron·*khee*·tis
constipation	Verstopfung	fer·*shtop*·fung
cough	Husten	*hoos*·ten
diarrhoea	Durchfall	*durkh*·fal
fever	Fieber	*fee*·ber
headache	Kopfschmerzen	*kopf*·shmer·tsen
heart condition	Herzbeschwerden	*herts*·be·shver·den
nausea	Übelkeit	*ew*·bel·kait
pain	Schmerzen	*shmer*·tsen
sore throat	Halsschmerzen	*hals*·shmer·tsen
toothache	Zahnschmerzen	*tsaan*·shmer·tsen

I'm allergic to ...	Ich bin allergisch gegen ...	ikh bin a·*lair*·gish *gey*·gen ...
antibiotics	Antibiotika	an·ti·bi·*aw*·ti·ka
anti-inflammatories	entzündungs-hemmende Mittel	en·*tsewn*·dungks-he·men·de *mi*·tel
aspirin	Aspirin	as·pi·*reen*
bees	Bienen	*bee*·nen
codeine	Kodein	ko·de·*een*
penicillin	Penizillin	pe·ni·tsi·*leen*

antiseptic	Antiseptikum n	an·ti·*zep*·ti·kum
bandage	Verband m	fer·*bant*
condoms	Kondom n	kon·*dawm*
contraceptives	Verhütungsmittel n	fer·*hew*·tungks·mi·tel
diarrhoea medicine	Mittel gegen Durchfall n	*mi*·tel *gey*·gen *durkh*·fal
insect repellent	Insektenschutzmittel n	in·*zek*·ten·shuts·mi·tel
laxatives	Abführmittel n	*ap*·fewr·mi·tel
painkillers	Schmerzmittel n	*shmerts*·mi·tel
rehydration salts	Kochsalzlösung n	kokh·zalts·*leu*·zung
sleeping tablets	Schlaftabletten f pl	*shlaaf*·ta·ble·ten

english–german dictionary

German nouns in this dictionary have their gender indicated by ⓜ (masculine), ⓕ (feminine) or ⓝ (neuter). If it's a plural noun, you'll also see pl. Words are also marked as n (noun), a (adjective), v (verb), sg (singular), pl (plural), inf (informal) and pol (polite) where necessary.

A

accident *Unfall* ⓜ un-fal
accommodation *Unterkunft* ⓕ un-ter-kunft
adaptor *Adapter* ⓜ a-dap-ter
address *Adresse* ⓕ a-dre-se
after *nach* naakh
air-conditioned *mit Klimaanlage* ⓕ
  mit klee-ma-an-laa-ge
airplane *Flugzeug* ⓝ flook-tsoyk
airport *Flughafen* ⓜ flook-haa-fen
alcohol *Alkohol* ⓜ al-ko-hawl
all a *alle* a-le
allergy *Allergie* ⓕ a-lair-gee
ambulance *Krankenwagen* ⓜ krang-ken-vaa-gen
and *und* unt
ankle *Knöchel* ⓜ kneu-khel
arm *Arm* ⓜ arm
ashtray *Aschenbecher* ⓜ a-shen-be-kher
ATM *Geldautomat* ⓜ gelt-ow-to-maat
Austria *Österreich* ⓝ eus-ter-raikh

B

baby *Baby* ⓝ bay-bi
back (body) *Rücken* ⓜ rew-ken
backpack *Rucksack* ⓜ ruk-zak
bad *schlecht* shlekht
bag *Tasche* ⓕ ta-she
baggage claim *Gepäckausgabe* ⓕ ge-pek-ows-gaa-be
bank *Bank* ⓕ bangk
bar *Lokal* ⓝ lo-kaal
bathroom *Badezimmer* ⓝ baa-de-tsi-mer
battery *Batterie* ⓕ ba-te-ree
beautiful *schön* sheun
bed *Bett* ⓝ bet
beer *Bier* ⓝ beer
before *vor* fawr
behind *hinter* hin-ter
Belgium ⓝ *Belgien* bel-gi-en

bicycle *Fahrrad* ⓝ faar-raat
big *groß* graws
bill *Rechnung* ⓕ rekh-nung
black *schwarz* shvarts
blanket *Decke* ⓕ de-ke
blood group *Blutgruppe* ⓕ bloot-gru-pe
blue *blau* blow
book (make a reservation) v *buchen* boo-khen
bottle *Flasche* ⓕ fla-she
bottle opener *Flaschenöffner* ⓜ fla-shen-euf-ner
boy *Junge* ⓜ yung-e
brakes (car) *Bremsen* ⓕ pl brem-zen
breakfast *Frühstück* ⓝ frew-shtewk
broken (faulty) *kaputt* ka-put
bus *Bus* ⓜ bus
business *Geschäft* ⓝ ge-sheft
buy *kaufen* kow-fen

C

café *Café* ⓝ ka-fey
camera *Kamera* ⓕ ka-me-ra
camp site *Zeltplatz* ⓜ tselt-plats
cancel *stornieren* shtor-nee-ren
can opener *Dosenöffner* ⓜ daw-zen-euf-ner
car *Auto* ⓝ ow-to
cash *Bargeld* ⓝ baar-gelt
cash (a cheque) v *(einen Scheck) einlösen*
  (ai-nen shek) ain-leu-zen
cell phone *Handy* ⓝ hen-di
centre *Zentrum* ⓝ tsen-trum
change (money) v *wechseln* vek-seln
cheap *billig* bi-likh
check (bill) *Rechnung* ⓕ rekh-nung
check-in *Abfertigungsschalter* ⓜ
  ap-fer-ti-gungks-shal-ter
chest *Brustkorb* ⓜ brust-korp
child *Kind* ⓝ kint
cigarette *Zigarette* ⓕ tsi-ga-re-te
city *Stadt* ⓕ shtat
clean a *sauber* zow-ber

closed *geschlossen* ge-*shlo*-sen
coffee *Kaffee* ⓜ *ka*-fey
coins *Münzen* ⓕ pl *mewn*-tsen
cold a *kalt* kalt
collect call *R-Gespräch* ⓝ *air*-ge-shpreykh
come *kommen* *ko*-men
computer *Computer* ⓜ kom-*pyoo*-ter
condom *Kondom* ⓝ kon-*dawm*
contact lenses *Kontaktlinsen* ⓕ pl kon-*takt*-lin-zen
cook v *kochen* *ko*-khen
cost *Preis* ⓜ prais
credit card *Kreditkarte* ⓕ kre-*deet*-kar-te
cup *Tasse* ⓕ *ta*-se
currency exchange *Geldwechsel* ⓜ *gelt*-vek-sel
customs (immigration) *Zoll* ⓜ tsol

D

dangerous *gefährlich* ge-*fair*-likh
date (time) *Datum* ⓝ *daa*-tum
day *Tag* ⓜ taak
delay n *Verspätung* ⓕ fer-*shpey*-tung
dentist *Zahnarzt/Zahnärztin* ⓜ/ⓕ
   tsaan-artst/tsaan-*erts*-tin
depart *abfahren* *ap*-faa-ren
diaper *Windel* ⓕ *vin*-del
dictionary *Wörterbuch* ⓝ *veur*-ter-bookh
dinner *Abendessen* ⓝ *aa*-bent-e-sen
direct *direkt* di-*rekt*
dirty *schmutzig* *shmu*-tsikh
disabled *behindert* be-*hin*-dert
discount n *Rabatt* ⓜ ra-*bat*
doctor *Arzt/Ärztin* ⓜ/ⓕ artst/*erts*-tin
double bed *Doppelbett* ⓝ *do*-pel-bet
double room *Doppelzimmer mit einem Doppelbett* ⓝ
   do-pel-tsi-mer mit ai-nem *do*-pel-bet
drink *Getränk* ⓝ ge-*trengk*
drive v *fahren* *faa*-ren
drivers licence *Führerschein* ⓜ *few*-rer-shain
drugs (illicit) *Droge* ⓕ *draw*-ge
dummy (pacifier) *Schnuller* ⓜ *shnu*-ler

E

ear *Ohr* ⓝ awr
east *Osten* ⓜ *os*-ten
eat *essen* *e*-sen
economy class *Touristenklasse* ⓕ tu-*ris*-ten-kla-se
electricity *Elektrizität* ⓕ e-lek-tri-tsi-*teyt*
elevator *Lift* ⓜ lift

email *E-Mail* e-mayl
embassy *Botschaft* ⓕ *bawt*-shaft
emergency *Notfall* ⓜ *nawt*-fal
English (language) *Englisch* ⓝ *eng*-lish
entrance *Eingang* ⓜ *ain*-gang
evening *Abend* ⓜ *aa*-bent
exchange rate *Wechselkurs* ⓜ *vek*-sel-kurs
exit *Ausgang* ⓜ *ows*-gang
expensive *teuer* *toy*-er
express mail *Expresspost* ⓕ eks-*pres*-post
eye *Auge* ⓝ *ow*-ge

F

far *weit* vait
fast *schnell* shnel
father *Vater* ⓜ *faa*-ter
film (camera) *Film* ⓜ film
finger *Finger* ⓜ *fing*-er
first-aid kit *Verbandskasten* ⓜ fer-*bants*-kas-ten
first class *erste Klasse* ⓕ *ers*-te *kla*-se
fish *Fisch* ⓜ fish
food *Essen* ⓝ *e*-sen
foot *Fuß* ⓜ foos
fork *Gabel* ⓕ *gaa*-bel
free (of charge) *gratis* *graa*-tis
friend *Freund/Freundin* ⓜ/ⓕ froynt/*froyn*-din
fruit *Frucht* ⓕ frukht
full *voll* fol
funny *lustig* *lus*-tikh

G

German (language) *Deutsch* ⓝ doytsh
Germany *Deutschland* ⓝ *doytsh*-lant
gift *Geschenk* ⓝ ge-*shengk*
girl *Mädchen* ⓝ *meyt*-khen
glass (drinking) *Glas* ⓝ glaas
glasses *Brille* ⓕ *bri*-le
go *gehen* *gey*-en
good *gut* goot
green *grün* grewn
guide *Führer* ⓜ *few*-rer

H

half *Hälfte* ⓕ *helf*-te
hand *Hand* ⓕ hant
handbag *Handtasche* ⓕ *hant*-ta-she
happy *glücklich* *glewk*-likh

have *haben* haa-ben

he er air

head *Kopf* ⓜ kopf

heart *Herz* ⓝ herts

heat n *Hitze* ⓕ hi-tse

heavy *schwer* shvair

help v *helfen* hel-fen

here *hier* heer

high *hoch* hawkh

highway *Autobahn* ⓕ ow-to-baan

hike v *wandern* van-dern

holiday *Urlaub* ⓜ oor-lowp

homosexual *homosexuell* haw-mo-zek-su-el

hospital *Krankenhaus* ⓝ krang-ken-hows

hot *heiß* hais

hotel *Hotel* ⓝ ho-tel

hungry *hungrig* hung-rikh

husband *Ehemann* ⓜ ey-e-man

I

I *ich* ikh

identification (card) *Personalausweis* ⓜ
  per-zo-naal-ows-vais

ill *krank* krangk

important *wichtig* vikh-tikh

included *inbegriffen* in-be-gri-fen

injury *Verletzung* ⓕ fer-le-tsung

insurance *Versicherung* ⓕ fer-zi-khe-rung

Internet *Internet* ⓝ in-ter-net

interpreter *Dolmetscher/Dolmetscherin* ⓜ/ⓕ
  dol-met-sher/dol-met-she-rin

J

jewellery *Schmuck* ⓜ shmuk

job *Arbeitsstelle* ⓕ ar-baits-shte-le

K

key *Schlüssel* ⓜ shlew-sel

kilogram *Kilogramm* ⓝ kee-lo-gram

kitchen *Küche* ⓕ kew-khe

knife *Messer* ⓝ me-ser

L

laundry (place) *Waschküche* ⓕ vash-kew-khe

lawyer *Rechtsanwalt/Rechtsanwältin* ⓜ/ⓕ
  rekhts-an-valt/rekhts-an-vel-tin

left (direction) *links* lingks

left-luggage office *Gepäckaufbewahrung* ⓕ
  ge-pek-owf-be-vaa-rung

leg *Bein* ⓝ bain

lesbian *Lesbierin* ⓕ les-bi-e-rin

less *weniger* vey-ni-ger

letter (mail) *Brief* ⓜ breef

lift (elevator) *Lift* ⓜ lift

light *Licht* ⓝ likht

like v *mögen* meu-gen

lock *Schloss* ⓝ shlos

long *lang* lang

lost *verloren* fer-law-ren

lost-property office *Fundbüro* ⓝ funt-bew-raw

love v *lieben* lee-ben

luggage *Gepäck* ⓝ ge-pek

lunch *Mittagessen* ⓝ mi-taak-e-sen

M

mail *Post* ⓕ post

man *Mann* ⓜ man

map *Karte* ⓕ kar-te

market *Markt* ⓜ markt

matches *Streichhölzer* ⓝ pl shtraikh-heul-tser

meat *Fleisch* ⓝ flaish

medicine *Medizin* ⓕ me-di-tseen

menu *Speisekarte* ⓕ shpai-ze-kar-te

message *Mitteilung* ⓕ mi-tai-lung

milk *Milch* ⓕ milkh

minute *Minute* ⓕ mi-noo-te

mobile phone *Handy* ⓝ hen-di

money *Geld* ⓝ gelt

month *Monat* ⓜ maw-nat

morning *Morgen* ⓜ mor-gen

mother *Mutter* ⓕ mu-ter

motorcycle *Motorrad* ⓝ maw-tor-raat

motorway *Autobahn* ⓕ ow-to-baan

mouth *Mund* ⓜ munt

music *Musik* ⓕ mu-zeek

N

name *Name* ⓜ naa-me

napkin *Serviette* ⓕ zer-vye-te

nappy *Windel* ⓕ vin-del

near *nahe* naa-e

neck *Hals* ⓜ hals

new *neu* noy

news *Nachrichten* ⓕ pl naakh-rikh-ten

newspaper *Zeitung* ① *tsai*-tung
night *Nacht* ① nakht
no *nein* nain
noisy *laut* lowt
nonsmoking *Nichtraucher* nikht-row-kher
north *Norden* ⓜ nor-den
nose *Nase* ① *naa*-ze
now *jetzt* yetst
number *Zahl* ① tsaal

O

oil (engine) *Öl* ⓝ eul
old *alt* alt
one-way ticket *einfache Fahrkarte* ①
  ain-fa-khe faar-kar-te
open a *offen* o-fen
outside *draußen* drow-sen

P

package *Paket* ⓝ pa-keyt
paper *Papier* ⓝ pa-*peer*
park (car) v *parken* par-ken
passport *(Reise)Pass* ⓜ (rai-ze-)pas
pay *bezahlen* be-tsaa-len
pen *Kugelschreiber* ⓜ koo-gel-shrai-ber
petrol *Benzin* ⓝ ben-*tseen*
pharmacy *Apotheke* ① a-po-*tey*-ke
phonecard *Telefonkarte* ① te-le-*fawn*-kar-te
photo *Foto* ⓝ *faw*-to
plate *Teller* ⓜ te-ler
police *Polizei* ① po-li-*tsai*
postcard *Postkarte* ① post-kar-te
post office *Postamt* ⓝ post-amt
pregnant *schwanger* shvang-er
price *Preis* ⓜ prais

Q

quiet *ruhig* roo-ikh

R

rain n *Regen* ⓜ *rey*-gen
razor *Rasierer* ⓜ ra-*zee*-rer
receipt *Quittung* ① *kvi*-tung
red *rot* rawt
refund *Rückzahlung* ① rewk-tsaa-lung
registered mail *Einschreiben* ⓝ ain-shrai-ben

rent v *mieten* mee-ten
repair v *reparieren* re-pa-*ree*-ren
reservation *Reservierung* ① re-zer-*vee*-rung
restaurant *Restaurant* ⓝ res-to-*raang*
return v *zurückkommen* tsu-rewk-ko-men
return ticket *Rückfahrkarte* ① rewk-faar-kar-te
right (direction) *rechts* rekhts
road *Straße* ① *shtraa*-se
room *Zimmer* ⓝ tsi-mer

S

safe a *sicher* zi-kher
sanitary napkin *Damenbinden* ① pl *daa*-men-bin-den
seat *Platz* ⓜ plats
send *senden* zen-den
service station *Tankstelle* ① tangk-shte-le
sex *Sex* ⓜ seks
shampoo *Shampoo* ⓝ *sham*-poo
share (a dorm) *teilen (mit)* tai-len (mit)
shaving cream *Rasiercreme* ① ra-*zeer*-kreym
she *sie* zee
sheet (bed) *Bettlaken* ⓝ bet-laa-ken
shirt *Hemd* ⓝ hemt
shoes *Schuhe* ⓝ pl *shoo*-e
shop n *Geschäft* ⓝ ge-*sheft*
short *kurz* kurts
shower *Dusche* ① *doo*-she
single room *Einzelzimmer* ⓝ ain-tsel-tsi-mer
skin *Haut* ① howt
skirt *Rock* ⓜ rok
sleep v *schlafen* shlaa-fen
slowly *langsam* lang-zaam
small *klein* klain
smoke (cigarettes) v *rauchen* row-khen
soap *Seife* ① zai-fe
some *einige* ai-ni-ge
soon *bald* balt
south *Süden* ⓜ zew-den
souvenir shop *Souvenirladen* ⓜ zu-ve-*neer*-laa-den
speak *sprechen* shpre-khen
spoon *Löffel* ⓜ leu-fel
stamp *Briefmarke* ① breef-mar-ke
stand-by ticket *Standby-Ticket* ⓝ stend-*bai*-ti-ket
station (train) *Bahnhof* ⓜ baan-hawf
stomach *Magen* ⓜ maa-gen
stop v *anhalten* an-hal-ten
stop (bus) *Bushaltestelle* ① bus-hal-te-shte-le
street *Straße* ① *shtraa*-se

student *Student/Studentin* ⓜ / ⓕ
  shtu-*dent*/shtu-*den*-tin
sun *Sonne* ⓕ *zo*-ne
sunscreen *Sonnencreme* ⓕ *zo*-nen-kreym
swim v *schwimmen* *shvi*-men
Switzerland *Schweiz* ⓕ shvaits

T

tampons *Tampons* ⓜ pl *tam*-pons
taxi *Taxi* ⓝ *tak*-si
teaspoon *Teelöffel* ⓜ *tey*-leu-fel
teeth *Zähne* ⓝ pl *tsey*-ne
telephone *Telefon* ⓝ te-le-*fawn*
television *Fernseher* ⓜ *fern*-zey-er
temperature (weather) *Temperatur* ⓕ tem-pe-ra-*toor*
tent *Zelt* ⓝ tselt
that (one) *jene* *yey*-ne
they *sie* zee
thirsty *durstig* *durs*-tikh
this (one) *diese* *dee*-ze
throat *Kehle* ⓕ *key*-le
ticket (transport) *Fahrkarte* ⓕ *faar*-kar-te
ticket (sightseeing) *Eintrittskarte* ⓕ *ain*-trits-kar-te
time *Zeit* ⓕ tsait
tired *müde* *mew*-de
tissues *Papiertaschentücher* ⓝ pl
  pa-*peer*-ta-shen-tew-kher
today *heute* *hoy*-te
toilet *Toilette* ⓕ to-a-*le*-te
tomorrow *morgen* *mor*-gen
tonight *heute Abend* *hoy*-te *aa*-bent
toothbrush *Zahnbürste* ⓕ *tsaan*-bewrs-te
toothpaste *Zahnpasta* ⓕ *tsaan*-pas-ta
torch (flashlight) *Taschenlampe* ⓕ *ta*-shen-lam-pe
tour *Tour* ⓕ toor
tourist office *Fremdenverkehrsbüro* ⓝ
  frem-den-fer-*kairs*-bew-raw
towel *Handtuch* ⓝ *hant*-tookh
train *Zug* ⓜ tsook
translate *übersetzen* ew-ber-*ze*-tsen
travel agency *Reisebüro* ⓝ *rai*-ze-bew-raw
travellers cheque *Reisescheck* ⓜ *rai*-ze-shek
trousers *Hose* ⓕ *haw*-ze
twin beds *zwei Einzelbetten* ⓝ pl tsvai *ain*-tsel-be-ten
tyre *Reifen* ⓜ *rai*-fen

U

underwear *Unterwäsche* ⓕ *un*-ter-ve-she
urgent *dringend* *dring*-ent

V

vacant *frei* frai
vacation *Ferien* pl *fair*-i-en
vegetable *Gemüse* ⓝ ge-*mew*-ze
vegetarian a *vegetarisch* ve-ge-*taa*-rish
visa *Visum* ⓝ *vee*-zum

W

waiter *Kellner/Kellnerin* ⓜ / ⓕ *kel*-ner/*kel*-ne-rin
walk v *gehen* *gey*-en
wallet *Brieftasche* ⓕ *breef*-ta-she
warm a *warm* varm
wash (something) *waschen* *va*-shen
watch *Uhr* ⓕ oor
water *Wasser* ⓝ *va*-ser
we *wir* veer
weekend *Wochenende* ⓝ *vo*-khen-en-de
west *Westen* ⓜ *ves*-ten
wheelchair *Rollstuhl* ⓜ *rol*-shtool
when *wann* van
where *wo* vaw
white *weiß* vais
who *wer* vair
why *warum* va-*rum*
wife *Ehefrau* ⓕ *ey*-e-frow
window *Fenster* ⓝ *fens*-ter
wine *Wein* ⓜ vain
with *mit* mit
without *ohne* *aw*-ne
woman *Frau* ⓕ frow
write *schreiben* *shrai*-ben

Y

yellow *gelb* gelp
yes *ja* yaa
yesterday *gestern* *ges*-tern
you sg inf *du* doo
you sg pol *Sie* zee
you pl *Sie* zee

Hungarian

hungarian alphabet

A a	Á á	B b	C c	Cs cs	D d	Dz dz	Dzs dzs
o	a	bey	tsey	chey	dey	dzey	jey
E e	É é	F f	G g	Gy gy	H h	I i	Í í
e	ey	ef	gey	dyey	ha	i	ee
J j	K k	L l	Ly ly	M m	N n	Ny ny	O o
yey	ka	el	ey	em	en	en'	aw
Ó ó	Ö ö	Ő ő	P p	Q q	R r	S s	Sz sz
áw	eu	eü	pey	ku	er	esh	es
T t	Ty ty	U u	Ú ú	Ü ü	Ű ű	V v	W w
tey	tyey	u	ű	ew	ēw	vey	du-plo-vey
X x	Y y	Z z	Zs zs				
iks	ip·sil·awn	zey	zhey				

MAGYAR

hungarian

HUNGARIAN

magyar

introduction

Hungarian (*magyar mo*-dyor) is a unique language. Though distantly related to Finnish, it has no significant similarities to any other language in the world. If you have some background in European languages you'll be surprised at just how different Hungarian is. English actually has more in common with Russian and Sinhala (from Sri Lanka) than it does with Hungarian – even though words like *goulash*, *paprika* and *vampire* came to English from this language.

So how did such an unusual language end up in the heart of the European continent? The answer lies somewhere beyond the Ural mountains in western Siberia, where the nomadic ancestors of today's Hungarian speakers began a slow migration west about 2000 years ago. At some point in the journey the group began to split. One group turned towards Finland, while the other continued towards the Carpathian Basin, arriving in the late 9th century. Calling themselves Magyars (derived from the Finno-Ugric words for 'speak' and 'man') they cultivated and developed the occupied lands. By AD 1000 the Kingdom of Hungary was officially established. Along the way Hungarian acquired words from languages like Latin, Persian, Turkish and Bulgarian, yet overall changed remarkably little.

With more than 14.5 million speakers worldwide, Hungarian is nowadays the official language of Hungary and a minority language in the parts of Eastern Europe which belonged to the Austro-Hungarian Empire before World War I – Slovakia, Croatia, the northern Serbian province of Vojvodina and parts of Austria, Romania and the Ukraine.

Hungarian is a language rich in grammar and expression. These characteristics can be both alluring and intimidating. Word order in Hungarian is fairly free, and it has been argued that this stimulates creative or experimental thinking. Some believe that the flexibility of the tongue, combined with Hungary's linguistic isolation, has encouraged the culture's strong tradition of poetry and literature. For the same reason, however, the language is resistant to translation and much of the nation's literary heritage is still unavailable to English speakers. Another theory holds that Hungary's extraordinary number of great scientists is also attributable to the language's versatile nature. Still, Hungarian needn't be intimidating and you won't need to look very far to discover the beauty of the language. You may even find yourself unlocking the poet or scientist within!

pronunciation

The Hungarian language may seem daunting with its long words and many accent marks, but it's surprisingly easy to pronounce. Like English, Hungarian isn't always written the way it's pronounced, but just stick to the coloured phonetic guides that accompany each phrase or word and you can't go wrong.

vowel sounds

Hungarian vowels sounds are similar to those found in the English words listed in the table below. The symbol ˘ over a vowel, like ă, means you say it as a long vowel sound. The letter y is always pronounced as in 'yes'.

symbol	english equivalent	hungarian example	transliteration
a	father	*hátizsák*	*ha*·ti·zhak
aw	law (but short)	*kor*	kawr
e	bet	*zsebkés*	*zheb*·keysh
ee	see	*cím*	tseem
eu	her	*zöld*	zeuld
ew	ee pronounced with rounded lips	*csütörtök*	*chew*·teur·teuk
ey	hey	*én*	eyn
i	bit	*rizs*	rizh
o	pot	*gazda*	*goz*·do
oy	toy	*megfojt, komoly*	*meg*·foyt, *kaw*·moy
u	put	*utas*	*u*·tosh

word stress

Accent marks over vowels don't influence word stress, which always falls on the first syllable of the word. The stressed syllables in our coloured pronunciation guides are always in italics.

consonant sounds

Always pronounce y like the 'y' in 'yes'. We've also used the ' symbol to show this y sound when it's attached to n, d, and t and at the end of a syllable. You'll also see double consonants like bb, dd or tt – draw them out a little longer than you would in English.

symbol	english equivalent	hungarian example	transliteration
b	bed	bajusz	bo-yus
ch	cheat	család	cho-lad
d	dog	dervis	der-vish
dy	during	magyar	mo-dyor
f	fat	farok	fo-rawk
g	go	gallér, igen	gol-leyr, i-gen
h	hat	hát	hat
j	joke	dzsem, hogy	jem, hawj
k	kit	kacsa	ko-cho
l	lot	lakat	lo-kot
m	man	most	mawsht
n	not	nem	nem
p	pet	pamut	po-mut
r	run (rolled)	piros	pi-rawsh
s	sun	kolbász	kawl-bas
sh	shot	tojást	taw-yasht
t	top	tag	tog
ty	tutor	kártya	kar-tyo
ts	hats	koncert	kawn-tsert
v	very	vajon	vo-yawn
y	yes	hajó, melyik	ho-yāw, me-yik
z	zero	zab	zob
zh	pleasure	zsemle	zhem-le
'	a slight y sound	poggyász, hány	pawd'-dyas, han'

basics

language difficulties

Do you speak English?
Beszél/Beszélsz angolul? pol/inf   be·seyl/be·seyls on·gaw·lul

Do you understand?
Érti/Érted? pol/inf   eyr·ti/eyr·ted

I (don't) understand.
(Nem) Értem.   (nem) eyr·tem

What does (*lángos*) mean?
Mit jelent az, hogy (lángos)?   mit ye·lent oz hawj (lan·gawsh)

How do you ...?	*Hogyan ...?*	haw·dyon ...
pronounce this	*mondja ki ezt*	mawnd·yo ki ezt
write (*útlevél*)	*írja azt, hogy*	eer·yo ozt hawj
	(útlevél)	(üt·le·veyl)

Could you please ...?	*..., kérem.*	... key·rem
repeat that	*Megismételné ezt*	meg·ish·mey·tel·ney ezt
speak more	*Tudna lassabban*	tud·no losh·shob·bon
slowly	*beszélni*	be·seyl·ni
write it down	*Leírná*	le·eer·na

essentials

Yes.	*Igen.*	i·gen
No.	*Nem.*	nem
Please.	*Kérem/Kérlek.* pol/inf	key·rem/keyr·lek
Thank you	*(Nagyon)*	(no·dyawn)
(very much).	*Köszönöm.*	keu·seu·neum
You're welcome.	*Szívesen.*	see·ve·shen
Excuse me.	*Elnézést kérek.*	el·ney·zeysht key·rek
Sorry.	*Sajnálom.*	shoy·na·lawm

numbers

0	nulla	nul·lo	16	tizenhat	ti·zen·hot
1	egy	ej	17	tizenhét	ti·zen·heyt
2	kettő	ket·tëü	18	tizennyolc	ti·zen·nyawlts
3	három	ha·rawm	19	tizenkilenc	ti·zen·ki·lents
4	négy	neyj	20	húsz	hüs
5	öt	eut	21	huszonegy	hu·sawn·ej
6	hat	hot	22	huszonkettő	hu·sawn·ket·tëü
7	hét	heyt	30	harminc	hor·mints
8	nyolc	nyawlts	40	negyven	nej·ven
9	kilenc	ki·lents	50	ötven	eut·ven
10	tíz	teez	60	hatvan	hot·von
11	tizenegy	ti·zen·ej	70	hetven	het·ven
12	tizenkettő	ti·zen·ket·tëü	80	nyolcvan	nyawlts·von
13	tizenhárom	ti·zen·ha·rawm	90	kilencven	ki·lents·ven
14	tizennégy	ti·zen·neyj	100	száz	saz
15	tizenöt	ti·zen·eut	1000	ezer	e·zer

time & dates

What time is it?	Hány óra?	han' āw·ra
It's one o'clock.	(Egy) óra van.	(ej) āw·ra von
It's (10) o'clock.	(Tíz) óra van.	(teez) āw·ra von
Quarter past (10).	Negyed (tizenegy).	ne·dyed (ti·zen·ej)
Half past (10).	Fél (tizenegy).	feyl (ti·zen·ej)
Quarter to (11).	Háromnegyed (tizenegy).	ha·rawm·ne·dyed (ti·zen·ej)
At what time ...?	Hány órakor ...?	han' āw·ro·kawr ...
At ...	... kor.	... kawr
am (morning)	délelőtt	deyl·e·lëütt
pm (afternoon)	délután	deyl·u·tan
pm (evening)	este	esh·te
Monday	hétfő	heyt·fëü
Tuesday	kedd	kedd
Wednesday	szerda	ser·do
Thursday	csütörtök	chew·teur·teuk
Friday	péntek	peyn·tek
Saturday	szombat	sawm·bot
Sunday	vasárnap	vo·shar·nop

January	január	yo·nu·ar
February	február	feb·ru·ar
March	március	mar·tsi·ush
April	április	ap·ri·lish
May	május	ma·yush
June	június	yū·ni·ush
July	július	yū·li·ush
August	augusztus	o·u·gus·tush
September	szeptember	sep·tem·ber
October	október	awk·tāw·ber
November	november	naw·vem·ber
December	december	de·tsem·ber

What date is it today?

Hányadika van ma?	ha·nyo·di·ko von mo

It's (18 October).

(Október tizennyolcadika) van.	(awk·tāw·ber ti·zen·nyawl·tso·di·ko) von

| since (May) | (május) óta | (ma·yush) āw·to |
| until (June) | (június)ig | (yū·ni·ush)·ig |

yesterday	tegnap	teg·nop
last night	tegnap éjjel	hawl·nop ey·yel
today	ma	mo
tonight	ma este	mo esh·te
tomorrow	holnap	hawl·nop

last/next ...	a múlt/a jövő ...	o mült/o yeu·vēū ...
week	héten	hey·ten
month	hónapban	hāw·nop·bon
year	évben	eyv·ben

yesterday/tomorrow ...	tegnap/holnap ...	teg·nop/hawl·nop ...
morning	reggel	reg·gel
afternoon	délután	deyl·u·tan
evening	este	esh·te

weather

What's the weather like?	Milyen az idő?	mi·yen oz i·dēū
It's ...		
cloudy	Az idő felhős.	oz i·dēū fel·hēūsh
cold	Az idő hideg.	oz i·dēū hi·deg
hot	Az idő nagyon meleg.	oz i·dēū no·dyawn me·leg
raining	Esik az eső.	e·shik oz e·shēū
snowing	Esik a hó.	e·shik o hāw
sunny	Az idő napos.	oz i·dēū no·pawsh
warm	Az idő meleg.	oz i·dēū me·leg
windy	Az idő szeles.	oz i·dēū se·lesh
spring	tavasz	to·vos
summer	nyár	nyar
autumn	ősz	ēūs
winter	tél	teyl

border crossing

I'm ...	... vagyok.	... vo·dyawk
in transit	Átutazóban	at·u·to·zāw·bon
on business	Üzleti úton	ewz·le·ti ü·tawn
on holiday	Szabadságon	so·bod·sha·gawn
I'm here for ...	... vagyok itt.	... vo·dyawk itt
(10) days	(Tíz) napig	(teez) no·pig
(two) months	(Két) hónapig	(keyt) hāw·no·pig
(three) weeks	(Három) hétig	(ha·rawm) hey·tig

I'm going to (Szeged).
(Szeged)re megyek. — (se·ged)·re me·dyek

I'm staying at (the Gellért Hotel).
A (Gellért)ben fogok lakni. — o (gel·leyrt)·ben faw·gawk lok·ni

I have nothing to declare.
Nincs elvámolnivalóm. — ninch el·va·mawl·ni·vo·lāwm

I have something to declare.
Van valami elvámolnivalóm. — von vo·lo·mi el·va·mawl·ni·vo·lāwm

That's (not) mine.
Az (nem) az enyém. — oz (nem) oz e·nyeym

transport

tickets & luggage

Where can I buy a ticket?
Hol kapok jegyet? hawl *ko*·pawk *ye*·dyet

Do I need to book a seat?
Kell helyjegyet váltanom? kell *he*·ye·dyet *val*·ta·nawm

One ... ticket	*Egy ... jegy*	ej ... yej
to (Eger), please.	*(Eger)be.*	(*e*·ger)·be
one-way	*csak oda*	chok *aw*·do
return	*oda-vissza*	*aw*·do·*vis*·so

I'd like to ... my	*Szeretném ...*	*se*·ret·neym ...
ticket, please.	*a jegyemet.*	o *ye*·dye·met
cancel	*törölni*	*teu*·reul·ni
change	*megváltoztatni*	*meg*·val·tawz·tot·ni
collect	*átvenni*	*at*·ven·ni
confirm	*megerősíteni*	*meg*·e·rēū·shee·te·ni

I'd like a ... seat,	*... helyet*	... *he*·yet
please.	*szeretnék.*	*se*·ret·neyk
nonsmoking	*Nemdohányzó*	*nem*·daw·han'·zāw
smoking	*Dohányzó*	*daw*·han'·zāw

How much is it?
Mennyibe kerül? men'·nyi·be *ke*·rewl

Is there air conditioning?
Van légkondicionálás? von *leyg*·kawn·di·tsi·aw·na·lash

Is there a toilet?
Van vécé? von *vey*·tsey

How long does the trip take?
Mennyi ideig tart az út? men'·nyi *i*·de·ig tort oz ūt

Is it a direct route?
Ez közvetlen járat? ez *keuz*·vet·len *ya*·rot

My luggage has been ...	*A poggyászom ...*	o *pawd'*·dya·sawm ...
damaged	*megsérült*	*meg*·shey·rewlt
lost	*elveszett*	*el*·ve·sett

My luggage has been stolen.
Ellopták a poggyászomat.   *el*-lawp-tak o *pawd*'-dya-saw-mot

Where can I find a luggage locker?
Hol találok egy poggyász-   hawl *to*-la-lawk ej *pawd*'-dyas-
megőrző automatát?   meg-ëür-zëü *o*-u-taw-mo-tat

getting around

Where does flight (BA15) arrive?
Hova érkezik a (BA tizenötös)   *haw*-vo eyr-ke-zik a (bey o *ti*-zen-eu-teush)
számú járat?   *sa*-mü *ya*-rot

Where does flight (BA26) depart?
Honnan indul a (BA huszonhatos)   *hawn*-non *in*-dul a (bey o *hu*-sawn-ho-tawsh)
számú járat?   *sa*-mü *ya*-rot

Where's (the) ...?	*Hol van ...?*	hawl von ...
arrivals hall	*az érkezési csarnok*	oz *eyr*-ke-zey-shi *chor*-nawk
departures hall	*az indulási csarnok*	oz *in*-du-la-shi *chor*-nawk
duty-free shop	*a vámmentes üzlet*	o *vam*-men-tesh *ewz*-let
gate (five)	*az (ötös) kapu*	oz *(eu*-teush) *ko*-pu

Which ... goes	*Melyik ... megy*	*me*-yik ... mej
to (Budapest)?	*(Budapest)re?*	*(bu*-do-pesht)-re
boat	*hajó*	*ho*-yāw
bus	*busz*	bus
plane	*repülőgép*	*re*-pew-lēü-geyp
train	*vonat*	*vaw*-not

What time's the	*Mikor megy ... (busz)?*	*mi*-kawr mej ... (bus)
... (bus)?		
first	*az első*	oz *el*-shēü
last	*az utolsó*	oz *u*-tawl-shāw
next	*a következő*	o *keu*-vet-ke-zēü

At what time does it arrive/leave?
Mikor érkezik/indul?   *mi*-kawr eyr-kez-ik/*in*-dul

How long will it be delayed?
Mennyit késik?   men'-nyit *key*-shik

What station/stop is this?
Ez milyen állomás/megálló?   ez *mi*-yen *al*-law-mash/*meg*-al-lāw

What's the next station/stop?

    Mi a következő állomás/megálló?   mi o *keu*·vet·ke·zēū *al*·law·mash/*még*·āl·lāw

Does it stop at (Visegrád)?

    Megáll (Visegrád)on?   *meg*·all (*vi*·she·grad)·on

Please tell me when we get to (Eger).

    Kérem, szóljon, amikor   *key*·rem *sāwl*·yawn o·mi·kawr
    (Eger)be érünk.   (e·ger)·be ey·rewnk

How long do we stop here?

    Mennyi ideig állunk itt?   *men*·nyi *i*·de·ig *al*·lunk itt

Is this seat available?

    Szabad ez a hely?   *so*·bod ez o *he*·y

That's my seat.

    Az az én helyem.   oz oz eyn *he*·yem

I'd like a taxi ...	*Szeretnék egy taxit ...*	se·ret·neyk ej *tok*·sit ...
at (9am)	*(reggel kilenc)re*	(*reg*·gel *ki*·lents)·re
now	*most*	mawsht
tomorrow	*holnapra*	*hawl*·nop·ro

Is this taxi available?

    Szabad ez a taxi?   *so*·bod ez o *tok*·si

How much is it to ...?

    Mennyibe kerül ...ba?   *men*·nyi·be ke·rewl ...·bo

Please put the meter on.

    Kérem, kapcsolja be az órát.   *key*·rem *kop*·chawl·yo be oz *āw*·rat

Please take me to (this address).

    Kérem, vigyen el (erre a címre).   *kay*·rem *vi*·dyen el (*er*·re o *tseem*·re)

Please ...	*Kérem, ...*	*key*·rem ...
slow down	*lassítson*	*losh*·sheet·shawn
stop here	*álljon meg itt*	*all*·yawn meg itt
here	*várjon itt*	*var*·yawn itt

car, motorbike & bicycle hire

I'd like to hire a ...	*Szeretnék egy ... bérelni.*	se·ret·neyk ej ... *bey*·rel·ni
bicycle	*biciklit*	*bi*·tsik·lit
car	*autót*	*o*·u·tāwt
motorbike	*motort*	*maw*·tawrt

with a driver	sofőrrel	shaw·feūr·rel
with air conditioning	lég-kondicionálóval	leyg·kawn·di·tsi·aw·na·lāw·vol
with antifreeze	fagyállóval	fod'·al·lāw·vol
with snow chains	hólánccal	hāw·lant'·tsol

How much	Mennyibe kerül	men'·nyi·be ke·rewl
for ... hire?	a kölcsönzés ...?	o keul·cheun·zeysh ...
hourly	óránként	āw·ran·keynt
daily	egy napra	ej nop·ro
weekly	egy hétre	ej heyt·re

air	levegő	le·ve·gēū
oil	olaj	aw·lo·y
petrol	benzin	ben·zin
tyres	gumi	gu·mi

I need a mechanic.
Szükségem van egy sewk·shey·gem von ej
autószerelőre. o·u·tāw·se·re·lēū·re

I've run out of petrol.
Kifogyott a benzinem. ki·faw·dyawtt o ben·zi·nem

I have a flat tyre.
Defektem van. de·fek·tem von

directions

Where's the ...?	Hol van a ...?	hawl von o ...
bank	bank	bonk
city centre	városközpont	va·rawsh·keuz·pawnt
hotel	szálloda	sal·law·do
market	piac	pi·ots
police station	rendőrség	rend·ēūr·sheyg
post office	postahivatal	pawsh·to·hi·vo·tol
public toilet	nyilvános vécé	nyil·va·nawsh vey·tsey
tourist office	turistairoda	tu·rish·to·i·raw·do

Is this the road to (Sopron)?
Ez az út vezet (Sopron)ba? ez oz üt ve·zet (shawp·rawn)·bo

Can you show me (on the map)?
Meg tudja mutatni nekem meg tud'·yo mu·tot·ni ne·kem
(a térképen)? (o teyr·key·pen)

What's the address?
  Mi a cím? mi o tseem

How far is it?
  Milyen messze van? mi·yen mes·se von

How do I get there?
  Hogyan jutok oda? haw·dyon yu·tawk aw·do

Turn ...	*Forduljon ...*	fawr·dul·yawn ...
at the corner	*a saroknál*	o sho·rawk·nal
at the traffic	*a közlekedési*	o keuz·le·ke·dey·shi
lights	*lámpánál*	lam·pa·nal
left/right	*balra/jobbra*	bol·ro/yawbb·ro

It's ...	*... van.*	... von
behind ...	*... mögött*	... meu·geutt
far away	*Messze*	mes·se
here	*Itt*	itt
in front of ...	*... előtt*	... e·lëütt
left	*Balra*	bol·ro
near ...	*... közelében*	... keu·ze·ley·ben
next to ...	*... mellett*	... mel·lett
on the corner	*A sarkon*	o shor·kawn
opposite ...	*... val szemben*	...·vol sem·ben
right	*Jobbra*	yawbb·ro
straight ahead	*Egyenesen előttünk*	e·dye·ne·shen e·lëüt·tewnk
there	*Ott*	ott

by bus	*busszal*	bus·sol
by taxi	*taxival*	tok·si·vol
by train	*vonattal*	vaw·not·tol
on foot	*gyalog*	dyo·lawg

north	*észak*	ey·sok
south	*dél*	deyl
east	*kelet*	ke·let
west	*nyugat*	nyu·got

Bejárat/Kijárat	be·ya·rot/ki·ya·rot	Entrance/Exit
Nyitva/Zárva	nyit·vo/zar·vo	Open/Closed
Van Üres Szoba	von ew·resh saw·bo	Rooms Available
Minden Szoba Foglalt	min·den saw·bo fawg·lolt	No Vacancies
Információ	in·fawr·ma·tsi·āw	Information
Rendőrség	rend·ēūr·sheyg	Police Station
Tilos	ti·lawsh	Prohibited
Mosdó	mawsh·dāw	Toilets
Férfiak	feyr·fi·ok	Men
Nők	nēūk	Women
Meleg/Hideg	me·leg/hi·deg	Hot/Cold

accommodation

finding accommodation

Where's a ...?	Hol van egy ...?	hawl von ej ...
camping ground	kemping	kem·ping
guesthouse	panzió	pon·zi·āw
hotel	szálloda	sal·law·do
youth hostel	ifjúsági szálló	if·yū·sha·gi sal·lāw

Can you recommend	Tud ajánlani	tud o·yan·lo·ni
somewhere ...?	egy ... helyet?	ej ... he·yet
cheap	olcsó	awl·chāw
good	jó	yāw
nearby	közeli	keu·ze·li

I'd like to book a	Szeretnék egy	se·ret·neyk ej
room, please.	szobát foglalni.	saw·bat fawg·lol·ni
I have a reservation.	Van foglalásom.	von fawg·lo·la·shawm
My name's ...	A nevem ...	o ne·vem ...

Do you have	Van Önnek kiadó	von eun·nek ki·o·dāw
a ... room?	egy ... szobája?	ed' ... saw·ba·yo
single	egyágyas	ej·a·dyosh
double	duplaágyas	dup·lo·a·dyosh
twin	kétágyas	keyt·a·dyosh

How much is it per ...?	*Mennyibe kerül egy ...?*	men'·nyi·be ke·rewl ej ...
night	*éjszakára*	ey·so·ka·ro
person	*főre*	feū·re

Can I pay by ...?	*Fizethetek ...?*	fi·zet·he·tek ...
credit card	*hitelkártyával*	hi·tel·kar·tya·vol
travellers cheque	*utazási csekkel*	u·to·za·shi chek·kel

I'd like to stay for (three) nights.
(Három) éjszakára. (ha·rawm) ey·so·ka·ro

From (July 2) to (July 6).
(Július kettő)től (július hat)ig. (yū·li·ush ket·tēū)·tēūl (yū·li·ush hot)·ig

Can I see it?
Megnézhetem? meg·neyz·he·tem

Am I allowed to camp here?
Táborozhatok itt? ta·baw·rawz·ho·tawk itt

Where can I find the camping ground?
Hol találom a kempinget? hawl to·la·lawm o kem·pin·get

requests & queries

When/Where is breakfast served?
Mikor/Hol van a reggeli? mi·kawr/hawl von o reg·ge·li

Please wake me at (seven).
Kérem, ébresszen fel (hét)kor. key·rem eyb·res·sen fel (heyt)·kawr

Could I have my key, please?
Megkaphatnám a kulcsomat, kérem? meg·kop·hot·nam o kul·chaw·mot key·rem

Can I get another (blanket)?
Kaphatok egy másik (takaró)t? kop·ho·tawk ej ma·shik (to·ko·rāw)t

Is there a/an ...?	*Van Önöknél ...?*	von eu·neuk·neyl ...
elevator	*lift*	lift
safe	*széf*	seyf

The room is too ...	*Túl ...*	tūl ...
expensive	*drága*	dra·go
noisy	*zajos*	zo·yawsh
small	*kicsi*	ki·chi

The ... doesn't work.	A ... nem működik.	o ... nem *mēw*·keu·dik
air conditioning	*légkondicionáló*	*leyg*·kawn·di·tsi·aw·na·lāw
fan	*ventilátor*	*ven*·ti·la·tawr
toilet	*vécé*	*vey*·tsey

This ... isn't clean.	Ez a ... nem tiszta.	ez o ... nem *tis*·to
sheet	*lepedő*	*le*·pe·dēū
towel	*törülköző*	*teu*·rewl·keu·zēū

checking out

What time is checkout?
Mikor kell kijelentkezni? — *mi*·kawr kell *ki*·ye·lent·kez·ni

Can I leave my luggage here?
Itt hagyhatom a csomagjaimat? — itt *hoj*·ho·tawm o *chaw*·mog·yo·i·mot

Could I have my ..., please?	Visszakaphatnám ..., kérem?	vis·so·kop·hot·nam ... *key*·rem
deposit	*a letétemet*	o *le*·tey·te·met
passport	*az útlevelemet*	oz *üt*·le·ve·le·met
valuables	*az értékeimet*	oz *eyr*·tey·ke·i·met

communications & banking

the internet

Where's the local Internet café?
Hol van a legközelebbi internet kávézó? — hawl von o *leg*·keu·ze·leb·bi *in*·ter·net *ka*·vey·zāw

How much is it per hour?
Mennyibe kerül óránként? — *men'*·nyi·be *ke*·rewl *āw*·ran·keynt

I'd like to check my email.
Szeretném megnézni az e-mailjeimet. — se·ret·neym *meg*·neyz·ni oz *ee*·meyl·ye·i·met

I'd like to ...	Szeretnék ...	se·ret·neyk ...
get Internet access	*rámenni az internetre*	*ra*·men·ni oz *in*·ter·net·re
use a printer	*használni egy nyomtatót*	*hos*·nal·ni ej *nyawm*·to·tāwt
use a scanner	*használni egy szkennert*	*hos*·nal·ni ej *sken*·nert

I'd like a ...	Szeretnék egy ...	se·ret·neyk ej ...
mobile/cell phone	mobiltelefont	maw·bil·te·le·fawnt
for hire	bérelni	bey·rel·ni
SIM card	SIM-kártyát	sim·kar·tyat
for your network	ennek a hálózatnak	en·nek o ha·lāw·zot·nok
What are the rates?	Milyen díjak vannak?	mi·yen dee·yok von·nok

telephone

What's your phone number?
 Mi a telefonszáma/   mi o te·le·fawn·sa·ma/
 telefonszámod? **pol/inf**   te·le·fawn·sa·mawd

The number is ...
 A szám ...   o sam ...

Where's the nearest public phone?
 Hol a legközelebbi   hawl o leg·keu·ze·leb·bi
 nyilvános telefon?   nyil·va·nawsh te·le·fawn

I'd like to buy a phonecard.
 Szeretnék telefonkártyát venni.   se·ret·neyk te·le·fawn·kar·tyat ven·ni

I want to make a reverse-charge call.
 'R' beszélgetést szeretnék kérni.   er·be·seyl·ge·teysht se·ret·neyk keyr·ni

I want to ...	Szeretnék ...	se·ret·neyk ...
call (Singapore)	(Szingapúr)ba	(sin·go·pür)·bo
	telefonálni	te·le·faw·nal·ni
make a local call	helyi telefon-	he·yi te·le·fawn-
	beszélgetést	be·seyl·ge·teysht
	folytatni	faw·y·tot·ni

How much	Mennyibe	men'·nyi·be
does ... cost?	kerül ...?	ke·rewl ...
a (three)-minute	egy (három)perces	ej (ha·rawm)·per·tsesh
call	beszélgetés	be·seyl·ge·teysh
each extra minute	minden további perc	min·den taw·vab·bi perts

(30) forints per (30) seconds.
 (Harminc) másodpercenként   (hor·mints) ma·shawd·per·tsen·keynt
 (harminc) forint.   (hor·mints) faw·rint

post office

I want to send a ...	... szeretnék küldeni.	... se·ret·neyk kewl·de·ni
fax	Faxot	fok·sawt
letter	Levelet	le·ve·let
parcel	Csomagot	chaw·mo·gawt
postcard	Képeslapot	key·pesh·lo·pawt

I want to buy a/an...	... szeretnék venni.	... se·ret·neyk ven·ni
envelope	Borítékot	baw·ree·tey·kawt
stamp	Bélyeget	bey·ye·get

Please send it to (Australia) by ...	Kérem, küldje ... (Ausztráliá)ba.	key·rem kewld·ye ... (o·ust·ra·li·a)·bo
airmail	légipostán	ley·gi·pawsh·tan
express mail	expresszel	eks·press·zel
registered mail	ajánlottan	o·yan·law·tton
surface mail	simán	shi·man

Is there any mail for me?	Van levelem?	von le·ve·lem

bank

Where's a/an ...?	Hol van egy ...?	hawl von ej ...
ATM	bankautomata	bonk·o·u·taw·mo·to
foreign exchange office	valutaváltó	vo·lu·to·val·tāw
	ügynökség	ewj·neuk·sheyg

I'd like to ...	Szeretnék ...	se·ret·neyk ...
Where can I ...?	Hol tudok ...?	hawl tu·dawk ...
arrange a transfer	pénzt átutalni	peynzt at·u·tol·ni
cash a cheque	beváltani egy csekket	be·val·to·ni ej chek·ket
change a travellers cheque	beváltani egy utazási csekket	be·val·to·ni ej u·to·za·shi chek·ket
change money	pénzt váltani	peynzt val·to·ni
get a cash advance	készpénzelőleget felvenni	keys·peynz·e·leū·le·get fel·ven·ni
withdraw money	pénzt kivenni	peynzt ki·ven·ni

What's the ...?	*Mennyi ...?*	*men'·nyi ...*
charge for that	*a díj*	*o dee·y*
exchange rate	*a valutaárfolyam*	*o vo·lu·to·ar·faw·yom*

It's (100) euros.	*(Száz) euró.*	*(saz) e·u·raw*
It's (500) forints.	*(Ötszáz) forint.*	*(eut·saz) faw·rint*
It's free.	*Ingyen van.*	*in·dyen von*

What time does the bank open?
Mikor nyit a bank? — *mi·kawr nyit o bonk*

Has my money arrived yet?
Megérkezett már a pénzem? — *meg·eyr·ke·zett mar o peyn·zem*

sightseeing

getting in

What time does it open/close?
Mikor nyit/zár? — *mi·kawr nyit/zar*

What's the admission charge?
Mennyibe kerül a belépőjegy? — *men'·nyi·be ke·rewl o be·ley·pēū·yej*

Is there a discount for students/children?
Van kedvezmény diákok/ gyerekek számára? — *von ked·vez·meyn' di·a·kawk/ dye·re·kek sa·ma·ro*

I'd like a ...	*Szeretnék egy ...*	*se·ret·neyk ej ...*
catalogue	*katalógust*	*ko·to·lāw·gusht*
guide	*idegenvezetőt*	*i·de·gen·ve·ze·tēūt*
local map	*itteni térképet*	*it·te·ni teyr·key·pet*

I'd like to see ...	*Szeretnék látni ...*	*se·ret·neyk lat·ni ...*
What's that?	*Az mi?*	*oz mi*
Can I take a photo?	*Fényképezhetek?*	*feyn'·key·pez·he·tek*

tours

When's the next ...?	*Mikor van a következő ...?*	*mi·kawr von o keu·vet·ke·zēū ...*
day trip	*egynapos kirándulás*	*ej·no·pawsh ki·ran·du·lash*
tour	*túra*	*tü·ro*

sightseeing

castle	vár	var
cathedral	székesegyház	sey-kesh-ej-haz
church	templom	temp-lawm
main square	fő tér	feū ter
monastery	kolostor	kaw-lawsh-tawr
monument	emlékmű	em-leyk-mēw
museum	múzeum	mū-ze-um
old city	óváros	āw-va-rawsh
palace	palota	po-law-to
ruins	romok	raw-mawk
stadium	stadion	shto-di-awn
statues	szobrok	saw-brawk

Is ... included?	Benne van az árban ...?	ben-ne von oz ar-bon ...
accommodation	a szállás	o sal-lash
the admission charge	a belépőjegy	o be-ley-pēū-yej
food	az ennivaló	oz en-ni-vo-lāw
transport	a közlekedés	o keuz-le-ke-deysh

How long is the tour?
Mennyi ideig tart a túra?   men'-nyi i-de-ig tort o tū-ra

What time should we be back?
Mikorra érünk vissza?   mi-kawr-ro ey-rewnk vis-so

shopping

enquiries

Where's a ...?	Hol van egy ...?	hawl von ej ...
bank	bank	bonk
bookshop	könyvesbolt	keun'-vesh-bawlt
camera shop	fényképezőgép-bolt	feyn'-key-pe-zēū-geyp-bawlt
department store	áruház	a-ru-haz
grocery store	élelmiszerbolt	ey-lel-mi-ser-bawlt
market	piac	pi-ots
newsagency	újságárus	ū-y-shag-a-rush
supermarket	élelmiszeráruház	ey-lel-mi-ser-a-ru-haz

Where can I buy (a padlock)?
Hol tudok venni (egy lakatot)?   hawl tu·dawk ven·ni (ej lo·ko·tawt)

I'm looking for …
Keresem a …   ke·re·shem o …

Can I look at it?
Megnézhetem?   meg·neyz·he·tem

Do you have any others?
Van másmilyen is?   von mash·mi·yen ish

Does it have a guarantee?
Van rajta garancia?   von ro·y·to go·ron·tsi·o

Can I have it sent overseas?
El lehet küldetni külföldre?   el le·het kewl·det·ni kewl·feuld·re

Can I have my … repaired?
Megjavíttathatnám itt …?   meg·yo·veet·tot·hot·nam itt …

It's faulty.
Hibás.   hi·bash

I'd like …, please.	*…, kérem.*	… key·rem
a bag	*Kaphatnék egy zacskót*	kop·hot·neyk ej zoch·kāwt
a refund	*Vissza szeretném*	vis·so se·ret·neym
	kapni a pénzemet	kop·ni o peyn·ze·met
to return this	*Szeretném*	se·ret·neym
	visszaadni ezt	vis·so·od·ni ezt

paying

How much is it?
Mennyibe kerül?   men'·nyi·be ke·rewl

Could you write down the price?
Le tudná írni az árat?   le tud·na eer·ni oz a·rot

That's too expensive.
Ez túl drága.   ez tül dra·go

Do you have something cheaper?
Van valami olcsóbb?   von vo·lo·mi awl·chāwbb

I'll give you (500 forints).
Adok Önnek (ötszáz forintot).   o·dawk eun·nek (eut·saz faw·rin·tawt)

There's a mistake in the bill.
Valami nem stimmel a számlával.   vo·lo·mi nem shtim·mel o sam·la·vol

Do you accept ...?	Elfogadnak ...?	el·faw·god·nok ...
credit cards	hitelkártyát	hi·tel·kar·tyat
debit cards	bankkártyát	bonk·kar·tyat
travellers cheques	utazási csekket	u·to·za·shi chek·ket

I'd like ..., please.	..., kérem.	... key·rem
a receipt	Kaphatnék egy nyugtát	kop·hot·neyk ej nyug·tat
my change	Szeretném megkapni	se·ret·neym meg·kop·ni
	a visszajáró pénzt	o vís·so·ya·ráw peynzt

clothes & shoes

Can I try it on?	Felpróbálhatom?	fel·práw·bal·ho·tawm
My size is (40).	A méretem	o mey·re·tem
	(negyvenes).	(nej·ve·nesh)
It doesn't fit.	Nem jó.	nem yáw

small	kicsi	ki·chi
medium	közepes	keu·ze·pesh
large	nagy	noj

books & music

I'd like a ...	Szeretnék egy ...	se·ret·neyk ej ...
newspaper	(angol)	(on·gawl)
(in English)	újságot	úy·sha·gawt
pen	tollat	tawl·lot

Is there an English-language bookshop?

Van valahol egy angol von vo·lo·hawl ej on·gawl
nyelvű könyvesbolt? nyel·véw keun'·vesh·bawlt

I'm looking for something by (Zsuzsa Koncz).

(Koncz Zsuzsá)tól (konts zhu·zha)·táwl
keresek valamit. ke·re·shek vo·lo·mit

Can I listen to this?

Meghallgathatom ezt? meg·holl·got·ho·tawm ezt

photography

Can you transfer photos from my camera to CD?
Át tudják vinni a képeket   at *tud*·yak *vin*·ni o *key*·pe·ket
a fényképezőgépemről CD-re?   o *feyn'*·key·pe·zēū·gey·pem·rēūl *tsey*·dey·re

Can you develop this film?
Elő tudják hívni ezt a filmet?   e·lēū *tud*·yak *heev*·ni ezt o *fil*·met

Can you load my film?
Bele tudják tenni a filmet   be·le *tud*·yak *ten*·ni o *fil*·met
a gépembe?   o *gey*·pem·be

I need a ... film for this camera.	... filmet szeretnék.	... fil·met se·ret·neyk
B&W	Fekete-fehér	fe·ke·te·fe·heyr
colour	Színes	see·nesh
slide	Dia	di·o
(200) speed	(Kétszáz)as fényérzékenységű	(keyt·saz)·osh feyn'·eyr·zey·ken'·shey·gēw

When will it be ready?   *Mikor lesz kész?*   *mi*·kawr les keys

meeting people

greetings, goodbyes & introductions

Hello.	Szervusz/Szervusztok. sg/pl	ser·vus/ser·vus·tawk
Hi.	Szia/Sziasztok. sg/pl	si·o/si·os·tawk
Good night.	Jó éjszakát.	yāw ey·y·so·kat
Goodbye.	Viszlát.	vis·lat
Bye.	Szia/Sziasztok. sg/pl	si·o/si·os·tawk

Mr	Úr	ūr
Mrs	Asszony	os·sawn'
Miss	Kisasszony	kish·os·sawn'

How are you?	Hogy van/vagy? pol/inf	hawj von/voj
Fine. And you?	Jól. És Ön/te? pol/inf	yāwl eysh eun/te
What's your name?	Mi a neve/neved? pol/inf	mi o ne·ve/ne·ved
My name is ...	A nevem ...	o ne·vem ...
I'm pleased to meet you.	Örvendek.	eur·ven·dek

This is my …	Ez …	ez …
boyfriend	a barátom	o bo·ra·tawm
brother (older)	a bátyám	o ba·tyam
brother (younger)	az öcsém	oz eu·cheym
daughter	a lányom	o la·nyawm
father	az apám	oz o·pam
friend	a barátom/barátnőm m/f	o bo·ra·tawm/bo·rat·nēūm
girlfriend	a barátnőm	o bo·rat·nēūm
husband	a férjem	o feyr·yem
mother	az anyám	oz o·nyam
partner (intimate)	a barátom/barátnőm m/f	o bo·ra·tawm/bo·rat·nēūm
sister (older)	a nővérem	o nēū·vey·rem
sister (younger)	a húgom	o hū·gawm
son	a fiam	o fi·om
wife	a feleségem	o fe·le·shey·gem

Here's my …	Itt van …	itt von …
address	a címem	o tsee·mem
email address	az e-mail címem	oz ee·meyl tsee·mem
fax number	a faxszámom	o foks·sa·mawm
phone number	a telefonszámom	o te·le·fawn·sa·mawm

What's your …?	Mi …?	mi …
address	a címe	o tsee·me
email address	az e-mail címe	oz ee·meyl tsee·me
fax number	a faxszáma	o foks·sa·ma
phone number	a telefonszáma	o te·le·fawn·sa·ma

occupations

What's your occupation?	Mi a foglalkozása/ foglalkozásod? pol/inf	mi o fawg·lol·kaw·za·sho/ fawg·lol·kaw·za·shawd
I'm a/an …	… vagyok.	… vo·dyawk
artist	Művész	mēw·veys
businessperson	Üzletember m	ewz·let·em·ber
	Üzletasszony f	ewz·let·os·sawn'
farmer	Gazda	goz·do
office worker	Irodai dolgozó	i·raw·do·i dawl·gaw·zāw
scientist	Természettudós	ter·mey·set·tu·dāwsh
student	Diák	di·ak
tradesperson	Kereskedő	ke·resh·ke·dēū

background

Where are you from?	Ön honnan jön? pol	eun *hawn*·non yeun
	Te honnan jössz? inf	te *hawn*·non yeuss
I'm from ...	Én ... jövök.	eyn ... *yeu*·veuk
Australia	Ausztráliából	o·ust·ra·li·a·bāwl
Canada	Kanadából	ko·no·da·bāwl
England	Angliából	ong·li·a·bāwl
New Zealand	Új-Zélandból	ū·y·zey·lond·bāwl
the USA	USAból	u·sho·bāwl
Are you married? m	Nős?	nēush
Are you married? f	Férjnél van?	*feyr*·y·neyl von
I'm ...	... vagyok.	... *vo*·dyawk
married	Nős/Férjnél m/f	nēush/*feyr*·y·neyl
single	Egyedülálló	e·dye·dewl·al·lāw

age

How old are you?	Hány éves? pol	han' *ey*·vesh
	Hány éves vagy? inf	han' *ey*·vesh voj
How old are your children?	Hány évesek a gyerekei/gyerekeid? pol/inf	han' *ey*·ve·shek o dye·re·ke·i/*dye*·re·ke·id
I'm ... years old.	... éves vagyok.	... *ey*·vesh *vo*·dyawk
He/She is ... years old.	... éves.	... *ey*·vesh

feelings

Are you ...?	... vagy?	... voj
happy	Boldog	bawl·dawg
hungry	Éhes	ey·hesh
sad	Szomorú	saw·maw·rū
thirsty	Szomjas	sawm·yosh
I'm ...	... vagyok.	... *vo*·dyawk
I'm not ...	Nem vagyok ...	nem *vo*·dyawk ...
happy	boldog	bawl·dawg
hungry	éhes	ey·hesh
sad	szomorú	saw·maw·rū
thirsty	szomjas	sawm·yosh

Are you cold?	Fázik/Fázol? pol/inf	fa·zik/fa·zawl
I'm (not) cold.	(Nem) Fázom.	(nem) fa·zawm
Are you hot?	Melege/Meleged van? pol/inf	me·le·ge/me·le·ged von
I'm hot.	Melegem van.	me·le·gem von
I'm not hot.	Nincs melegem.	ninch me·le·gem

entertainment

going out

Where can I find ...?	Hol találok ...?	hawl to·la·lawk ...
clubs	klubokat	klu·baw·kot
gay venues	meleg	me·leg
	szórakozóhelyeket	sáw·ro·kaw·záw·he·ye·ket
pubs	pubokat	po·baw·kot

I feel like going	Szeretnék	se·ret·neyk
to a/the ...	elmenni egy ...	el·men·ni ej ...
concert	koncertre	kawn·tsert·re
movies	moziba	maw·zi·bo
party	partira	por·ti·ro
restaurant	étterembe	eyt·te·rem·be
theatre	színházba	seen·haz·bo

interests

Do you like ...?	Szereted ...?	se·re·ted ...
I (don't) like ...	(Nem) Szeretem ...	(nem) se·re·tem ...
art	a művészetet	o mēw·vey·se·tet
movies	a filmeket	o fil·me·ket
sport	a sportot	o shpawr·tawt

Do you like ...?	Szeretsz ...?	se·rets ...
I (don't) like ...	(Nem) Szeretek ...	(nem) se·re·tek ...
cooking	főzni	fēūz·ni
nightclubs	diszkóba járni	dis·káw·bo yar·ni
reading	olvasni	awl·vosh·ni
shopping	vásárolni	va·sha·rawl·ni
travelling	utazni	u·toz·ni

dance	*Táncolsz?*	*taan-tsawls*
go to concerts	*Jársz koncertre?*	*yars kawn-tsert-re*
listen to music	*Hallgatsz zenét?*	*holl-gots ze-neyt*

food & drink

finding a place to eat

Can you recommend	*Tud/Tudsz ajánlani*	tud/tuds *o-yan-lo-ni*
a ...?	*egy ...?* pol/inf	ej ...
bar	*bárt*	bart
café	*kávézót*	*ka-vey-zāwt*
restaurant	*éttermet*	*eyt-ter-met*
I'd like ...	*Szeretnék ...*	*se-ret-neyk ...*
a table for (five)	*egy asztalt (öt)*	ej *os-tolt* (eut)
	személyre	*se-mey-re*

ordering food

breakfast	*reggeli*	*reg-ge-li*
lunch	*ebéd*	*e-beyd*
dinner	*vacsora*	*vo-chaw-ro*
snack	*snack*	snekk
today's special	*napi ajánlat*	*no-pi oy-an-lot*

How long is the wait?
Mennyi ideig kell várni?   *men'-nyi i-de-ig kell vaar-ni*

What would you recommend?
Mit ajánlana?   *mit o-yan-lo-no*

I'd like (the) ...	*... szeretném.*	*... se-ret-neym*
bill	*A számlát*	o *sam-lat*
drink list	*Az itallapot*	oz *i-tol-lo-pawt*
menu	*Az étlapot*	oz *eyt-lo-pawt*
that dish	*Azt az ételt*	ozt oz *ey-telt*

drinks

(cup of) coffee ...	(csésze) kávé ...	(chey·se) ka·vey ...
(cup of) tea ...	(csésze) tea ...	(chey·se) te·o ...
with milk	tejjel	ey·yel
without sugar	cukor nélkül	tsu·kawr neyl·kewl
... mineral water	... ásványvíz	... ash·van'·veez
sparkling	szénsavas	seyn·sho·vosh
still	szénsavmentes	seyn·shov·men·tesh
orange juice	narancslé	no·ronch·ley
soft drink	üdítőital	ew·dee·tēū·i·tal
(boiled) water	(forralt) víz	(fawr·rolt) veez

in the bar

I'll have ...	... kérek.	... key·rek
I'll buy you a drink.	Fizetek neked egy italt.	fi·ze·tek ne·ked ej i·tolt
What would you like?	Mit kérsz?	mit keyrs
Cheers! (to one person)	Egészségedre!	e·geys·shey·ged·re
Cheers! (to more than one person)	Egészségetekre!	e·geys·shey·ge·tek·re
brandy	brandy	bren·di
champagne	pezsgő	pezh·gēū
cocktail	koktél	kawk·teyl
a bottle/glass of (beer)	egy üveg/pohár (sör)	ej ew·veg/paw·har (sheur)
a shot of (whisky)	egy kupica (whisky)	ej ku·pi·tso (vís·ki)
a bottle/glass of ... wine	egy üveg/pohár ... bor	ej ew·veg/paw·har ... bawr
red	vörös	veu·reush
sparkling	pezsgő	pezh·gēū
white	fehér	fe·heyr

What's the local speciality?
Mi az itteni specialitás?   mi oz it·te·ni shpe·tsi·o·li·tash

What's that?
Az mi?   oz mi

How much is (a kilo of cheese)?
Mennyibe kerül (egy kiló sajt)?   men'·nyi·be ke·rewl (ej ki·lāw shoyt)

I'd like ...	*Kérek ...*	key·rek ...
200 grams	*húsz dekát*	hūs de·kat
a kilo	*egy kilót*	ej ki·lāwt
a piece	*egy darabot*	ej do·ro·bawt
a slice	*egy szeletet*	ej se·le·tet

Less.	*Kevésbé.*	ke·veysh·bey
Enough.	*Elég.*	e·leyg
More.	*Több.*	teubb

special diets & allergies

Is there a vegetarian restaurant near here?
Van a közelben   von o keu·zel·ben
vegetáriánus étterem?   ve·ge·ta·ri·a·nush eyt·te·rem

Do you have vegetarian food?
Vannak Önöknél   von·nok eu·neuk·neyl
vegetáriánus ételek?   ve·ge·ta·ri·a·nush ey·te·lek

Could you prepare	*Tudna készíteni*	tud·no key·see·te·ni
a meal without ...?	*egy ételt ... nélkül?*	ej ey·telt ... neyl·kewl
butter	*vaj*	vo·y
eggs	*tojás*	taw·yash
meat stock	*húsleveskocka*	hūsh·le·vesh·kawts·ko

I'm allergic to ...	*Allergiás vagyok a ...*	ol·ler·gi·ash vo·dyawk o ...
dairy produce	*tejtermékekre*	te·y·ter·mey·kek·re
gluten	*sikérre*	shi·keyr·re
MSG	*monoszódium*	maw·naw·sāw·di·um
	glutamátra	glu·to·mat·ro
nuts	*diófélékre*	di·āw·fey·leyk·re
seafood	*tenger gyümölcseire*	ten·ger yew·meul·che·i·re

bableves csülökkel	*bob*·le·vesh *chew*·leuk·kel	*bean soup with smoked pork*
csúsztatott palacsinta	*chūs*·to·tawtt *po*·lo·chin·to	*pancakes in a stack sprinkled with chocolate*
dobostorta	*daw*·bawsh·tawr·to	*sponge cake with chocolate cream, with a glazed sponge layer on top*
gombaleves	*gom*·bo·le·vesh	*mushroom & onion soup seasoned with paprika*
grenadírmas	*gre*·no·deer·morsh	*potatoes with sweet paprika, onion & pasta, served with sour gherkins*
gulyásleves	*gu*·yash·le·vesh	*beef soup with vegetables & pasta*
halászlé vegyes halból	*ho*·las·ley ve·dyesh *hol*·bāwl	*fish soup with onion, tomato & a dose of paprika*
hortobágyi ürügulyás	*hawr*·taw·ba·dyi *ew*·rew·gu·yash	*mutton stew*
kacsapecsenye	*ko*·cho·pe·che·nye	*roasted duck with apples, quinces & marjoram*
korhelyleves	*kawr*·he·y·le·vesh	*stew of smoked ham, sauerkraut & sliced sausage*
kürtőskalács	*kewr*·tēūsh·ko·lach	*dough wrapped around a roller, coated with honey & almonds or walnuts & roasted on a spit*
lángos	*lan*·gawsh	*deep-fried potato cakes topped with cabbage, ham, cheese or sour cream*
lecsó	*le*·chāw	*stewed tomatoes, peppers, onions & paprika*
lekváros szelet	*lek*·va·rawsh se·let	*sponge cake layered with strawberry jam*

májgaluska	mü·y·go·lush·ko	*fried egg dumplings made from chicken, veal or pork livers*
mákos tészta	ma·kawsh teys·to	*sweet pasta with poppy seeds*
meggyes rétes	mej·dyesh rey·tesh	*cherry & walnut strudel*
meggyleves	mejj·le·vesh	*chilled soup with cherries, sour cream & red wine*
palóc leves	po·lāwts le·vesh	*soup made from cubed leg of mutton or beef & vegetables*
paprikás	pop·ri·kash	*veal, chicken or rabbit stew*
pörkölt	peur·keult	*diced meat stew with a paprika gravy*
sonkás kocka	shawn·kash kots·ko	*chopped ham mixed with sour cream & pasta, then baked*
sonkával töltött gomba	shawn·ka·vol teul·teutt gawm·bo	*mushrooms stuffed with smoked ham in cheese sauce & grilled*
székely gulyás	sey·ke·y gu·yash	*stew of sautéed pork, bacon, sauerkraut & sour cream*
szilvás gombóc	sil·vash gawm·bāwts	*boiled potato-based dumplings filled with pitted plums*
tokány	taw·kan'	*meat stewed in white wine, tomato paste & seasonings*
töltött káposzta	teul·teutt ka·paws·to	*cabbage leaves stuffed with rice & ground pork*
töltött paprika	teul·teutt pop·ri·ko	*capsicums stuffed with rice & ground pork*
tűzdelt fácán	tēwz·delt fa·tsan	*pheasant larded with smoked bacon & roasted in red wine gravy*
vargabéles	vor·go·bey·lesh	*layered pasta & dough topped with a custard-like mixture*
zöldbabfőzelék	zeuld·bob·fēū·ze·leyk	*cooked green beans with sour cream & seasonings*

emergencies

basics

Help!	Segítség!	she-geet-sheyg
Stop!	Álljon meg!	all-yawn meg
Go away!	Menjen innen!	men-yen in-nen
Thief!	Tolvaj!	tawl-voy
Fire!	Tűz!	tēwz
Watch out!	Vigyázzon!	vi-dyaz-zawn

Call a doctor!	Hívjon orvost!	heev-yawn awr-vawsht
Call an ambulance!	Hívja a mentőket!	heev-yo o men-tēū-ket
Call the police!	Hívja a rendőrséget!	heev-yo o rend-ēūr-shey-get

It's an emergency!
Sürgős esetről van szó.　　　shewr-gēūsh e-shet-rēūl von sāw

Could you help me, please?
Tudna segíteni?　　　tud-no she-gee-te-ni

Can I use your phone?
Használhatom a telefonját?　　　hos-nal-ho-tawm o te-le-fawn-yat

I'm lost.
Eltévedtem.　　　el-tey-ved-tem

Where are the toilets?
Hol a vécé?　　　hawl o vey-tsey

police

Where's the police station?
Hol a rendőrség?　　　hawl o rend-ēūr-sheyg

I want to report an offence.
Bűncselekményt szeretnék
bejelenteni.　　　bēwn-che-lek-meynt se-ret-neyk
be-ye-len-te-ni

I have insurance.
Van biztosításom.　　　von biz-taw-shee-ta-shawm

I've been ...		
assaulted	Megtámadtak.	meg-ta-mod-tok
raped	Megerőszakoltak.	meg-e-rēū-so-kawl-tok
robbed	Kiraboltak.	ki-ro-bawl-tok

I've lost my ...	Elvesztettem ...	el·ves·tet·tem ...
My was/were stolen.	Ellopták ...	ĕl·lawp·tak ...
backpack	a hátizsákomat	o ha·ti·zha·kaw·mot
bags	a csomagjaimat	o chaw·mog·yo·i·mot
credit card	a hitelkártyámat	o hi·tel·kar·tya·mot
handbag	a kézitáskámat	o key·zi·tash·ka·mot
jewellery	az ékszereimet	oz eyk·se·re·i·met
money	a pénzemet	o peyn·ze·met
passport	az útlevelemet	oz üt·le·ve·le·met
travellers cheques	az utazási csekkjeimet	oz u·to·za·shi chekk·ye·i·met
wallet	a tárcámat	o tar·tsa·mot

I want to contact my embassy/consulate.

Kapcsolatba akarok lépni a követségemmel/ konzulátusommal.

kop·chaw·lot·bo o·ko·rawk leyp·ni o keu·vet·shey·gem·mel/ kawn·zu·la·tu·shawm·mol

health

medical needs

Where's the nearest ...?	Hol a legközelebbi ...?	hawl o leg·keu·ze·leb·bi ...
dentist	fogorvos	fawg·awr·vawsh
doctor	orvos	awr·vawsh
hospital	kórház	káwr·haz
(night) pharmacist	(éjszaka nyitvatartó) gyógyszertár	(ey·so·ko nyit·vo·tor·táw) dyáwj·ser·tar

I need a doctor (who speaks English).

(Angolul beszélő) Orvosra van szükségem.

(on·gaw·lul be·sey·lēū) awr·vawsh·ro von sewk·shey·gem

Could I see a female doctor?

Beszélhetnék egy orvosnővel?

be·seyl·het·neyk ej awr·vawsh·nēū·vel

I've run out of my medication.

Elfogyott az orvosságom.

el·faw·dyawtt oz awr·vawsh·sha·gawm

symptoms, conditions & allergies

I'm sick.	Rosszul vagyok.	raws·sul vo·dyawk
It hurts here.	Itt fáj.	itt fa·y

I have a ...		
cough	Köhögök.	keu·heu·geuk
headache	Fáj a fejem.	fa·y o fe·yem
sore throat	Fáj a torkom.	fa·y o tawr·kawm
toothache	Fáj a fogam.	fa·y o faw·gom

I have (a) ...	... van.	... von
asthma	Asztmám	ost·mam
bronchitis	Hörghurutom	heurg·hu·rut·awm
constipation	Székrekedésem	seyk·re·ke·dey·shem
diarrhoea	Hasmenésem	hosh·me·ney·shem
fever	Lázam	la·zom
heart condition	Szívbetegségem	seev·be·teg·sheyg·em
nausea	Hányingerem	han'·in·ge·rem
pain	Fájdalmam	fay·dol·mom

I'm allergic to ...	Allergiás vagyok ...	ol·ler·gi·ash vo·dyawk ...
antibiotics	az antibiotikumokra	oz on·ti·bi·aw·ti·ku·mawk·ro
anti-inflammatories	a gyulladásgátlókra	o dyul·lo·dash·gat·lāwk·ro
aspirin	az aszpirinre	oz os·pi·rin·re
bees	a méhekre	o mey·hek·re
codeine	a kodeinre	o ko·de·in·re
penicillin	a penicillinre	o pe·ni·tsil·lin·re

antiseptic n	fertőzésgátló	fer·tēū·zeysh·gat·lāw
bandage	kötés	keu·teysh
condoms	óvszer	āwv·ser
contraceptives	fogamzásgátló	faw·gom·zash·gat·lāw
diarrhoea medicine	hasmenés gyógyszer	hosh·men·eysh dyāwd'·ser
insect repellent	rovarirtó	raw·vor·ir·tāw
laxatives	hashajtó	hosh·ho·y·tāw
painkillers	fájdalomcsillapító	fa·y·do·lawm·chil·lo·pee·tāw
rehydration salts	folyadékpótló sók	faw·yo·deyk·pāwt·lāw shāwk
sleeping tablets	altató	ol·to·tāw

In this dictionary, words are marked as n (noun), a (adjective), v (verb), sg (singular), pl (plural), inf (informal) or pol (polite) where necessary.

A

accident *baleset* bol-e-shet
accommodation *szállás* sal-lash
adaptor *adapter* o-dop-ter
address n *cím* tseem
after *után* u-tan
air-conditioned *légkondicionált* leyg-kawn-di-tsi-aw-nalt
airplane *repülőgép* re-pew-lëü-geyp
airport *repülőtér* re-pew-lëü-teyr
alcohol *alkohol* ol-kaw-hawl
all *minden* min-den
allergy *allergia* ol-ler-gi-o
ambulance *mentő* men-tëü
and *és* eysh
ankle *boka* baw-ko
arm *kar* kor
ashtray *hamutartó* ho-mu-tor-täw
ATM *bankautomata* bonk-o-u-taw-mo-to

B

baby *baba* bo-bo
back (body) *hát* hat
backpack *hátizsák* ha-ti-zhak
bad *rossz* rawss
bag *táska* tash-ko
baggage claim *poggyászkiadó* pawd'-dyas-ki-o-däw
bank *bank* bonk
bar *bár* bar
bathroom *fürdőszoba* fewr-dëü-saw-bo
battery *elem* e-lem
beautiful *szép* seyp
bed *ágy* aj
beer *sör* sheur
before *előtt* e-lëütt
behind *mögött* meu-geutt
bicycle *bicikli* bi-tsik-li
big *nagy* noj
bill *számla* sam-lo
black *fekete* fe-ke-te

blanket *takaró* to-ko-räw
blood group *vércsoport* veyr-chaw-pawrt
blue *kék* keyk
boat (big) *hajó* ho-yàw
boat (small) *csónak* chäw-nok
book (make a reservation) v *lefoglal* le-fawg-lol
bottle *üveg* ew-veg
bottle opener *sörnyitó* sheur-nyi-täw
boy *fiú* fi-ü
brake (car) *fék* feyk
breakfast *reggeli* reg-ge-li
broken (faulty) *hibás* hi-bash
bus *busz* bus
business *üzlet* ewz-let
buy *vesz* ves

C

café *kávézó* ka-vey-zäw
camera *fényképezőgép* feyn'-key-pe-zëü-geyp
camp site *táborhely* ta-bawr-he-y
cancel *töröl* teu-reul
can opener *konzervnyitó* kawn-zerv-nyi-täw
car *autó* o-u-täw
cash n *készpénz* keys-peynz
cash (a cheque) v *bevált csekket* be-valt chek-ket
cell phone *mobil telefon* maw-bil te-le-fawn
centre n *központ* keuz-pawnt
change (money) v *pénzt vált* peynzt valt
cheap *olcsó* awl-chäw
check (bill) *számla* sam-lo
check-in n *bejelentkezés* be-ye-lent-ke-zeysh
chest *mellkas* mell-kosh
child *gyerek* dye-rek
cigarette *cigaretta* tsi-go-ret-to
city *város* va-rawsh
clean a *tiszta* tis-to
closed *zárva* zar-vo
coffee *kávé* ka-vey
coins *pénzérmék* peynz-eyr-meyk
cold a *hideg* hi-deg
collect call *'R' beszélgetés* er-be-seyl-ge-teysh
come *jön* yeun

computer *számítógép sa*-mee-täw-geyp
condom *óvszer* äwv-ser
contact lenses *kontaktlencse* kawn-tokt-len-che
cook v *főz* feüz
cost n *ár* ar
credit card *hitelkártya* hi-tel-kar-tyo
cup *csésze* chey-se
currency exchange *valutaátváltás* vo-lu-to-at-val-tash
customs (immigration) *vám* vam

D

dangerous *veszélyes* ve-sey-yesh
date (time) *dátum* da-tum
day *nap* nop
delay n *késés* key-sheysh
dentist *fogorvos* fawg-awr-vawsh
depart *elutazik* el-u-to-zik
diaper *pelenka* pe-len-ko
dictionary *szótár* säw-tar
dinner *vacsora* vo-chaw-ro
direct *közvetlen* keuz-vet-len
dirty *piszkos* pis-kawsh
disabled *mozgássérült* mawz-gash-shey-rewlt
discount n *árengedmény* ar-en-ged-meyn'
doctor *orvos* awr-vawsh
double bed *dupla ágy* dup-lo aj
double room *duplaágyas szoba* dup-lo-a-dyosh saw-bo
drink n *ital* i-tol
drive v *vezet* ve-zet
drivers licence *jogosítvány* yaw-gaw-sheet-van'
drug (illicit) *kábítószerek* ka-bee-täw-se-rek
dummy (pacifier) *cumi* tsu-mi

E

ear *fül* fewl
east *kelet* ke-let
eat *eszik* e-sik
economy class *turistaosztály* tu-rish-to-aws-ta-y
electricity *villany* vil-lon'
elevator *lift* lift
email *e-mail* ee-meyl
embassy *nagykövetség* noj-keu-vet-sheyg
emergency *vészhelyzet* veys-he-y-zet
English (language) *angol* on-gawl
entrance *bejárat* be-ya-rot
evening *este* esh-te
exchange rate *átváltási árfolyam* at-val-ta-shi ar-faw-yom

exit n *kijárat* ki-ya-rot
expensive *drága* dra-go
express mail *expressz posta* eks-press pawsh-to
eye *szem* sem

F

far *messze* mes-se
fast *gyors* dyawrsh
father *apa* o-po
film (camera) *film* film
finger *ujj* u-y
first-aid kit *elsősegély-láda* el-shëü-she-gey-la-do
first class *első osztály* el-shëü aws-ta-y
fish n *hal* hol
food *ennivaló* en-ni-vo-läw
foot *lábfej* lab-fe-y
fork *villa* vil-lo
free (of charge) *ingyenes* in-dye-nesh
friend (female) *barátnő* bo-rat-nëü
friend (male) *barát* bo-rat
fruit *gyümölcs* dyew-meulch
full *tele* te-le
funny *mulatságos* mu-lot-sha-gawsh

G

gift *ajándék* o-yan-deyk
girl *lány* lan'
glass (drinking) *üveg* ew-veg
glasses *szemüveg* sem-ew-veg
go *megy* mej
good *jó* yäw
green *zöld* zeuld
guide n *idegenvezető* i-de-gen-ve-ze-tëü

H

half n *fél* feyl
hand *kéz* keyz
handbag *kézitáska* key-zi-tash-ko
happy *boldog* bawl-dawg
have *van neki* von ne-ki
he *ő* ëü
head *fej* fe-y
heart *szív* seev
heat n *forróság* fawr-räw-shag
heavy *nehéz* ne-heyz
help v *segít* she-geet
here *itt* itt

high *magas* mo-gosh
highway *országút* awr-sag-út
hike v *kirándul* ki-rán-dul
holiday *szabadság* so-bod-shag
homosexual n *homoszexuális* haw-maw-sek-su-a-lish
hospital *kórház* káwr-haz
hot *forró* fawr-ráw
hotel *szálloda* sal-law-do
Hungarian (language) *magyar* mo-dyor
Hungary *Magyarország* mo-dyor-awr-sag
hungry *éhes* ey-hesh
husband *férj* feyr-y

I

I *én* eyn
identification (card) *személyi igazolvány* se-mey-yi i-go-zawl-van'
ill *beteg* be-teg
important *fontos* fawn-tawsh
included *beleértve* be-le-eyrt-ve
injury *sérülés* shey-rew-leysh
insurance *biztosítás* biz-taw-shee-tash
Internet *Internet* in-ter-net
interpreter *tolmács* tawl-mach

J

jewellery *ékszerek* eyk-se-rek
job *állás* al-lash

K

key *kulcs* kulch
kilogram *kilogramm* ki-láw-gromm
kitchen *konyha* kawn'-ho
knife *kés* keysh

L

laundry (place) *mosoda* maw-shaw-do
lawyer *jogász* yaw-gas
left (direction) *balra* bol-ro
left-luggage office *csomagmegőrző* chaw-mog-meg-éür-zéü
leg *láb* lab
lesbian n *leszbikus* les-bi-kush
less *kevésbé* ke-veysh-bey
letter (mail) *levél* le-veyl
lift (elevator) *lift* lift

light n *fény* feyn'
like v *szeret* se-ret
line *sor* shor
long *hosszú* haws-sú
lost *elveszett* el-ve-sett
lost-property office *talált tárgyak hivatala* to-lalt tar-dyok hi-vo-to-lo
love v *szeret* se-ret
luggage *poggyász* pawd'-dyas
lunch *ebéd* e-beyd

M

mail n *posta* pawsh-to
man *férfi* feyr-fi
map *térkép* teyr-keyp
market *piac* pi-ots
matches *gyufa* dyu-fo
meat *hús* húsh
medicine *orvosság* awr-vawsh-shag
menu *étlap* eyt-lop
message *üzenet* ew-ze-net
milk *tej* te-y
minute *perc* perts
mobile phone *mobil telefon* maw-bil te-le-fawn
money *pénz* peynz
month *hónap* háw-nop
morning *reggel* reg-gel
mother *anya* o-nyo
motorcycle *motorbicikli* maw-tawr-bi-tsik-li
motorway *autópálya* o-u-táw-pa-yo
mouth *száj* sa-y
music *zene* ze-ne

N

name *keresztnév* ke-rest-neyv
napkin *szalvéta* sol-vey-to
nappy *pelenka* pe-len-ko
near *közelében* keu-ze-ley-ben
neck *nyak* nyok
new *új* ú-y
news *hírek* hee-rek
newspaper *újság* ú-y-shag
night *éjszaka* ey-so-ko
no *nem* nem
noisy *zajos* zo-yawsh
nonsmoking *nemdohányzó* nem-daw-han'-záw
north *észak* ey-sok
nose *orr* awrr
now *most* mawsht
number *szám* sam

O

oil (engine) *olaj* aw-lo-y
old (person/thing) *öreg/régi* eu-reg/rey-gi
one-way ticket *csak oda jegy* chok aw-do yej
open a *nyitva* nyit-vo
outside *kint* kint

P

package *csomag* chaw-mog
paper *papír* po-peer
park (a car) v *parkol* por-kawl
passport *útlevél* üt-le-veyl
pay *fizet* fi-zet
pen *golyóstoll* gaw-yäwsh-tawll
petrol *benzin* ben-zin
pharmacy *gyógyszertár* dyäwj-ser-tar
phonecard *telefonkártya* te-le-fawn-kar-tyo
photo *fénykép* feyn'-keyp
plate *tányér* ta-nyeyr
police *rendőrség* rend-eür-sheyg
postcard *levelezőlap* le-ve-le-zëü-lop
post office *postahivatal* pawsh-to-hi-vo-tol
pregnant *terhes* ter-hesh
price *ár* ar

Q

quiet *csendes* chen-desh

R

rain n *eső* e-shëü
razor *borotva* baw-rawt-vo
receipt n *nyugta* nyug-to
red *piros* pi-rawsh
refund n *visszatérítés* vis-so-tey-ree-teysh
registered mail *ajánlott levél* o-yan-lawtt le-veyl
rent v *bérel* bey-rel
repair v *megjavít* meg-yo-veet
reservation *foglalás* fawg-lo-lash
restaurant *étterem* eyt-te-rem
return v *visszatér* vis-so-teyr
return ticket *oda-vissza jegy* aw-do-vis-so yej
right (direction) *jobbra* yawbb-ro
road *út* üt
room *szoba* saw-bo

S

safe a *biztonságos* biz-tawn-sha-gawsh
sanitary napkin *egészségügyi törlőkendő*
e-geys-sheyg-ew-dyi teur-lëü-ken-dëü
seat *ülés* ew-leysh
send *küld* kewld
service station *benzinkút* ben-zin-küt
sex *szex* seks
shampoo *sampon* shom-pawn
share (a dorm) *ben/ban lakik* -ben/-ban lo-kik
shaving cream *borotvakrém* baw-rawt-vo-kreym
she *ő* ëü
sheet (bed) *lepedő* le-pe-dëü
shirt *ing* ing
shoes *cipők* tsi-pëük
shop n *üzlet* ewz-let
short *alacsony* o-lo-chawn'
shower *zuhany* zu-hon'
single room *egyágyas szoba* ej-a-dyosh saw-bo
skin *bőr* bëür
skirt *szoknya* sawk-nyo
sleep v *alszik* ol-sik
slowly *lassan* losh-shon
small *kicsi* ki-chi
smoke (cigarettes) v *dohányzik* daw-han'-zik
soap *szappan* sop-pawn
some *néhány* ney-han'
soon *hamarosan* ho-mo-raw-shon
south *dél* deyl
souvenir shop *ajándékbolt* o-yan-deyk-bawlt
speak *beszél* be-seyl
spoon *kanál* ko-nal
stamp n *bélyeg* bey-yeg
stand-by ticket *készenléti jegy* key-sen-ley-ti yej
station (train) *állomás* al-law-mash
stomach *gyomor* dyaw-mawr
stop v *abbahagy* ob-bo-hoj
stop (bus) n *megálló* meg-al-läw
street *utca* ut-tso
student *diák* di-ak
sun *nap* nop
sunscreen *napolaj* nop-aw-lo-y
swim v *úszik* ü-sik

T

tampons *tampon* tom-pawn
taxi *taxi* tok-si
teaspoon *teáskanál* te-ash-ko-nal
teeth *fogak* faw-gok
telephone n *telefon* te-le-fawn

television *televízió* te-le-vee-zi-áw
temperature (weather) *hőmérséklet* héü-mevr-sheyk-let
tent *sátor* sha-tawr
that (one) *az* oz
they *ők* eük
thirsty *szomjas* sawm-yosh
this (one) *ez* ez
throat *torok* taw-rawk
ticket *jegy* yej
time *idő* i-déü
tired *fáradt* fa-rott
tissues *szövetek* seu-ve-tek
today *ma* mo
toilet *vécé* vey-tsey
tomorrow *holnap* hawl-nop
tonight *ma este* mo esh-te
toothbrush *fogkefe* fawg-ke-fe
toothpaste *fogkrém* fawg-kreym
torch (flashlight) *zseblámpa* zheb-lam-po
tour n *túra* tú-ro
tourist office *turistairoda* tu-rish-to-i-raw-do
towel *törülköző* teu-rewl-keu-zëü
train *vonat* vaw-not
translate *fordít* fawr-deet
travel agency *utazási iroda* u-to-za-shi i-raw-do
travellers cheque *utazási csekk* u-to-za-shi chekk
trousers *nadrág* nod-rag
twin beds *két ágy* keyt aj
tyre *autógumi* o-u-táw-gu-mi

U

underwear *alsónemű* ol-sháw-ne-mêw
urgent *sürgős* shewr-gëüsh

V

vacant *üres* ew-resh
vacation *vakáció* vo-ka-tsi-áw

vegetable n *zöldség* zeuld-sheyg
vegetarian a *vegetáriánus* ve-ge-ta-ri-a-nush
visa *vízum* vee-zum

W

waiter *pincér* pin-tseyr
walk v *sétál* shey-tal
wallet *tárca* tar-tsa-mot
warm a *meleg* me-leg
wash (something) *megmos* meg-mawsh
watch n *óra* áw-ro
water *víz* veez
we *mi* mi
weekend *hétvége* heyt-vey-ge
west *nyugat* nyu-got
wheelchair *rokkantkocsi* rawk-kont-kaw-chi
when *mikor* mi-kawr
where *hol* hawl
white *fehér* fe-heyr
who *ki* ki
why *miért* mi-eyrt
wife *feleség* fe-le-sheyg
window *ablak* ob-lok
wine *bor* bawr
with *-val/-vel* -vol/-vel
without *nélkül* neyl-kewl
woman *nő* nëü
write *ír* eer

Y

yellow *sárga* shar-go
yes *igen* i-gen
yesterday *tegnap* teg-nop
you sg inf *te* te
you pl inf *ti* ti
you sg pol *Ön* eun
you pl pol *Önök* eu-neuk

Polish

polish alphabet

A a a	*Ą ą* om/on	*B b* be	*C c* tse	*Ć ć* che	*D d* de
E e e	*Ę ę* em/en	*F f* ef	*G g* gye	*H h* kha	*I i* ee
J j yot	*K k* ka	*L l* el	*Ł ł* ew	*M m* em	*N n* en
Ń ń en'	*O o* o	*Ó ó* oo	*P p* pe	*R r* er	*S s* es
Ś ś esh	*T t* te	*U u* oo	*W w* woo	*Y y* i	*Z z* zet
Ż ż zhet	*Ż ż* zhyet				

polish

POLSKI

introduction

Ask most English speakers what they know about Polish (*polski* *pol*-skee), the language which donated the words *horde*, *mazurka* and *vodka* to English, and they will most likely dismiss it as an unpronounceable language. Who could pronounce an apparently vowel-less word like *szczyt* shchit (peak), for example? To be put off by this unfairly gained reputation, however, would be to miss out on a rich and rewarding language. The mother tongue of Copernicus, Chopin, Marie Curie and Pope John Paul II has a fascinating and turbulent past and symbolises the resilience of the Polish people in the face of domination and adversity.

The Polish tribes who occupied the basins of the Oder and Vistula rivers in the 6th century AD spoke a range of West Slavic dialects, which over time evolved into Polish. The closest living relatives of Polish are Czech and Slovak which also belong to the wider West Slavic family of languages. The language reached the apex of its influence during the era of the Polish Lithuanian Commonwealth (1569–1795). The Commonwealth covered a swath of territory from what are now Poland and Lithuania through Belarus, Ukraine and Latvia and part of Western Russia. Polish became a lingua franca throughout much of Central and Eastern Europe at this time due to the political, cultural, scientific and military might of this power.

When Poland was wiped off the map of Europe from 1795 to 1918 after three successive partitions in the second half of the 18th century (when it was carved up between Russia, Austria and Prussia), the language suffered attempts at both Germanisation and Russification. Later, after WWII, Poland became a satellite state of the Soviet Union and the language came under the renewed influence of Russian. Polish showed impressive resistance in the face of this oppression. The language not only survived these onslaughts but enriched itself by borrowing many words from both Russian and German. The works of Poland's greatest literary figures who wrote in exile — the Romantic poet Adam Mickiewicz, and, during Communist rule, the Nobel Prize winner Czesław Miłosz — are testament to this fact.

Today, Poland is linguistically one of the most homogenous countries in Europe — over 95% of the population speaks Polish as their first language. There are significant Polish-speaking minorities in the western border areas of Ukraine, Belarus and in southern Lithuania, with smaller populations in other neighbouring countries.

pronunciation

vowel sounds

Polish vowels are generally pronounced short, giving them a 'clipped' quality.

symbol	english equivalent	polish example	transliteration
a	run	*tak*	tak
ai	aisle	*tutaj*	*too*·tai
e	bet	*bez*	bes
ee	see	*wino*	*vee*·no
ey	hey	*kolejka*	ko·*ley*·ka
i	bit	*czy*	chi
o	pot	*woda*	*vo*·da
oo	zoo	*zakupy, mój*	za·*koo*·pi, mooy
ow	how	*migdał*	*meeg*·dow
oy	toy	*ojciec*	*oy*·chets

Polish also has nasal vowels, pronounced as though you're trying to force the air out of your nose rather than your mouth. Nasal vowels are indicated in written Polish by the letters ą and ę. Depending upon the letters that follow these vowels, they're pronounced with either an 'm' or an 'n' sound following the vowel.

symbol	english equivalent	polish example	transliteration
em	like the 'e' in 'get' plus nasal consonant sound	*wstęp*	fstemp
en		*mięso*	*myen*·so
om	like the 'o' in 'not' plus nasal consonant sound	*kąpiel*	*kom*·pyel
on		*wąsy*	*von*·si

word stress

In Polish, stress almost always falls on the second-last syllable. In our coloured pronunciation guides, the stressed syllable is italicised.

consonant sounds

Most Polish consonant sounds are also found in English, with the exception of the kh sound (pronounced as in the Scottish word *loch)* and the rolled r sound.

symbol	english equivalent	polish example	transliteration
b	**bed**	*babka*	*bap*·ka
ch	**cheat**	*cień, czas, ćma*	chen', chas, chma
d	**dog**	*drobne*	*drob*·ne
f	**fat**	*fala*	*fa*·la
g	**go**	*garnek*	*gar*·nek
j	**joke**	*dzieci*	*je*·chee
k	**kit**	*kac*	kats
kh	**loch**	*chata, hałas*	*kha*·ta, *kha*·was
l	**lot**	*lato*	*la*·to
m	**man**	*malarz*	*ma*·lash
n	**not**	*nagle*	*na*·gle
p	**pet**	*palec*	*pa*·lets
r	**run** (rolled)	*róg*	roog
s	**sun**	*samolot*	sa·*mo*·lot
sh	**shot**	*siedem, śnieg, szlak*	*shye*·dem, shnyek, shlak
t	**top**	*targ*	tark
v	**very**	*widok*	*vee*·dok
w	**win**	*złoto*	*zwo*·to
y	**yes**	*zajęty*	za·*yen*·ti
z	**zero**	*zachód*	*za*·khoot
zh	**pleasure**	*zima, żart, rzeźba*	*zhee*·ma, zhart, *zhezh*·ba
'	a slight y sound	*kwiecień*	*kfye*·chen'

basics

language difficulties

Do you speak English?
Czy pan/pani mówi
po angielsku? m/f pol

chi pan/*pa*·nee *moo*·vee
po an·*gyel*·skoo

Do you understand?
Czy pan/pani rozumie? m/f pol

chi pan/*pa*·nee ro·*zoo*·mye

I (don't) understand.
(Nie) Rozumiem.

(nye) ro·*zoo*·myem

What does (nieczynne) mean?
Co to znaczy (nieczynne)?

tso to *zna*·chi (nye·*chi*·ne)

How do you ...?   Jak się ...?   yak shye ...
   pronounce this   to wymawia   to vi·*mav*·ya
   write (pierogi)   pisze (pierogi)   *pee*·she (pye·*ro*·gee)

Could you please ...?   Proszę ...   *pro*·she ...
   repeat that   to powtórzyć   to po v·*too*·zhich
   speak more   mówić trochę   *moo*·veech *tro*·khe
   slowly   wolniej   *vol*·nyey
   write it down   to napisać   to na·*pee*·sach

essentials

Yes.	Tak.	tak
No.	Nie.	nye
Please.	Proszę.	*pro*·she
Thank you (very much).	Dziękuję (bardzo).	jyen·*koo*·ye (*bar*·dzo)
You're welcome.	Proszę.	*pro*·she
Excuse me.	Przepraszam.	pshe·*pra*·sham
Sorry.	Przepraszam.	pshe·*pra*·sham

0	zero	ze·ro	15	piętnaście	pyent·nash·chye
1	jeden m	ye·den	16	szesnaście	shes·nash·chye
	jedna f	yed·na	17	siedemnaście	shye·dem·nash·chye
	jedno n	yed·no	18	osiemnaście	o·shem·nash·chye
2	dwa m	dva	19	dziewiętnaście	jye·vyet·nash·chye
	dwie f	dvye	20	dwadzieścia	dva·jyesh·chya
	dwoje n	dvo·ye	21	dwadzieścia	dva·jyesh·chya
3	trzy	tshi		jeden	ye·den
4	cztery	chte·ri	22	dwadzieścia	dva·jyesh·chya
5	pięć	pyench		dwa	dva
6	sześć	sheshch	30	trzydzieści	tshi·jyesh·chee
7	siedem	shye·dem	40	czterdzieści	chter·jyesh·chee
8	osiem	o·shyem	50	pięćdziesiąt	pyen·jye·shont
9	dziewięć	jye·vyench	60	sześćdziesiąt	shesh·jye·shont
10	dziesięć	jye·shench	70	siedemdziesiąt	shye·dem·jye·shont
11	jedenaście	ye·de·nash·chye	80	osiemdziesiąt	o·shem·jye·shont
12	dwanaście	dva·nash·chye	90	dziewięćdziesiąt	jye·vyen·jye·shont
13	trzynaście	tshi·nash·chye	100	sto	sto
14	czternaście	chter·nash·chye	1000	tysiąc	ti·shonts

time & dates

What time is it?	Która jest godzina?	ktoo·ra yest go·jee·na
It's one o'clock.	Pierwsza.	pyerf·sha
It's (10) o'clock.	Jest (dziesiąta).	yest (jye·shon·ta)
Quarter past (10).	Piętnaście po (dziesiątej).	pyent·nash·chye po (jye·shon·tey)
Half past (10).	Wpół do (jedenastej).	fpoow do (ye·de·nas·tey)
Quarter to (11).	Za piętnaście (jedenasta).	za pyent·nash·chye (ye·de·nas·ta)
At what time ...?	O której godzinie ...?	o ktoo·rey go·jee·nye ...
At ...	O ...	o ...
in the morning	rano	ra·no
in the afternooon	po południu	po po·wood·nyoo
in the evening (6pm–10pm)	wieczorem	vye·cho·rem
at night (11pm–3am)	w nocy	v no·tsi

Monday	*poniedziałek*	po·nye·*jya*·wek
Tuesday	*wtorek*	*fto*·rek
Wednesday	*środa*	*shro*·da
Thursday	*czwartek*	*chfar*·tek
Friday	*piątek*	*pyon*·tek
Saturday	*sobota*	so·*bo*·ta
Sunday	*niedziela*	nye·*jye*·la

January	*styczeń*	*sti*·chen'
February	*luty*	*loo*·ti
March	*marzec*	*ma*·zhets
April	*kwiecień*	*kfye*·chen'
May	*maj*	mai
June	*czerwiec*	*cher*·vyets
July	*lipiec*	*lee*·pyets
August	*sierpień*	*shyer*·pyen'
September	*wrzesień*	*vzhe*·shyen'
October	*październik*	pazh·*jyer*·neek
November	*listopad*	lees·*to*·pat
December	*grudzień*	*groo*·jyen'

What date is it today?	*Którego jest dzisiaj?*	ktoo·*re*·go yest *jee*·shai
It's (18 October).	*Jest (osiemnastego października).*	yest (o·shem·nas·*te*·go pazh·*jyer·nee*·ka)
last night	*wczoraj wieczorem*	*fcho*·rai vye·*cho*·rem

last/next ...	*w zeszłym/przyszłym ...*	v *zesh*·wim/*pshish*·wim ...
week	*tygodniu*	ti·*god*·nyoo
month	*miesiącu*	mye·*shon*·tsoo
year	*roku*	*ro*·koo

yesterday/ tomorrow ...	*wczoraj/ jutro ...*	*fcho*·rai/ *yoo*·tro ...
morning	*rano*	*ra*·no
afternoon	*po południu*	po po·*wood*·nyoo
evening	*wieczorem*	vye·*cho*·rem

weather

What's the weather like?	Jaka jest pogoda?	ya·ka yest po·go·da

It's ...

cloudy	Jest pochmurnie.	yest pokh·moor·nye
cold	Jest zimno.	yest zheem·no
hot	Jest gorąco.	yest go·ron·tso
raining	Pada deszcz.	pa·da deshch
snowing	Pada śnieg.	pa·da shnyeg
sunny	Jest słonecznie.	yest swo·nech·nye
warm	Jest ciepło.	yest chyep·wo
windy	Jest wietrznie.	yest vyetzh·nye

spring	wiosna f	vyos·na
summer	lato n	la·to
autumn	jesień f	ye·shyen'
winter	zima f	zhee·ma

border crossing

I'm ...

in transit	w tranzycie	v tran·zi·chye
on business	służbowo	swoozh·bo·vo
on holiday	na wakacjach	na va·kats·yakh

Jestem ...   yes·tem ...

I'm here for ...

(10) days	(dziesięć) dni	(jye·shench) dnee
(three) weeks	(trzy) tygodnie	(tshi) ti·god·nye
(two) months	(dwa) miesiące	(dva) mye·shon·tse

Będę tu przez ...   ben·de too pshes ...

I'm going to (Kraków).
Jadę do (Krakowa).   ya·de do (kra·ko·va)

I'm staying at the (Pod Różą Hotel).
Zatrzymuję się w (hotelu 'pod Różą').   za·tshi·moo·ye shye v (ho·te·loo pod roo·zhom)

I have nothing to declare.
Nie mam nic do zgłoszenia.   nye mam neets do zgwo·she·nya

I have something to declare.
Mam coś do zgłoszenia.   mam tsosh do zgwo·she·nya

That's (not) mine.
To (nie) jest moje.   to (nye) yest mo·ye

transport

tickets

Where can I buy a ticket?
Gdzie mogę kupić bilet? gjye mo·ge koo·peech bee·let

Do I need to book a seat?
Czy muszę rezerwować? chi moo·she re·zer·vo·vach

One ... ticket	*Proszę bilet ...*	pro·she bee·let ...
(to Katowice), please.	*(do Katowic).*	do (ka·to·veets)
one-way	*w jedną stronę*	v yed·nom stro·ne
return	*powrotny*	po·vro·tni

I'd like to ...	*Chcę ... mój bilet.*	khtse ... mooy bee·let
my ticket, please.		
cancel	*odwołać*	od·vo·wach
change	*zmienić*	zmye·neech
collect	*odebrać*	o·de·brach
confirm	*potwierdzić*	po·tvyer·jyeech

How much is it?
Ile kosztuje? ee·le kosh·too·ye

Is there air conditioning?
Czy jest tam klimatyzacja? chi yest tam klee·ma·ti·za·tsya

Is there a toilet?
Czy jest tam toaleta? chi yest tam to·a·le·ta

How long does the trip take?
Ile trwa podróż? ee·le trfa po·droosh

Is it a direct route?
Czy to jest bezpośrednie połączenie? chi to yest bes·po·shred·nye po·won·che·nye

luggage

Where can I find a luggage locker?
Gdzie jest schowek na bagaż? gjye yest skho·vek na ba·gazh

My luggage	*Mój bagaż*	mooy *ba*·gazh
has been ...	*został ...*	*zos*·tow ...
damaged	*uszkodzony*	oosh·ko·*dzo*·ni
lost	*zagubiony*	za·goo·*byo*·ni
stolen	*skradziony*	skra·*jyo*·ni

getting around

Where does flight (LO125) arrive/depart?
Skąd przylatuje/odlatuje   skont pshi·la·*too*·ye/od·la·*too*·ye
lot (LO125)?   lot (el o sto dva·*jyesh*·chya pyench)

Where's (the) ...?	*Gdzie jest ...?*	gjye yest ...
arrivals hall	*hala przylotów*	*kha*·la pshi·*lo*·toof
departures hall	*hala odlotów*	*kha*·la od·*lo*·toof
duty-free shop	*sklep wolnocłowy*	sklep vol·no·*tswo*·vi
gate (five)	*wejście*	*veysh*·chye
	(numer pięć)	(*noo*·mer pyench)

Is this the ...	*Czy to jest ...*	chi to yest ...
to (Wrocław)?	*do (Wrocławia)?*	do (vrots·*wa*·vya)
bus	*autobus*	ow·*to*·boos
plane	*samolot*	sa·*mo*·lot
train	*pociąg*	*po*·chonk

When's the ... bus?	*Kiedy jest ... autobus?*	*kye*·di yest ... ow·*to*·boos
first	*pierwszy*	*pyerf*·shi
last	*ostatni*	os·*tat*·nee
next	*następny*	nas·*temp*·ni

At what time does it arrive/leave?
O której godzinie przyjeżdża/   o *ktoo*·rey go·*jee*·nye pshi·*yezh*·ja/
odjeżdża?   ot·*yezh*·ja

How long will it be delayed?
Jakie będzie opóźnienie?   *ya*·kye *ben*·jye o·poozh·*nye*·nye

What's the next station?
Jaka jest następna stacja?   *ya*·ka yest nas·*temp*·na *sta*·tsya

What's the next stop?
Jaki jest następny przystanek?   *ya*·kee yest nas·*tem*·pni pshi·*sta*·nek

Does it stop at (Kalisz)?
Czy on się zatrzymuje w (Kaliszu)? chi on shye za tshi moo ye f (ka loo shoo)

Please tell me when we get to (Krynica).
Proszę mi powiedzieć gdy pro·she mee po·vye·jyech gdi
dojedziemy do (Krynicy). do·ye·jye·mi do (kri·nee·tsi)

How long do we stop here?
Na jak długo stoję tu zatrzymamy? na yak dwoo·go shye too za·tshi·ma·mi

Is this seat available?
Czy to miejsce jest wolne? chi to myeys·tse yest vol·ne

That's my seat.
To jest moje miejsce. to yest mo·ye myeys·tse

I'd like a taxi ...	*Chcę zamówić*	khtse za·moo·veech
	taksówkę na ...	tak·soof·ke na ...
now	*teraz*	te·ras
tomorrow	*jutro*	yoo·tro
at (9am)	*(dziewiątą rano)*	(jye·vyon·tom ra·no)

Is this taxi available?
Czy ta taksówka jest wolna? chi ta tak·soof·ka yest vol·na

How much is it to (Szczecin)?
Ile kosztuje do (Szczecina)? ee·le kosh·too·ye (do shche·chee·na)

Please put the meter on.
Proszę włączyć taksometr. pro·she vwon·chich tak·so·metr

Please take me to (this address).
Proszę mnie zawieźć pod (ten adres). pro·she mnye za·vyeshch pod (ten ad·res)

Please ...	*Proszę ...*	pro·she ...
slow down	*zwolnić*	zvol·neech
stop here	*się tu zatrzymać*	shye too za·tshi·mach
wait here	*tu zaczekać*	too za·che·kach

car, motorbike & bicycle hire

I'd like to hire a ...	*Chcę wypożyczyć ...*	khtse vi·po·zhi·chich ...
bicycle	*rower*	ro·ver
car	*samochód*	sa·mo·khoot
motorbike	*motocykl*	mo·to·tsikl

with ...	z ...	z ...
air conditioning	*klimatyzacją*	klee·ma·ti·za·tsyom
a driver	*kierowcą*	kye·*rof*·tsom
antifreeze	*płynem nie*	*pwi*·nem nye
	zamarzającym	za·mar·za·*yon*·tsim
snow chains	*łańcuchami*	wan'·tsoo·*kha*·mee
	śnieżnymi	shnezh·*ni*·mee

How much for	*Ile kosztuje*	ee·le kosh·*too*·ye
... hire?	*wypożyczenie na ...?*	vi·po·zhi·*che*·nye na ...
hourly	*godzinę*	go·*jee*·ne
daily	*dzień*	jyen'
weekly	*tydzień*	*ti*·jyen'

air	*powietrze* n	po·*vye*·tshe
oil	*olej* m	*o*·ley
petrol	*benzyna* f	ben·*zi*·na
tyre	*opona* f	o·*po*·na

I need a mechanic.
 Potrzebuję mechanika. po·tshe·*boo*·ye me·kha·*nee*·ka

I've run out of petrol.
 Zabrakło mi benzyny. za·*bra*·kwo mee ben·*zi*·ni

I have a flat tyre.
 Złapałem/Złapałam gumę. m/f zwa·*pa*·wem/zwa·*pa*·wam *goo*·me

directions

Where's the ...?	*Gdzie jest ...?*	gjye yest ...
bank	*bank*	bank
city centre	*centrum miasta*	*tsen*·troom *myas*·ta
hotel	*hotel*	*ho*·tel
market	*targ*	tark
police station	*komisariat*	ko·mee·*sar*·yat
	policji	po·*leets*·yee
post office	*urząd pocztowy*	*oo*·zhond poch·*to*·vi
public toilet	*toaleta publiczna*	to·a·*le*·ta poo·*bleech*·na
tourist office	*biuro turystyczne*	*byoo*·ro too·ris·*tich*·ne

Is this the road to (Malbork)?
 Czy to jest droga do (Malborka)? chi to yest *dro*·ga do (mal·*bor*·ka)

Can you show me (on the map)?
*Czy może pan/pani
mi pokazać (na mapie)?* m/f

chi *mo*-zhe pan/pa nee
mee po-*ka*-zach (na ma pye)

What's the address?
Jaki jest adres?

ya-kee yest *ad*-res

How far is it?
Jak daleko to jest?

yak da-*le*-ko to yest

How do I get there?
Jak tam mogę się dostać?

yak tam *mo*-ge shye *dos*-tach

Turn ...	*Proszę skręcić ...*	pro-she skren-*cheech* ...
at the corner	*na rogu*	na *ro*-goo
at the traffic lights	*na światłach*	na *shfyat*-wakh
left/right	*w lewo/prawo*	v *le*-vo/*pra*-vo

It's ...	*To jest ...*	to yest ...
behind ...	*za ...*	za ...
far away	*daleko*	da-*le*-ko
here	*tu*	too
in front of ...	*przed ...*	pshet ...
left	*po lewej*	po *le*-vey
near	*blisko*	*blees*-ko
next to ...	*obok ...*	*o*-bok ...
on the corner	*na rogu*	na *ro*-goo
opposite ...	*naprzeciwko ...*	nap-she-*cheef*-ko ...
right	*po prawej*	po *pra*-vey
straight ahead	*na wprost*	na fprost
there	*tam*	tam

by bus	*autobusem*	ow-to-*boo*-sem
by taxi	*taksówką*	tak-*soof*-kom
by train	*pociągiem*	po-*chon*-gyem
on foot	*pieszo*	*pye*-sho

north	*północ*	*poow*-nots
south	*południe*	po-*wood*-nye
east	*wschód*	fskhoot
west	*zachód*	*za*-khoot

Wjazd/Wyjazd	vyazd/*vi*-yazd	**Entrance/Exit**
Otwarte/Zamknięte	ot-*far*-te/zamk-*nyen*-te	**Open/Closed**
Wolne pokoje	*vol*-ne po-*ko*-ye	**Rooms Available**
Brak wolnych miejsc	brak *vol*-nikh myeysts	**No Vacancies**
Informacja	een-for-*ma*-tsya	**Information**
Komisariat policji	ko-mee-*sar*-yat po-*lee*-tsyee	**Police Station**
Zabroniony	za-bro-*nyo*-ni	**Prohibited**
Toalety	to-a-*le*-ti	**Toilets**
Męskie	*mens*-kye	**Men**
Damskie	*dams*-kye	**Women**
Zimna/Gorąca	*zheem*-na/go-*ron*-tsa	**Hot/Cold**

accommodation

finding accommodation

Where's a ...?	*Gdzie jest ...?*	gjye yest ...
camping ground	*kamping*	*kam*-peeng
guesthouse	*pokoje gościnne*	po-*ko*-ye gosh-*chee*-ne
hotel	*hotel*	*ho*-tel
youth hostel	*schronisko*	skhro-*nees*-ko
	młodzieżowe	mwo-jye-*zho*-ve
Can you recommend	*Czy może pan/pani*	chi *mo*-zhe pan/*pa*-nee
somewhere ...?	*polecić coś ...?* m/f	po-*le*-cheech tsosh ...
cheap	*taniego*	ta-*nye*-go
good	*dobrego*	do-*bre*-go
nearby	*coś w pobliżu*	tsosh f po-*blee*-zhoo

I'd like to book a room, please.
Chcę zarezerwować pokój. khtse za-re-zer-*vo*-vach *po*-kooy

I have a reservation.
Mam rezerwację. mam re-zer-*va*-tsye

My name's ...
Nazywam się ... na-*zi*-vam shye ...

Do you have a … room?	Czy jest pokój …?	chi yest po-kooy …
single	jednoosobowy	yad-no-o-so-bo-vy
double	z podwójnym łóżkiem	z pod-vooy-nim woozh-kyem
twin	z dwoma łóżkami	z dvo-ma wozh-ka-mee

How much is it per …?	Ile kosztuje za …?	ee-le kosh-too-ye za …
night	noc	nots
person	osobę	o-so-be

Can I pay …?	Czy mogę zapłacić …?	chi mo-ge za-pwa-cheech …
by credit card	kartą kredytową	kar-tom kre-di-to-vom
with a travellers cheque	czekami podróżnymi	che-ka-mee po-droozh-ni-mee

For (three) nights/weeks.
Na (trzy) noce/tygodnie. — na (tshi) no-tse/ti-god-nye

From (2 July) to (6 July).
Od (drugiego lipca) do (szóstego lipca). — od (droo-gye-go leep-tsa) do (shoos-te-go leep-tsa)

Can I see it?
Czy mogę go zobaczyć? — chi mo-ge go zo-ba-chich

Am I allowed to I camp here?
Czy mogę się tutaj rozbić? — chi mo-ge shye too-tai roz-beech

Where can I find the camping ground?
Gdzie jest pole kampingowe? — gjye yest po-le kam-peen-go-ve

requests & queries

When's breakfast served?
O której jest śniadanie? — o ktoo-rey yest shnya-da-nye

Where's breakfast served?
Gdzie jest śniadanie? — gjye yest shnya-da-nye

Please wake me at (seven).
Proszę obudzić mnie o (siódmej). — pro-she o-boo-jeech mnye o (shyood-mey)

Could I have my key, please?
Czy mogę prosić o klucz? — chi mo-ge pro-sheech o klooch

Can I get another (blanket)?
Czy mogę prosić o jeszcze jeden (koc)? — chi mo-ge pro-sheech o yesh-che ye-den (kots)

Is there an elevator/a safe?
Czy jest winda/sejf? — chi yest *veen*·da/seyf

This (towel) isn't clean.
Ten (ręcznik) nie jest czysty. — ten (*rench*·neek) nye yest *chis*·ti

It's too ...	Jest zbyt ...	yest zbit ...
expensive	drogi	*dro*·gee
noisy	głośny	*gwosh*·ni
small	mały	*ma*·wi

The ... doesn't work.	... nie działa.	... nye *jya*·wa
air conditioner	Klimatyzator	klee·ma·ti·*za*·tor
fan	Wentylator	ven·ti·*la*·tor
toilet	Ubikacja	oo·bee·*kats*·ya

checking out

What time is checkout?
O której godzinie — o *ktoo*·rey go·*jye*·nye
muszę się wymeldować? — *moo*·she shye vi·mel·*do*·vach

Can I leave my luggage here?
Czy mogę tu zostawić — chi *mo*·ge too zo·*sta*·veech
moje bagaże? — *mo*·ye ba·*ga*·zhe

Could I have	Czy mogę prosić	chi *mo*·ge *pro*·sheech
my ..., please?	o mój/moje ...? sg/pl	o mooy/*mo*·ye ...
deposit	depozyt sg	de·*po*·zit
passport	paszport sg	*pash*·port
valuables	kosztowności pl	kosh·tov·*nosh*·chee

communications & banking

the internet

Where's the local Internet café?
Gdzie jest kawiarnia internetowa? — gjye yest ka·*vyar*·nya een·ter·ne·*to*·va

How much is it per hour?
Ile kosztuje za godzinę? — *ee*·le kosh·*too*·ye za go·*jee*·ne

I'd like to ...	Chciałem/Chciałam ... m/f	khchow·em/khchow·am ...
check my email	sprawdzić mój email	sprav·jeech mooy ee·mayl
get Internet access	podłączyć się do internetu	pod·won·chich shye do een·ter·ne·too
use a printer	użyć drukarki	oo·zhich droo·kar·kee
use a scanner	użyć skaner	oo·zhich ska·ner

mobile/cell phone

I'd like a ...	Chciałem/Chciałam ... m/f	khchow·em/khchow·am ...
mobile/cell phone for hire	wypożyczyć telefon komórkowy	vi·po·zhi·chich te·le·fon ko·moor·ko·vi
SIM card for your network	kartę SIM na waszą sieć	kar·te seem na va·shom shyech

What are the rates?	Jakie są stawki za rozmowy?	ya·kye som staf·kee za roz·mo·vi

telephone

What's your phone number?
Jaki jest pana/pani
numer telefonu? m/f pol
ya·kee yest pa·na/pa·nee
noo·mer te·le·fo·noo

The number is ...
Numer jest ...
noo·mer yest ...

Where's the nearest public phone?
Gdzie jest najbliższy telefon?
gjye yest nai·bleezh·shi te·le·fon

I'd like to buy a chip phonecard.
Chciałem/Chciałam kupić
czipową kartę telefoniczną. m/f
khchow·em/khchow·am koo·peech
chee·po·vom kar·te te·le·fo·neech·nom

I want to ...	Chciałem/Chciałam ... m/f	khchow·em/khchow·am ...
call (Singapore)	zadzwonić do (Singapuru)	zad·zvo·neech do (seen·ga·poo·roo)
make a local call	zadzwonić pod lokalny numer	zad·zvo·neech pod lo·kal·ni noo·mer
reverse the charges	zamówić rozmowę na koszt odbiorcy	za·moo·veech roz·mo·ve na kosht od·byor·tsi

How much does ... cost?	Ile kosztuje ...?	ee·le kosh·too·ye ...
a (three)-minute call	rozmowa (trzy) minutowa	roz·mo·va (tshi) mee·noo·to·va
each extra minute	każda dodatkowa minuta	kazh·da do·dat·ko·va mee·noo·ta
(Two złotys) per (30) seconds.	(Dwa złote) za (trzydzieści) sekund.	(dva zwo·te) za (tshi·jyesh·chee) se·koond

post office

I want to send a ...	Chciałem/Chciałam wysłać ... m/f	khchow·em/khchow·am vis·wach ...
fax	faks	faks
letter	list	leest
parcel	paczkę	pach·ke
postcard	pocztówkę	poch·toof·ke
I want to buy a/an ...	Chciałem/Chciałam kupić ... m/f	khchow·em/khchow·am koo·peech ...
envelope	kopertę	ko·per·te
stamp	znaczek	zna·chek
Please send it (to Australia) by ...	Proszę wysłać to ... (do Australii).	pro·she vis·wach to ... (do ows·tra·lyee)
airmail	pocztą lotniczą	poch·tom lot·nee·chom
express mail	pocztą ekspresową	poch·tom eks·pre·so·vom
registered mail	pocztą poleconą	poch·tom po·le·tso·nom
surface mail	pocztą lądową	poch·tom lon·do·vom
Is there any mail for me?	Czy jest dla mnie jakaś korespondencja?	chi yest dla mnye ya·kash ko·res·pon·den·tsya

bank

Where's a/an ...?	Gdzie jest ...?	gjye yest ...
ATM	bankomat	ban·ko·mat
foreign exchange office	kantor walut	kan·tor va·loot

I'd like to ...	Chciałem/Chciałam ... m/f	khchow·em/khchow·am ...
Where can I ...?	Gdzie mogę ...?	gjye mo ge
cash a cheque	wymienić czek	vi·mye·neech chek
	na gotówkę	na go·toof·ke
change a travellers cheque	wymienić czek podróżny	vi·mye·neech chek po·droozh·ni
change money	wymienić pieniądze	vi·mye·neech pye·nyon·dze
get a cash advance	dostać zaliczkę na moją kartę kredytową	dos·tach za·leech·ke na mo·yom kar·te kre·di·to·vom
withdraw money	wypłacić pieniądze	vi·pwa·cheech pye·nyon·dze

What's the ...?	Jaki/Jaka jest ...? m/f	ya·kee/ya·ka yest ...
charge for that	prowizja f	pro·veez·ya
exchange rate	kurs wymiany m	koors vi·mya·ni

It's (12) złotys.
To kosztuje (dwanaście) złotych. to kosh·too·ye (dva·nash·chye) zwo·tikh

It's free.
Jest bezpłatny. yest bes·pwat·ni

What time does the bank open?
W jakich godzinach jest bank otwarty? v ya·keekh go·jee·nakh yest bank ot·far·ti

Has my money arrived yet?
Czy doszły już moje pieniądze? chi dosh·wi yoosh mo·ye pye·nyon·dze

sightseeing

getting in

What time does it open/close?
O której godzinie jest otwarte/zamknięte? o ktoo·rey go·jee·nye yest ot·far·te/zam·knyen·te

What's the admission charge?
Ile kosztuje wstęp? ee·le kosh·too·ye fstemp

Is there a discount for students/children?

Czy jest zniżka dla studentów/dzieci? — chi yest *zneezh*-ka dla stoo-*den*-toof/*jye*-chee

I'd like to see ...

Chciałem/Chciałam obejrzeć ... m/f — *khchow*-em/*khchow*-am o-*bey*-zhech ...

What's that?

Co to jest? — tso to yest

Can I take a photo?

Czy mogę zrobić zdjęcie? — chi *mo*-ge *zro*-beech *zdyen*-chye

I'd like a ...	*Chciałem/Chciałam ...* m/f	*khchow*-em/*khchow*-am ...
catalogue	*broszurę*	bro-*shoo*-re
guide	*przewodnik*	pshe-*vod*-neek
local map	*mapę okolic*	*ma*-pe o-*ko*-leets

tours

When's the next ...?	*Kiedy jest następna ...?*	*kye*-di yest nas-*temp*-na ...
day trip	*wycieczka jednodniowa*	vi-*chyech*-ka yed-no-*dnyo*-va
tour	*tura*	*too*-ra

Is ... included?	*Czy ... wliczone/a?* n&pl/f	chi ... vlee-*cho*-ne/na
accommodation	*noclegi są* pl	nots-*le*-gee som
the admission charge	*opłata za wstęp jest* f	o-*pwa*-ta za fstemp yest
food	*wyżywienie jest* n	vi-zhi-*vye*-nye yest

Is transport included?

Czy transport jest wliczony? — chi *trans*-port yest vlee-*cho*-ne

How long is the tour?

Jak długo trwa wycieczka? — yak *dwoo*-go trfa vi-*chyech*-ka

What time should we be back?

O której godzinie powinniśmy wrócić? — o *ktoo*-rey go-*jee*-nye po-vee-*neesh*-mi *vroo*-cheech

castle	*zamek* m	*za-*mek
cathedral	*katedra* f	*ka-te-*dra
church	*kościół* m	*kosh-*chyoow'
main square	*rynek główny* m	*ri-*nek *gwoov-*ni
monastery	*klasztor* m	*klash-*tor
monument	*pomnik* m	*pom-*neek
museum	*muzeum* n	moo-*ze-*oom
old city	*stare miasto* n	*sta-*re *myas-*to
palace	*pałac* m	*pa-*wats
ruins	*ruiny* f pl	roo-*ee-*ni
stadium	*stadion* m	*sta-*dyon
statue	*pomnik* m	*pom-*neek

shopping

enquiries

Where's a ...?	*Gdzie jest ...?*	*gjye yest ...*
bank	*bank*	bank
bookshop	*księgarnia*	kshyen-*gar-*nya
camera shop	*sklep fotograficzny*	sklep fo-to-gra-*feech-*ni
department store	*dom towarowy*	dom to-va-*ro-*vi
grocery store	*sklep spożywczy*	sklep spo-*zhiv-*chi
market	*targ*	tark
newsagency	*kiosk*	kyosk
supermarket	*supermarket*	soo-per-*mar-*ket

Where can I buy (a padlock)?
Gdzie mogę kupić (kłódkę)?   *gjye mo-ge koo-*peech (*kwoot-*ke)

I'm looking for ...
Szukam ...   *shoo-*kam

Can I look at it?
Czy mogę to zobaczyć?   chi *mo-*ge to zo-*ba-*chich

Do you have any others?
Czy są jakieś inne?   chi som *ya-*kyesh *ee-*ne

Does it have a guarantee?
Czy to ma gwarancję?   chi to ma gva-*ran-*tsye

Can I have it sent overseas?
Czy mogę to wysłać za granicę?   chi *mo*·ge to *vis*·wach za gra·*nee*·tse

Can I have my ... repaired?
Czy mogę tu oddać ... do naprawy?   chi *mo*·ge too *ot*·dach ... do na·*pra*·vi

It's faulty.
To jest wadliwe.   to yest vad·*lee*·ve

I'd like to return this, please.
Chciałem/Chciałam to zwrócić. m/f   *khchow*·em/*khchow*·am to zvroo·cheech

I'd like a ..., please.	*Proszę o ...*	pro·she o ...
bag	*torbę*	*tor*·be
refund	*zwrot pieniędzy*	zvrot pye·*nyen*·dzi

paying

How much is it?
Ile to kosztuje?   *ee*·le to kosh·*too*·ye

Can you write down the price?
Proszę napisać cenę.   pro·she na·*pee*·sach *tse*·ne

That's too expensive.
To jest za drogie.   to yest za *dro*·gye

What's your final price?
Jaka jest pana/pani   *ya*·ka yest *pa*·na/*pa*·nee
ostateczna cena? m/f   os·ta·*tech*·na *tse*·na

I'll give you (10 złotys).
Dam panu/pani (dziesięć złotych). m/f   dam *pa*·noo/*pa*·nee (*jye*·shench *zwo*·tikh)

There's a mistake in the bill.
Na czeku jest pomyłka.   na *che*·koo yest po·*miw*·ka

Do you accept ...?	*Czy mogę zapłacić ...?*	chi *mo*·ge za·*pwa*·cheech ...
credit cards	*kartą kredytową*	*kar*·tom kre·di·*to*·vom
debit cards	*kartą debetową*	*kar*·tom de·be·*to*·vom
travellers	*czekami*	che·*ka*·mee
cheques	*podróżnymi*	pod·roozh·*ni*·mee

I'd like ..., please.	*Proszę o ...*	pro·she o ...
a receipt	*rachunek*	ra·*khoo*·nek
my change	*moją resztę*	*mo*·yom *resh*·te

clothes & shoes

Can I try it on?	*Czy mogę przymierzyć?*	chi *mo*·ge pshi·*mye*·zhich
My size is (40).	*Noszę rozmiar*	*no*·she *roz*·myar
	(czterdzieści).	(chter·*jyesh*·chee)
It doesn't fit.	*Nie pasuje.*	nye pa·*soo*·ye
large/medium/small	*L/M/S*	*el*·ke/*em*·ke/*es*·ke

books & music

I'd like a ...	*Chciałem/Chciałam* ... m/f	khchow·em/khchow·am ...
newspaper	*gazetę (w języku*	ga·*ze*·te (v yen·zi·koo
(in English)	*angielskim)*	an·*gyel*·skeem)
pen	*długopis*	dwoo·*go*·pees

Is there an English-language bookshop?
Czy jest tu księgarnia angielska?   chi yest too kshyen·*gar*·nya an·*gyel*·ska

I'm looking for something by (Górecki).
Szukam czegoś (Góreckiego).   *shoo*·kam *che*·gosh (goo·rets·*kye*·go)

Can I listen to this?
Czy mogę tego posłuchać?   chi *mo*·ge *te*·go pos·*woo*·khach

photography

Can you ...?	*Czy może pan/pani* ...? m/f	chi *mo*·zhe pan/*pa*·nee ...
develop this film	*wywołać ten film*	vi·*vo*·wach ten film
load my film	*założyć film*	za·*wo*·zhich film
transfer photos	*skopiować zdjęcia*	sko·*pyo*·vach *zdyen*·chya
from my camera	*z mojego aparatu*	z mo·ye·go a·pa·*ra*·too
to CD	*na płytę kompaktową*	na *pwi*·te kom·pak·*to*·vom

I need a/an ... film	*Potrzebuję film* ...	po·tshe·*boo*·ye film ...
for this camera.	*do tego aparatu.*	do *te*·go a·pa·*ra*·too
APS	*APS*	a pe es
B&W	*panchromatyczny*	pan·khro·ma·*tich*·ni
colour	*kolorowy*	ko·lo·*ro*·vi
slide	*do slajdów*	do *slai*·doof
(200) speed	*(dwieście) ASA*	(*dvyesh*·chye) *a*·sa

When will it be ready?   *Na kiedy będzie gotowe?*   na *kye*·di *ben*·jye go·*to*·ve

meeting people

greetings, goodbyes & introductions

Hello/Hi.	*Cześć.*	cheshch
Good night.	*Dobranoc.*	do-*bra*-nots
Goodbye.	*Do widzenia.*	do vee-*dze*-nya
Bye.	*Pa.*	pa
See you later.	*Do zobaczenia.*	do zo-ba-*che*-nya
Mr/Mrs/Miss	*Pan/Pani/Panna*	pan/*pa*-nee/*pa*-na
How are you?	*Jak pan/pani*	yak pan/*pa*-nee
	się miewa? m/f pol	shye *mye*-va
	Jak się masz? inf	yak shye mash
Fine. And you?	*Dobrze. A pan/pani?* m/f pol	*dob*-zhe a pan/*pa*-nee
	Dobrze. A ty? inf	*dob*-zhe a ti
What's your name?	*Jak się pan/pani*	yak shye pan/*pa*-nee
	nazywa? m/f pol	na-*zi*-va
	Jakie się nazywasz? inf	yak shye na-*zi*-vash
My name is ...	*Nazywam się ...*	na-*zi*-vam shye ...
I'm pleased to	*Miło mi pana/panią*	*mee*-wo mee *pa*-na/*pa*-nyom
meet you.	*poznać.* m/f pol	*po*-znach
	Miło mi ciebie poznać. inf	*mee*-wo mee *chye*-bye *po*-znach
This is my ...	*To jest mój/moja ...* m/f	to yest mooy/*mo*-ya ...
boyfriend	*chłopak*	*khwo*-pak
brother	*brat*	brat
daughter	*córka*	*tsoor*-ka
father	*ojciec*	*oy*-chyets
friend	*przyjaciel* m	pzhi-*ya*-chyel
	przyjaciółka f	pzhi-*ya*-chyoow-ka
girlfriend	*dziewczyna*	jyev-*chi*-na
husband	*mąż*	monzh
mother	*matka*	*mat*-ka
partner (intimate)	*partner/partnerka* m/f	*part*-ner/*part*-ner-ka
sister	*siostra*	*shyos*-tra
son	*syn*	sin
wife	*żona*	*zho*-na

Here's my ...	Tu jest mój	too yest mooy ...
What's your ...?	Jaki jest pana/	ya·kee yest pa·na/
	pani ...? m/f pol	pa·nee ...
(email) address	adres (emailowy)	ad·res (e·mai·lo·vi)
fax number	numer faksu	noo·mer fak·soo
phone number	numer telefonu	noo·mer te·le·fo·noo

occupations

What's your occupation?	Jaki jest pana/pani zawód? m/f pol	ya·kee yest pa·na/pa·nee za·vood
I'm a/an ...	Jestem ...	yes·tem ...
artist	artystą/artystką m/f	ar·tis·tom/ar·tist·kom
farmer	rolnikiem m&f	rol·nee·kyem
manual worker	pracownikiem fizycznym m&f	pra·tsov·nee·kyem fee·zich·nim
office worker	pracownikiem biurowym m&f	pra·tsov·nee·kyem byoo·ro·vim
scientist	naukowcem m&f	now·kov·tsem
tradesperson	rzemieślnikiem m&f	zhe·mye·shlnee·kyem

background

Where are you from?	Skąd pan/pani jest? m/f pol	skont pan/pa·nee yest
I'm from ...	Jestem z ...	yes·tem z ...
Australia	Australii	ow·stra·lyee
Canada	Kanady	ka·na·di
England	Anglii	ang·lee
New Zealand	Nowej Zelandii	no·vey ze·lan·dyee
the USA	USA	oo es a

Are you married? (to a man)
Czy jest pan żonaty? pol — chi yest pan zho·na·ti

Are you married? (to a woman)
Czy jest pani zamężna? pol — chi yest pa·nee za·menzh·na

I'm married.
Jestem żonaty/zamężna. m/f — yes·tem zho·na·ti/za·menzh·na

I'm single.
Jestem nieżonaty/niezamężna. m/f — nye·zho·na·ti/nye·za·menzh·na

age

How old is your ...?	Ile lat ma pana/ pani ...? m/f pol	*ee*·le lat ma *pa*·na/ *pa*·nee ...
daughter	córka	*tsoor*·ka
son	syn	sin
How old are you?	Ile pan/pani ma lat? m/f pol	*ee*·le pan/*pa*·nee ma lat
	Ile masz lat? inf	*ee*·le mash lat
I'm ... years old.	Mam ... lat.	mam ... lat
He/She is ... years old.	On/Ona ma ... lat.	on/*o*·na ma ... lat

feelings

I'm (not) ...	(Nie) Jestem ...	(nye) *yes*·tem ...
Are you ...?	Czy jest pan/pani ...? m/f pol	chi yest pan/*pa*·nee ...
cold	zmarznięty/a m/f	zmar·*znyen*·ti/a
happy	szczęśliwy/a m/f	shchen·*shlee*·vi/a
hungry	głodny/a m/f	*gwod*·ni/a
sad	smutny/a m/f	*smoot*·ni/a
thirsty	spragniony/a m/f	sprag·*nyo*·ni/a

entertainment

going out

Where can I find ...?	Gdzie mogę znaleźć ...?	gjye *mo*·ge *zna*·lezhch ...
clubs	kluby nocne	*kloo*·bi *nots*·ne
gay venues	kluby dla gejów	*kloo*·bi dla *ge*·yoof
pubs	puby	*pa*·bi
I feel like going to a/the ...	Mam ochotę pójść ...	mam o·*kho*·te *pooy*·shch ...
concert	na koncert	na *kon*·tsert
movies	na film	na feelm
party	na imprezę	na eem·*pre*·ze
restaurant	do restauracji	do res·tow·*ra*·tsyee
theatre	na sztukę	na *shtoo*·ke

Do you like ...?	Czy lubisz ...? inf	chi loo·beesh ...
I like ...	Lubię ...	loo·bye ...
cooking	gotować	go·to·vach
movies	oglądać filmy	o·glon·dach feel·mi
reading	czytać	chi·tach
sport	sport	sport
travelling	podróżować	po·droo·zho·vach
Do you like art?	Czy lubisz sztukę? inf	chi loo·beesh shtoo·ke
I like art.	Lubię sztukę.	loo·bye shtoo·ke
Do you ...?	Czy ...? inf	chi ...
dance	tańczysz	tan'·chish
go to concerts	chodzisz na koncerty	kho·jeesh na kon·tser·ti
listen to music	słuchasz muzyki	swoo·khash moo·zi·kee

food & drink

finding a place to eat

Can you	Czy może pan/pani	chi mo·zhe pan/pa·nee
recommend a ...?	polecić ...? m/f	po·le·cheech ...
bar	bar	bar
café	kawiarnię	ka·vyar·nye
restaurant	restaurację	res·tow·rats·ye
I'd like ..., please.	Proszę ...	pro·she ...
a table for (five)	o stolik na (pięć) osób	o sto·leek na (pyench) o·soob

ordering food

breakfast	śniadanie n	shnya·da·nye
lunch	obiad m	o·byad
dinner	kolacja f	ko·la·tsya
snack	przekąska f	pshe·kons·ka

What would you recommend?

Co by pan polecił? m		tso bi pan po·*le*·cheew
Co by pani poleciła? f		tso bi *pa*·nee po·le·*chee*·wa

I'd like (the) …, please.	*Proszę …*	*pro*·she …
bill	*o rachunek*	o ra·*khoo*·nek
drink list	*o spis napojów*	o spees na·*po*·yoof
menu	*o jadłospis*	o ya·*dwo*·spees
that dish	*to danie*	to *da*·nye

drinks

(cup of) coffee …	*(filiżanka) kawy …*	(fee·lee·*zhan*·ka) *ka*·vi …
(cup of) tea …	*(filiżanka) herbaty …*	(fee·lee·*zhan*·ka) her·*ba*·ti …
with milk	*z mlekiem*	z *mle*·kyem
without sugar	*bez cukru*	bez *tsoo*·kroo
(orange) juice	*sok (pomarańczowy)* m	sok (po·ma·ran'·*cho*·vi)
soft drink	*napój* m	*na*·pooy
… water	*woda …*	*vo*·da …
hot	*gorąca*	go·*ron*·tsa
mineral	*mineralna*	mee·ne·*ral*·na

in the bar

I'll have …	*Proszę …*	*pro*·she …
I'll buy you a drink.	*Kupię ci drinka.* inf	koo·pye chee *dreen*·ka
What would you like?	*Co zamówić dla ciebie?* inf	tso za·*moo*·veech dla *chye*·bye
Cheers!	*Na zdrowie!*	na *zdro*·vye
brandy	*brandy* m	*bren*·di
champagne	*szampan* m	*sham*·pan
a shot of (vodka)	*kieliszek (wódki)*	kye·*lee*·shek (*vood*·kee)
a bottle/glass of beer	*butelka/szklanka piwa*	boo·*tel*·ka/*shklan*·ka *pee*·va
a bottle/glass	*butelka/kieliszek*	boo·*tel*·ka/kye·*lee*·shek
of … wine	*wina …*	*vee*·na …
red	*czerwonego*	cher·vo·*ne*·go
sparkling	*musującego*	moo·soo·yon·*tse*·go
white	*białego*	bya·*we*·go

What's the local speciality?

Co jest miejscową — tso yest myeys·*tso*·vom
specjalnością? — spe·tsyal·*nosh*·chyom

What's that?

Co to jest? — tso to yest

How much (is a kilo of cheese)?

Ile kosztuje (kilogram sera)? — ee·le kosh·*too*·ye (kee·*lo*·gram *se*·ra)

I'd like …	*Proszę …*	*pro·she …*
200 grams	*dwadzieścia deko*	dva·*jyesh*·chya *de*·ko
(two) kilos	*(dwa) kilo*	(dva) *kee*·lo
(three) pieces	*(trzy) kawałki*	(tshi) ka·*vow*·kee
(six) slices	*(sześć) plasterków*	(sheshch) plas·*ter*·koof

Less.	*Mniej.*	mney
Enough.	*Wystarczy.*	vis·*tar*·chi
More.	*Więcej.*	*vyen*·tsey

special diets & allergies

Is there a vegetarian restaurant near here?

Czy jest tu gdzieś restauracja — chi yest too gjyesh res·tow·*ra*·tsya
wegetariańska? — ve·ge·ta·*ryan'*·ska

Do you have vegetarian food?

Czy jest żywność wegetariańska? — chi yest zhiv·noshch ve·ge·tar·*yan'*·ska

Could you prepare	*Czy można przygotować*	chi *mo*·zhna pshi·go·*to*·vach
a meal without …?	*jedzenie bez …?*	ye·*dze*·nye bes …
butter	*masła*	*mas*·wa
eggs	*jajek*	*yai*·ek
meat stock	*wywaru mięsnego*	vi·*va*·roo myens·*ne*·go

I'm allergic to …	*Mam uczulenie na …*	mam oo·choo·*le*·nye na …
dairy produce	*produkty mleczne*	pro·*dook*·ti *mlech*·ne
gluten	*gluten*	*gloo*·ten
MSG	*glutaminian sodu*	gloo·ta·*mee*·nyan *so*·doo
nuts	*orzechy*	o·*zhe*·khi
seafood	*owoce morza*	o·*vo*·tse *mo*·zha

menu decoder

barszcz biały m	barshch *bya*-wi	thick sourish wheat & potato-starch soup with marjoram
barszcz czerwony m	barshch cher-*vo*-ni	beetroot soup with dumplings, hard-boiled egg slices or beans
bigos m	*bee*-gos	sauerkraut, cabbage & meat stew, simmered with mushrooms & prunes & flavoured with red wine
bliny m pl	*blee*-ni	small thick pancakes made from wheat or buckwheat flour & yeast
budyń m	*boo*-din'	milk-based cream dessert in a range of flavours (eg strawberry, vanilla or chocolate)
chłodnik m	*khwod*-neek	baby beetroot soup with yogurt & fresh vegetables, served cold
ćwikła f	*chfeek*-wa	boiled & grated beetroot with horseradish, served with roast or smoked meat & sausages
drożdżówka f	drozh-*joof*-ka	brioche (sweet yeast bun)
flaczki m pl	*flach*-kee	seasoned tripe & vegetables cooked in bouillon
galareta f	ga-la-*re*-ta	appetiser of meat or fish encased in aspic • sweet flavoured jelly
gofry m pl	*go*-fri	thick rectangular waffles served with toppings such as whipped cream, chocolate or jam
golonka f	go-*lon*-ka	boiled pigs' hocks served with sauerkraut or puréed yellow peas
gołąbki m pl	go-*womb*-kee	cabbage leaves stuffed with minced beef & rice
grahamka f	gra-*kham*-ka	small wholemeal roll
grochówka f	gro-*khoof*-ka	lentil soup

jabłecznik m	ya-bwoch-neek	apple strudel
kapuśniak m	ka-poosh-nyak	sauerkraut soup
kisiel m	kee-shyel	jelly-type dessert made with potato starch
klopsiki m pl	klop-shee-kee	meatballs made with ground beef, pork and/or veal
knedle m pl	kned-le	dumplings stuffed with plums, cherries or apples
kopytka n pl	ko-pit-ka	potato dumplings similar to gnocchi
łosoś wędzony m	wo-sosh ven-dzo-ni	smoked salmon
makowiec m	ma-ko-vyets	poppy-seed strudel
melba f	mel-ba	ice cream, fruit & whipped cream
mizeria f	mee-zer-ya	sliced cucumber in sour cream
naleśniki m pl	na-lesh-nee-kee	crêpes • pancakes
nóżki w galarecie n pl	noosh-kee v ga-la-re-chye	jellied pigs' knuckles
pierogi m pl	pye-ro-gee	ravioli-like dumplings made from noodle dough, usually stuffed with mincemeat, sauerkraut, mushroom, cheese & potato
rosół z makaronem m	ro-soow z ma-ka-ro-nem	bouillon with noodles
sałatka jarzynowa f	sa-wat-ka ya-zhi-no-va	salad made with potato, vegetables & mayonnaise
sernik m	ser-neek	cheesecake
szaszłyk m	shash-wik	shish kebab
śledź w śmietanie m	shlej v shmye-ta-nye	herring in sour cream
tatar m	ta-tar	minced sirloin served raw with onion, raw egg yolk & chopped dill cucumber
zapiekanka f	za-pye-kan-ka	half a bread roll filled with cheese & mushrooms, baked & served hot

emergencies

basics

Help!	*Na pomoc!*	na *po*·mots
Stop!	*Stój!*	stooy
Go away!	*Odejdź!*	o·deyj
Thief!	*Złodziej!*	zwo·jyey
Fire!	*Pożar!*	po·zhar
Watch out!	*Uważaj!*	oo·*va*·zhai
Call ...!	*Zadzwoń po ...!*	zad·zvon' po ...
a doctor	*lekarza*	le·*ka*·zha
an ambulance	*karetkę*	ka·*ret*·ke
the police	*policję*	po·*lee*·tsye

It's an emergency.
To nagły wypadek.   to *nag*·wi vi·*pa*·dek

Could you help me, please?
Czy może pan/pani mi pomóc? m/f   chi *mo*·zhe pan/*pa*·nee mee *po*·moots

Can I use the telephone?
Czy mogę użyć telefon?   chi *mo*·ge *oo*·zhich te·*le*·fon

I'm lost.
Zgubiłem/Zgubiłam się. m/f   zgoo·*bee*·wem/zgoo·*bee*·wam shye

Where are the toilets?
Gdzie są toalety?   gjye som to·a·*le*·ti

police

Where's the police station?
Gdzie jest posterunek policji?   gje yest pos·te·*roo*·nek po·*lee*·tsyee

I want to report an offence.
Chciałem/Chciałam zgłosić   khchow·em/khchow·am zgwo·sheech
przestępstwo. m/f   pshe·*stemps*·tfo

I have insurance.
Mam ubezpieczenie.   mam oo·bes·pye·*che*·nye

I've been ...	Zostałem/Zostałam ... m/f	zo-stow-em/zo-stow-am ...
assaulted	napadnięty/a m/f	na-pad-nyen-ti/a
raped	zgwałcony/a m/f	zgvow-tso-ni/a
robbed	okradziony/a m/f	o-kra-jyo-ni/a

I've lost my ...	Zgubiłem/ Zgubiłam ... m/f	zgoo-bee-wem/ zgoo-bee-wam ...
backpack	plecak	ple-tsak
bag	torbę	tor-be
credit card	kartę kredytową	kar-te kre-di-to-vom
handbag	torebkę	to-rep-ke
jewellery	biżuterię	bee-zhoo-ter-ye
money	pieniądze	pye-nyon-dze
passport	paszport	pash-port
wallet	portfel	port-fel

I want to contact my ...	Chcę się skontaktować z ...	khtse shye skon-tak-to-vach z ...
consulate	moim konsulatem	mo-yeem kon-soo-la-tem
embassy	moją ambasadą	mo-yom am-ba-sa-dom

health

medical needs

Where's the nearest ...?	Gdzie jest najbliższy/a ...? m/f	gjye yest nai-bleezh-shi/a ...
dentist	dentysta m	den-tis-ta
doctor	lekarz m	le-kash
hospital	szpital m	shpee-tal
(night) pharmacist	apteka (nocna) f	ap-te-ka (nots-na)

I need a doctor (who speaks English).
Szukam lekarza (który mówi po angielsku).
shoo-kam le-ka-zha (ktoo-ri moo-vee po an-gyel-skoo)

Could I see a female doctor?
Czy mogę się widzieć z lekarzem kobietą?
chi mo-ge shye vee-jyech z le-ka-zhem ko-bye-tom

I've run out of my medication.
Skończyły mi się lekarstwa.
skon-chi-wi mee shye le-kars-tfa

symptoms, conditions & allergies

I'm sick.	*Jestem chory/a.* m/f	*yes*-tem *kho*-ri/a
It hurts here.	*Tutaj boli.*	*too*-tai *bo*-lee
I have (a) ...	*Mam ...*	mam ...
asthma	*astma* f	*ast*-ma
constipation	*zatwardzenie* n	zat-far-*dze*-nye
cough	*kaszel* m	*ka*-shel
diarrhoea	*rozwolnienie* n	roz-vol-*nye*-nye
fever	*gorączka* f	go-*ronch*-ka
headache	*ból głowy* m	bool *gwo*-vi
heart condition	*stan serca* m	stan *ser*-tsa
nausea	*mdłości* pl	*mdwosh*-chee
pain	*ból* m	bool
sore throat	*ból gardła* m	bool *gar*-dwa
toothache	*ból zęba* m	bool *zem*-ba
I'm allergic to ...	*Mam alergię na ...*	mam a-ler-*gye* na ...
antibiotics	*antybiotyki*	an-ti-byo-*ti*-kee
anti-inflammatories	*leki przeciwzapalne*	*le*-kee pshe-cheef-za-*pal*-ne
aspirin	*aspirynę*	as-pee-*ri*-ne
bees	*pszczoły*	*pshcho*-wi
codeine	*kodeinę*	ko-de-*ee*-ne
penicillin	*penicylinę*	pe-nee-tsi-*lee*-ne
antiseptic	*środki odkażające* pl	*shrod*-kee od-ka-zha-*yon*-tse
bandage	*bandaż* m	*ban*-dash
condoms	*kondom* pl	*kon*-dom
contraceptives	*środki antykoncepcyjne* pl	*shrod*-kee an-ti-kon-tsep-*tsiy*-ne
diarrhoea medicine	*rozwolnienie*	ros-vol-*nye*-nye
insect repellent	*środek na owady* m	*shro*-dek na o-*va*-di
laxatives	*środek przeczyszczający* m	*shro*-dek pshe-chish-cha-*yon*-tsi
painkillers	*środki przeciwbólowe* pl	*shrod*-kee pshe-cheef-boo-*lo*-ve
rehydration salts	*sole fizjologiczne* pl	*so*-le fee-zyo-lo-*geech*-ne
sleeping tablets	*pigułki nasenne* pl	pee-*goow*-kee na-*se*-ne

english-polish dictionary

Polish nouns in this dictionary have their gender indicated by ⓜ (masculine), ⓕ (feminine) or ⓝ (neuter). If it's a plural noun, you'll also see pl. Adjectives are given in the masculine form only. Words are also marked as a (adjective), v (verb), sg (singular), pl (plural), inf (informal) or pol (polite) where necessary.

A

accident *wypadek* ⓜ vi-*pa*-dek
accommodation *nocleg* ⓜ *nots*-leg
adaptor *zasilacz* ⓜ za-*shee*-lach
address *adres* ⓜ *a*-dres
after *po* • za po • za
air conditioning *klimatyzacja* ⓕ klee-ma-ti-*za*-tsya
airplane *samolot* ⓜ sa-*mo*-lot
airport *lotnisko* ⓝ lot-*nees*-ko
alcohol *alkohol* ⓜ al-*ko*-khol
all *wszystko* fshist-ko
allergy *alergia* ⓕ a-*ler*-gya
ambulance *karetka pogotowia* ⓕ ka-*ret*-ka po-go-*to*-vya
and *i* ee
ankle *kostka* ⓕ *kost*-ka
arm *ręka* ⓕ *ren*-ka
ashtray *popielniczka* ⓕ po-pyel-*neech*-ka
ATM *bankomat* ⓜ ban-*ko*-mat

B

baby *niemowlę* ⓝ nye-*mov*-le
back (body) *plecy* pl *ple*-tsi
backpack *plecak* ⓜ *ple*-tsak
bad *zły* zwi
bag *torba* ⓕ *tor*-ba
baggage claim *odbiór bagażu* ⓜ *od*-byoor ba-*ga*-zhoo
bank *bank* ⓜ bank
bar *bar* ⓜ bar
bathroom *łazienka* ⓕ wa-*zhyen*-ka
battery *bateria* ⓕ ba-*te*-rya
beautiful *piękny* pyen-kni
bed *łóżko* ⓝ *woozh*-ko
beer *piwo* ⓝ *pee*-vo
before *przed* pshet
behind *za* za
bicycle *rower* ⓜ *ro*-ver
big *duży* doo-zhi
bill *rachunek* ⓜ ra-*khoo*-nek
black *czarny* char-ni
blanket *koc* ⓜ kots

blood group *grupa krwi* ⓕ *groo*-pa krfee
blue *niebieski* nye-*byes*-kee
boat *łódź* ⓕ wooj
book (make a reservation) v *rezerwować* re-zer-vo-vach
bottle *butelka* ⓕ boo-*tel*-ka
bottle opener *otwieracz do butelek* ⓜ ot-*fye*-rach do boo-*te*-lek
boy *chłopiec* ⓜ *khwo*-pyets
brakes (car) *hamulce* pl ha-*mool*-tse
breakfast *śniadanie* ⓝ shnya-*da*-nye
broken (faulty) *połamany* po-wa-*ma*-ni
bus *autobus* ⓜ *ow*-to-boos
business *firma* ⓕ *feer*-ma
buy *kupować* koo-*po*-vach

C

café *kawiarnia* ⓕ ka-*vyar*-nya
camera *aparat* ⓜ a-*pa*-rat
camp site *kamping* ⓜ *kam*-peeng
cancel *unieważniać* oo-nye-*vazh*-nyach
can opener *otwieracz do konserw* ⓜ ot-*fye*-rach do kon-*serf*
car *samochód* ⓜ sa-*mo*-khoot
cash *gotówka* ⓕ go-*toof*-ka
cash (a cheque) v *zrealizować czek* zre-a-lee-*zo*-vach chek
cell phone *telefon komórkowy* ⓜ te-*le*-fon ko-moor-*ko*-vi
centre *środek* ⓜ *shro*-dek
change (money) v *rozmieniać* roz-*mye*-nyach
cheap *tani* ta-nee
check (bill) *sprawdzenie* ⓝ sprav-*dze*-nye
check-in *zameldowanie* ⓝ za-mel-do-*va*-nye
chest *klatka piersiowa* ⓕ *klat*-ka pyer-*shyo*-va
child *dziecko* ⓝ *jye*-tsko
cigarette *papieros* ⓜ pa-*pye*-ros
city *miasto* ⓝ *myas*-to
clean a *czysty* chi-sti
closed *zamknięty* zam-*knyen*-ti
coffee *kawa* ⓕ *ka*-va
coins *monety* ⓕ pl mo-*ne*-ti
cold a *zimny* zheem-ni

collect call *rozmowa opłacona przez odbierającego* ⓘ
roz-*mo*-va o-*pwa-tso*-na pshes od-bye-ra-yon-*tse*-go
come (by vehicle) *przyjść* pshiyshch
come (on foot) *przychodzić* pshi-*kho*-jeech
computer *komputer* ⓜ kom-*poo*-ter
condom *kondom* ⓜ kon-dom
contact lenses *soczewki kontaktowe* ⓕ pl
so-*chef*-kee kon-tak-*to*-ve
cook v *gotować* go-*to*-vach
cost *koszt* ⓜ kosht
credit card *karta kredytowa* ⓕ *kar*-ta kre-di-*to*-va
cup *filiżanka* ⓕ fee-lee-*zhan*-ka
currency exchange *kantor* ⓜ *kan*-tor
customs (immigration) *urząd celny* ⓜ
oo-zhont *tsel*-ni

D

dangerous *niebezpieczny* nye-bes-*pyech*-ni
date (time) *data* ⓕ *da*-ta
day *dzień* jyen´
delay *opóźnienie* ⓝ o-poozh-*nye*-nye
dentist *dentysta* ⓜ den-*tis*-ta
depart *odjeżdżać* od-*yezh*-jach
diaper *pieluszka* ⓕ pye-*loosh*-ka
dictionary *słownik* ⓜ *swov*-neek
dinner *kolacja* ⓕ ko-*la*-tsya
direct *bezpośredni* bes-po-*shred*-nee
dirty *brudny* brood-ni
disabled *niepełnosprawny* nye-pew-no-*sprav*-ni
discount *zniżka* ⓕ zneesh-ka
doctor *lekarz* ⓜ *le*-kash
double bed *łóżko małżeńskie* ⓝ
woozh-ko mow-*zhen´*-skye
double room *pokój dwuosobowy* ⓜ
po-kooy dvoo-o-so-*bo*-vi
drink *napój* ⓜ *na*-pooy
drive v *kierować* kye-ro-vach
drivers licence *prawo jazdy* ⓝ *pra*-vo yaz-di
drugs (illicit) *narkotyki* ⓝ pl nar-ko-*ti*-kee
dummy (pacifier) *smoczek* ⓜ *smo*-chek

E

ear *ucho* ⓝ *oo*-kho
east *wschód* ⓜ vskhood
eat *jeść* yeshch
economy class *klasa oszczędnościowa* ⓕ
kla-sa osh-chend-nosh-*chyo*-va
electricity *elektryczność* ⓕ e-lek-*trich*-noshch
elevator *winda* ⓕ *veen*-da
email *email* ⓜ e-mail

embassy *ambasada* ⓕ am-ba-*sa*-da
emergency *nagły przypadek* ⓜ *nag*-wi pshi-*pa*-dek
English (language) *angielski* an-*gyel*-skee
entrance *wejście* ⓝ *veysh*-chye
evening *wieczór* ⓜ *vye*-choor
exchange rate *kurs wymiany* ⓜ koors vi-*mya*-ni
exit *wyjście* ⓝ *viysh*-chye
expensive *drogi* *dro*-gee
express mail *list ekspresowy* ⓜ leest eks-pre-*so*-vi
eye *oko* ⓝ *o*-ko

F

far *daleki* da-*le*-kee
fast *szybki* shib-kee
father *ojciec* ⓜ *oy*-chyets
film (camera) *film* ⓜ feelm
finger *palec* ⓜ *pa*-lets
first-aid kit *apteczka pierwszej pomocy* ⓕ
ap-*tech*-ka pyerf-shey po-*mo*-tsi
first class *pierwsza klasa* ⓕ pyerf-sha *kla*-sa
fish *ryba* ⓕ ri-ba
food *żywność* ⓕ zhiv-noshch
foot *stopa* ⓕ *sto*-pa
fork *widelec* ⓜ vee-*de*-lets
free (of charge) *bezpłatny* bes-*pwat*-ni
friend *przyjaciel/przyjaciółka* ⓜ/ⓕ
pshi-ya-chyel/pshi-ya-*choow*-ka
fruit *owoc* ⓜ *o*-vots
full *pełny* pew-ni
funny *zabawny* za-*bav*-ni

G

gift *prezent* ⓜ *pre*-zent
girl *dziewczyna* ⓕ jyev-*chi*-na
glass (drinking) *szklanka* ⓕ *shklan*-ka
glasses *okulary* pl o-koo-*la*-ri
go (by vehicle) *jechać* ye-khach
go (on foot) *iść* eeshch
good *dobry* do-bri
green *zielony* zhye-*lo*-ni
guide *przewodnik* ⓜ pshe-*vod*-neek

H

half *połówka* ⓕ po-*woof*-ka
hand *ręka* ⓕ *ren*-ka
handbag *torebka* ⓕ to-*rep*-ka
happy *szczęśliwy* shchen-*shlee*-vi
have *mieć* myech
he *on* on

head *głowa* ① gwo-va
heart *serce* ⓝ ser-tse
heat *upał* ⓜ oo-pow
heavy *ciężki* ⓐ chyensh-kee
help v *pomagać* po-ma-gach
here *tutaj* too-tai
high *wysoki* vi-so-kee
highway *szosa* ① sho-sa
hike v *wędrować* ven-dro-vach
homosexual n *homoseksualista* ⓜ
  ho-mo-sek-soo-a-lees-ta
hospital *szpital* ⓜ shpee-tal
hot *gorący* go-ron-tsi
hotel *hotel* ⓜ ho-tel
hungry *głodny* gwo-dni
husband *mąż* ⓜ monzh

I

I *ja* ya
identification (card) *dowód tożsamości* ⓜ
  do-vood tozh-sa-mosh-chee
ill *chory* kho-ri
important *ważny* vazh-ni
included *wliczony* vlee-cho-ni
injury *rana* ① ra-na
insurance *ubezpieczenie* ⓝ oo-bes-pye-che-nye
Internet *internet* ⓜ een-ter-net
interpreter *tłumacz/tłumaczka* ⓜ / ①
  twoo-mach/twoo-mach-ka

J

jewellery *biżuteria* ① bee-zhoo-ter-ya
job *praca* ① pra-tsa

K

key *klucz* klooch
kilogram *kilogram* ⓜ kee-lo-gram
kitchen *kuchnia* ① kookh-nya
knife *nóż* ⓜ noosh

L

laundry (place) *pralnia* ① pral-nya
lawyer *prawnik* ⓜ prav-neek
left (direction) *lewy* ⓜ le-vi
left-luggage office *przechowalnia bagażu* ①
  pshe-kho-val-nya ba-ga-zhoo

leg *noga* ① no-ga
lesbian n *lesbijka* ① les-beey-ka
less *mniej* mnyey
letter (mail) *list* ⓜ leest
lift (elevator) *winda* ① veen-da
light *światło* ⓝ shyat-wo
like v *lubić* loo-beech
lock *zamek* ⓜ za-mek
long *długi* dwoo-gee
lost *zgubiony* zgoo-byo-ni
lost-property office *biuro rzeczy znalezionych* ⓝ
  byoo-ro zhe-chi zna-le-zhyo-nikh
love v *kochać* ko-khach
luggage *bagaż* ⓜ ba-gash
lunch *lunch* ⓜ lanch

M

mail (letters) *list* ⓜ leest
mail (postal system) *poczta* ① poch-ta
man *mężczyzna* ⓜ menzh-chiz-na
map (of country) *mapa* ① ma-pa
map (of town) *plan* ⓜ plan
market *rynek* ⓜ ri-nek
matches *zapałki* ① pl za-pow-kee
meat *mięso* ⓝ myen-so
medicine *lekarstwo* ⓝ le-karst-fo
menu *jadłospis* ⓜ ya-dwo-spees
message *wiadomość* ① vya-do-moshch
milk *mleko* ⓝ mle-ko
minute *minuta* ① mee-noo-ta
mobile phone *telefon komórkowy* ⓜ
  te-le-fon ko-moor-ko-vi
money *pieniądze* ⓝ pl pye-nyon-dze
month *miesiąc* ⓜ mye-shonts
morning *rano* ⓝ ra-no
mother *matka* ① mat-ka
motorcycle *motor* ⓜ mo-tor
motorway *autostrada* ① ow-to-stra-da
mouth *usta* pl oos-ta
music *muzyka* ① moo-zi-ka

N

name *imię* ⓝ ee-mye
napkin *serwetka* ① ser-vet-ka
nappy *pieluszka* ① pye-loosh-ka
near *bliski* blees-kee
neck *szyja* ① shi-ya
new *nowy* no-vi
news *wiadomości* ① vya-do-mosh-chee
newspaper *gazeta* ① ga-ze-ta
night *noc* ① nots

no *nie* nye
noisy *hałaśliwy* ha-wa-*shlee*-vi
nonsmoking *niepalący* nye-pa-*lon*-tsi
north *północ* ① *poow*-nots
nose *nos* ⓜ nos
now *teraz* te-ras
number *numer* ⓜ *noo*-mer

O

oil (engine) *olej* ⓜ o-ley
old *stary* sta-ri
one-way ticket *bilet w jedną stronę* ⓜ
  bee-let v yed-nom *stro*-ne
open a *otwarty* ot-*far*-ti
outside *na zewnątrz* na zev-nontsh

P

package *paczka* ① *pach*-ka
paper *papier* ⓜ pa-pyer
park (car) v *parkować* par-*ko*-vach
passport *paszport* ⓜ *pash*-port
pay *płacić* pwa-cheech
pen *długopis* ⓜ dwoo-*go*-pees
petrol *benzyna* ① ben-*zi*-na
pharmacy *apteka* ① ap-*te*-ka
phonecard *karta telefoniczna* ① *kar*-ta te-le-fo-*neech*-na
photo *zdjęcie* ⓝ *zdyen*-chye
plate *talerz* ⓜ *ta*-lesh
Poland *Polska* ① *pol*-ska
police *policja* ① po-*lee*-tsya
Polish (language) *polski* ⓜ *pol*-skee
postcard *pocztówka* ① poch-*toof*-ka
post office *urząd pocztowy* ⓜ *oo*-zhond poch-*to*-vi
pregnant *w ciąży* v chyon-zhi
price *cena* ① *tse*-na

Q

quiet *cichy* chee-khi

R

rain *deszcz* ⓜ deshch
razor *brzytwa* ① *bzhit*-fa
receipt *rachunek* ⓜ ra-*khoo*-nek
red *czerwony* cher-*vo*-ni
refund *zwrot pieniędzy* ⓜ zvrot pye-*nyen*-dzi
registered mail *list polecony* ⓜ leest po-le-*tso*-ni
rent v *wynająć* vi-*na*-yonch

repair v *naprawić* na-*pra*-veech
reservation *rezerwacja* ① re-zer-*va*-tsya
restaurant *restauracja* ① res-tow-*ra*-tsya
return v *wracać* *vra*-tsach
return ticket *bilet powrotny* ⓜ *bee*-let po-*vro*-tni
right (direction) *prawoskrętny* pra-vo-*skrent*-ni
road *droga* ① *dro*-ga
room *pokój* ⓜ *po*-kooy

S

safe a *bezpieczny* bes-*pyech*-ni
sanitary napkin *podpaski higieniczne* ① pl
  pod-*pas*-kee hee-gye-*neech*-ne
seat *miejsce* ⓝ *myeys*-tse
send *wysyłać* vi-*si*-wach
service station *stacja obsługi* ① *sta*-tsya ob-*swoo*-gee
sex *seks* ⓜ seks
shampoo *szampon* ⓜ *sham*-pon
share (a dorm) v *mieszkać z kimś* *myesh*-kach z keemsh
shaving cream *krem do golenia* ⓜ krem do go-*le*-nya
she *ona* o-na
sheet (bed) *prześcieradło* ⓝ pshesh-chye-*ra*-dwo
shirt *koszula* ① ko-*shoo*-la
shoes *buty* ⓜ pl *boo*-ti
shop *sklep* ⓜ sklep
short *krótki* *kroot*-kee
shower *prysznic* ⓜ *prish*-neets
single room *pokój jednoosobowy* ⓜ
  po-kooy ye-dno-o-so-*bo*-vi
skin *skóra* ① *skoo*-ra
skirt *spódnica* ① spood-*nee*-tsa
sleep v *spać* spach
slowly *powoli* po-*vo*-lee
small *mały* *ma*-wi
smoke (cigarettes) v *palić* pa-leech
soap *mydło* ⓝ *mid*-wo
some *kilka* *keel*-ka
soon *wkrótce* fkroot-tse
south *południe* ⓝ po-*wood*-nye
souvenir shop *sklep z pamiątkami* ⓜ
  sklep z pa-*myont*-ka-mi
speak *mówić* *moo*-veech
spoon *łyżka* ① *wish*-ka
stamp *znaczek* ⓜ *zna*-chek
stand-by ticket *bilet z listy rezerwowej* ⓜ
  bee-let z lees-ti re-zer-*vo*-vey
station (train) *stacja* ① *sta*-tsya
stomach *żołądek* ⓜ zho-*won*-dek
stop v *przestać* *pshes*-tach
stop (bus) *przystanek* ① pshis-*ta*-nek
street *ulica* ① oo-*lee*-tsa
student *student* ⓜ *stoo*-dent

O

sun *słońce* ⓜ *swon'-tse*
sunscreen *krem przeciwsłoneczny* ⓜ
  krem pshe-cheef-swo-nech-ni
swim v *pływać* *pwi-vach*

T

tampon *tampon* ⓜ *tam-pon*
taxi *taksówka* ① *tak-soof-ka*
teaspoon *łyżeczka* ① *wi-zhech-ka*
teeth *zęby* ⓜ pl *zem-bi*
telephone *telefon* ⓜ *te-le-fon*
television *telewizja* ① *te-le-veez-ya*
temperature (weather) *temperatura* ①
  tem-pe-ra-too-ra
tent *namiot* ⓜ *na-myot*
that (one) *który* *ktoo-ri*
they *oni* *o-nee*
thirsty *spragniony* *sprag-nyo-ni*
this (one) *ten* ⓜ *ten*
throat *gardło* *gard-wo*
ticket *bilet* ⓜ *bee-let*
time *czas* ⓜ *chas*
tired *zmęczony* *zmen-cho-ni*
tissues *chusteczki* ① pl *khoos-tech-kee*
today *dzisiaj* *jee-shyai*
toilet *toaleta* ① *to-a-le-ta*
tomorrow *jutro* *yoo-tro*
tonight *dzisiaj wieczorem* *jee-shyai vye-cho-rem*
toothbrush *szczotka do zębów* ① *shchot-ka do zem-boof*
toothpaste *pasta do zębów* ① *pas-ta do zem-boof*
torch (flashlight) *latarka* ① *la-tar-ka*
tour *wycieczka* ① *vi-chyech-ka*
tourist office *biuro turystyczne* ⓝ *byoo-ro too-ris-tich-ne*
towel *ręcznik* ⓜ *rench-neek*
train *pociąg* ⓜ *po-chyonk*
translate *przetłumaczyć* *pshe-twoo-ma-chich*
travel agency *biuro podróży* ⓝ *byoo-ro po-droo-zhi*
travellers cheques *czeki podróżne* ⓜ pl
  che-kee po-droozh-ne
trousers *spodnie* pl *spo-dnye*
twin beds *dwa łóżka* ⓝ pl *dva woosh-ka*
tyre *opona* ① *o-po-na*

U

underwear *bielizna* ① *bye-leez-na*
urgent *pilny* *peel-ni*

V

vacant *wolny* *vol-ni*
vacation *wakacje* pl *va-ka-tsye*
vegetable *warzywo* ⓝ *va-zhi-vo*
vegetarian a *wegetariański* *ve-ge-tar-yan'-skee*
visa *wiza* ① *vee-za*

W

waiter *kelner* ⓜ *kel-ner*
walk v *spacerować* *spa-tse-ro-vach*
wallet *portfel* ⓜ *port-fel*
warm a *ciepły* *chyep-wi*
Warsaw *Warszawa* ① *var-sha-va*
wash (something) *prać* *prach*
watch *zegarek* ⓜ *ze-ga-rek*
water *woda* ① *vo-da*
we *my* *mi*
weekend *weekend* ⓜ *wee-kend*
west *zachód* ⓜ *za-khood*
wheelchair *wózek inwalidzki* ⓜ
  voo-zek een-va-leets-kee
when *kiedy* *kye-di*
where *gdzie* *gjye*
white *biały* *bya-wi*
who *kto* *kto*
why *dlaczego* *dla-che-go*
wife *żona* ① *zho-na*
window *okno* ⓝ *ok-no*
wine *wino* ⓝ *vee-no*
with *z* *z*
without *bez* *bes*
woman *kobieta* ① *ko-bye-ta*
write *pisać* *pee-sach*

Y

yellow *żółty* *zhoow-ti*
yes *tak* *tak*
yesterday *wczoraj* *fcho-rai*
you sg inf *ty* *ti*
you sg pol *pan/pani* ⓜ/① *pan/pa-nee*
you pl inf *wy* *vi*
you pl pol *panowie/panie* ⓜ/① *pa-no-vye/pa-nye*
you pl pol *państwo* ⓜ&① *pan'-stfo*

Slovak

slovak alphabet

A a uh	*Á á* *dl*-hair a	*Ä ä* *shi*-ro-kair e	*B b* bair	*C c* tsair	*Č č* ch
D d dair	*Ď ď* dy	*Dz dz* dz	*Dž dž* j	*E e* e	*É é* *dl*-hair air
F f ef	*G g* gair	*H h* ha	*Ch ch* kh	*I i* i	*Í í* *dl*-hair ee
J j yair	*K k* ka	*L l* el	*Ĺ ĺ* *dl*-hair el	*Ľ ľ* ly	*M m* em
N n en	*Ň ň* ny	*O o* o	*Ó ó* *dl*-hair aw	*Ô ô* wo	*P p* pair
Q q quair	*R r* er	*Ŕ ŕ* *dl*-hair er	*S s* es	*Š š* sh	*T t* tair
Ť ť ty	*U u* u	*Ú ú* *dl*-hair oo	*V v* vair	*W w* *dvo*-yi-tair vair	*X x* iks
Y y *ip*-si-lon	*Ý ý* ee	*Z z* zet	*Ž ž* zh		

SLOVENČINA

slovak

introduction

The cosy position of the Slovak language (*slovenčina* slo·ven·chi·na) in Central Europe makes it a perfect base for learning or understanding the languages of other Slavic nations. It shares certain features with its close relatives in the West Slavic group – Czech and Polish. To a lesser extent, Slovak is similar to the South Slavic languages (particularly Slovene, from which it was distanced by the arrival of the Hungarians to their present day homeland in the 9th century). There are even similarities between Slovak and Ukrainian, which represents the East Slavic branch.

Not surprisingly, however, the language that bears the closest resemblance to Slovak is Czech, since ties between the two now independent countries date back to the 9th century and the Great Moravian Empire. More recently, the 20th-century Czechoslovakian affair established even closer relations between Czech and Slovak, to the extent that the two languages are mutually intelligible (although less so in the colloquial form or among the younger generation). Hungarian influence on Slovak (mainly in the vocabulary) is a result of the centuries during which Slovaks formed first part of the Kingdom of Hungary, and later the Austro-Hungarian Empire.

The literary standard of Slovak emerged in the mid-19th century, during a national revival movement, marked on the linguistic front by the work of L'udovít Štúr. In earlier times, it was mostly a spoken language, subordinated in writing to Latin and Czech, although texts with elements of Slovak or written entirely in Slovak can be traced back to the 15th century. The Great Moravian Empire was originally the place of St Cyril and Methodius' mission, which used the Glagolitic script, the precursor of the Cyrillic alphabet, for Old Church Slavonic literature. However, the West Slavic languages, including Slovak, soon adopted the Roman alphabet due to the influence of the Catholic Church.

Since 1993, Slovak has stepped out of the shadow of its larger neighbour, Czech, with which it shared official status during the Czechoslovakian days. It is now the official language of about 5 million speakers in Slovakia and there are Slovak speaking minorities in Poland, Hungary, Romania, Ukraine, the northern Serbian province of Vojvodina, and of course, the Czech Republic.

Even if you don't speak Slovak, be sure to look up your name in the official Slovak calendar – in which each day corresponds to a personal name and entitles people to celebrate their 'name day' (*sviatok* svyuh·tok or *meniny* me·nyi·ni) with equal pomp as their birthday!

pronunciation

vowel sounds

Slovak is rich in vowels, including a number of vowel combinations (or 'diphthongs').

symbol	english equivalent	slovak example	transliteration
a	father	*pán*	pan
ai	aisle	*raňajky*	ruh·nyai·ki
air	hair	*voľné*	voľ·nair
aw	law	*pól*	pawl
e	bet	*sestra, mäso*	ses·truh, me·so
ee	see	*prosím, bývať*	pro·seem, bee·vuhť
ey	hey	*olej*	o·ley
i	bit	*izba, byt*	iz·buh, bit
o	pot	*meno*	me·no
oh	oh	*zmesou*	zme·soh
oo	zoo	*pavúk*	puh·vook
ow	how	*auto*	ow·to
oy	toy	*ahoj*	a·hoy
uh	run	*matka*	muht·kuh
wo	quote	*môžem*	mwo·zhem

word stress

In Slovak, stress always falls on the first syllable, but it's quite light.

consonant sounds

Slovak consonants are shown opposite. Most have equivalents in English.

172

symbol	english equivalent	slovak example	transliteration
b	bed	*obed*	o·bed
ch	cheat	*večer*	ve·cher
d	dog	*adresa*	uh·dre·suh
dy	during	*ďaleko, džem*	dyuh·le·ko, dyem
dz	adds	*prichádza*	pri·kha·dzuh
f	fat	*fotka*	fot·kuh
g	go	*margarín*	muhr·guh·reen
h	hat	*hlava*	hluh·vuh
k	kit	*oko*	o·ko
kh	loch	*chorý*	kho·ree
l	lot	*lampa*	luhm·puh
ly	million	*doľava*	do·lyuh·vuh
m	man	*matka*	muht·kuh
n	not	*noviny*	no·vi·ni
ny	canyon	*kuchyňa*	ku·khi·nyuh
p	pet	*pero*	pe·ro
r	run	*ráno*	ra·no
s	sun	*sukňa*	suk·nyuh
sh	shot	*štyri*	shti·ri
t	top	*tri*	tri
ts	hats	*anglicky*	uhng·lits·ki
ty	tutor	*ťava*	tyuh·vuh
v	very	*vízum, watt*	vee·zum, vuht
y	yes	*ja*	yuh
z	zero	*zub*	zub
zh	pleasure	*manžel*	muhn·zhel
'	a slight y sound	*meď*	med'

language difficulties

Do you speak English?
Hovoríte po anglicky? ho·vo·ree·tye po *uhng*·lits·ki

Do you understand?
Rozumiete? ro·zu·mye·tye

I understand.
Rozumiem. ro·zu·myem

I don't understand.
Nerozumiem. nye·ro·zu·myem

What does (*jablko*) mean?
Čo znamená (jablko)? cho *znuh*·me·na (*yuh*·bl·ko)

How do you ...? *Ako sa ...?* *uh*·ko suh ...
  pronounce this *toto vyslovuje* *to*·to *vi*·slo·vu·ye
  write (*cesta*) *píše (cesta)* *pee*·she (*tses*·tuh)

Could you please ...? *Môžete prosím ...?* *mwo*·zhe·tye *pro*·seem ...
  repeat that *to zopakovať* *to* zo·puh·ko·vuht'
  speak more slowly *hovoriť pomalšie* ho·vo·rit' *po*·muhl·shye
  write it down *to napísať* to *nuh*·pee·suht'

essentials

Yes.	*Áno.*	*a*·no
No.	*Nie.*	*ni*·ye
Please.	*Prosím.*	*pro*·seem
Thank you	*Ďakujem*	*dyuh*·ku·yem
(very much).	*(veľmi pekne).*	(*veľ*·mi *pek*·nye)
You're welcome.	*Prosím.*	*pro*·seem
Excuse me.	*Prepáčte.*	pre·*pach*·tye
Sorry.	*Prepáčte.*	pre·*pach*·tye

numbers

0	*nula*	*nu·luh*	15	*pätnásť*	*pet·nast'*
1	*jeden* m	*ye·den*	16	*šestnásť*	*shes·nast'*
	jedna f	*yed·na*	17	*sedemnásť*	*se·dyem·nast'*
	jedno n	*yed·no*	18	*osemnásť*	*o·sem·nast'*
2	*dva* m	*dvuh*	19	*deväťnásť*	*dye·vet·nast'*
	dve n/f	*dve*	20	*dvadsať*	*dvuh·tsuht'*
3	*tri*	*tri*	21	*dvadsať–*	*dvuh·tsuht'·*
4	*štyri*	*shti·ri*		*jeden*	*ye·den*
5	*päť*	*pet'*	22	*dvadsaťdva*	*dvuh·tsuht'·dvuh*
6	*šesť*	*shest'*	30	*tridsať*	*tri·tsuht'*
7	*sedem*	*se·dyem*	40	*štyridsať*	*shti·ri·tsuht'*
8	*osem*	*o·sem*	50	*päťdesiat*	*pe·dye·syuht*
9	*deväť*	*dye·vet'*	60	*šesťdesiat*	*shes·dye·syuht*
10	*desať*	*dye·suht'*	70	*sedemdesiat*	*se·dyem·dye·syuht*
11	*jedenásť*	*ye·de·nast'*	80	*osemdesiat*	*o·sem·dye·syuht*
12	*dvanásť*	*dvuh·nast'*	90	*deväťdesiat*	*dye·ve·dye·syuht*
13	*trinásť*	*tri·nast'*	100	*sto*	*sto*
14	*štrnásť*	*shtr·nast'*	1000	*tisíc*	*tyi·seets*

time & dates

What time is it?	*Koľko je hodín?*	*koľ·ko ye ho·dyeen*
It's one o'clock.	*Je jedna hodina.*	*ye yed·nuh ho·dyi·nuh*
It's (two) o'clock.	*Sú (dve) hodiny.*	*soo (dve) ho·dyi·ni*
Quarter past (one).	*Štvrť na (dve).*	*shtvrt' nuh (dve)*
Half past (one).	*Pól (druhej).*	*pol (dru·hey)*
	(lit: half two)	
Quarter to (eight).	*Tritštvrte na (osem).*	*tri·shtvr·tye nuh (o·sem)*
At what time ...?	*O kolkej ...?*	*o koľ·key ...*
At ...	*O ...*	*o ...*
am (before 10)	*ráno*	*ra·no*
pm (10 to 12)	*dobedu*	*do·be·du*
pm	*pobede*	*po·be·dye*

Monday	pondelok	pon·dye·lok
Tuesday	utorok	u·to·rok
Wednesday	streda	stre·duh
Thursday	štvrtok	shtvr·tok
Friday	piatok	pyuh·tok
Saturday	sobota	so·bo·tuh
Sunday	nedeľa	nye·dye·lyuh
January	januar	yuh·nu·ar
February	februar	feb·ru·ar
March	marec	muh·rets
April	apríl	uhp·reel
May	máj	mai
June	jún	yoon
July	júl	yool
August	august	ow·gust
September	september	sep·tem·ber
October	október	ok·taw·ber
November	november	no·vem·ber
December	december	de·tsem·ber

What date is it today?
Koľkého je dnes?   kol·kair·ho ye dnyes

It's (15 December).
Je (pätnásteho decembra).   ye (pet·nas·te·ho de·tsem·bruh)

since (May)	od (mája)	od (ma·yuh)
until (June)	do (júna)	do (yoo·nuh)
last night	minulú noc	mi·nu·loo nots
last/next ...	minulý/budúci ...	mi·nu·lee/bu·doo·tsi ...
week	týždeň	teezh·dyen'
month	mesiac	me·syuhts
year	rok	rok
yesterday/tomorrow ...	včera/zajtra ...	vche·ruh/zai·truh ...
morning	ráno	ra·no
afternoon	popoludnie	po·po·lud·ni·ye
evening	večer	ve·cher

weather

What's the weather like?	Aké je počasie?	uh·kair ye po·chuh·si·ye
It's ...		
cloudy	Je zamračené.	ye zuh·mruh·che·nair
cold	Je zima.	ye zi·muh
hot	Je horúco.	ye ho·roo·tso
raining	Prší.	pr·shee
snowing	Sneží.	sne·zhee
sunny	Je slnečno.	ye sl·nyech·no
warm	Je teplo.	ye tyep·lo
windy	Je veterno.	ye ve·tyer·no
spring	jar f	yuhr
summer	leto n	le·to
autumn	jeseň f	ye·sen'
winter	zima f	zi·muh

border crossing

I'm here ...	Som tu ...	som tu ...
on business	v obchodnej	v ob·khod·ney
	záležitosti	za·le·zhi·tos·tyi
on holiday	na dovolenke	nuh do·vo·len·ke
I'm here for ...	Som tu na ...	som tu nuh ...
(10) days	(desať) dni	(dye·suht') dnyee
(two) months	(dva) mesiace	(dvuh) me·syuh·tse
(three) weeks	(tri) týždne	(tri) teezhd·nye

I'm going to (Bratislava).
Idem do (Bratislavy).   i·dyem do (bruh·tyi·sluh·vi)

I'm staying at the (Hotel Grand).
Zostávam v (hoteli Grand).   zo·sta·vuhm v (ho·te·li gruhnd)

I have nothing to declare.
Nemám nič na preclenie.   nye·mam nyich nuh prets·le·ni·ye

I have something to declare.
Mám niečo na preclenie.   mam ni·ye·cho nuh prets·le·ni·ye

That's (not) mine.
To (nie) je moje.   to (ni·ye) ye mo·ye

transport

tickets & luggage

Where can I buy a ticket?
Kde si môžem kúpiť
cestovný lístok?

kdye si *mwo*-zhem *koo*-pit'
tses-tov-nee *lees*-tok

Do I need to book a seat?
Potrebujem si rezervovať
miestenku?

po-tre-bu-yem si *re*-zer-vo-vuht'
myes-tyen-ku

One ... ticket	Jeden ... lístok	ye-den ... lees-tok
(to Poprad), please.	(do Popradu), prosím.	(do pop-ruh-du) pro-seem
one-way	jednosmerný	yed-no-smer-nee
return	spiatočný	spyuh-toch-nee

I'd like to ... my	Chcel/Chcela by som ...	khtsel/khtse-luh bi som ...
ticket, please.	môj lístok, prosím. m/f	mwoy lees-tok pro-seem
cancel	zrušiť	zru-shit'
change	zmeniť	zme-nyit'
collect	vyzdvihnúť	vizd-vih-noot'
confirm	potvrdiť	po-tvr-dyit'

I'd like a ... seat, please.	Prosím si ... miesto.	pro-seem si ... mye-sto
nonsmoking	nefajčiarske	nye-fai-chyuhr-ske
smoking	fajčiarske	fai-chyuhr-ske

How much is it?
Koľko to stojí?

kol'-ko to *sto*-yee

Is there air conditioning?
Je tam klimatizácia?

ye tuhm *kli*-muh-ti-za-tsi-yuh

Is there a toilet?
Je tam toaleta?

ye tuhm *to*-uh-le-tuh

How long does the trip take?
Koľko trvá cesta?

kol'-ko *tr*-va *tses*-tuh

Is it a direct route?
Je to priamy smer?

ye to *pryuh*-mi smer

I'd like a luggage locker.
Chcel/Chcela by som skrinku
na batožinu. m/f

khtsel/khtse-luh bi som *skrin*-ku
nuh *buh*-to-zhi-nu

My luggage has been ...	Moja batožina ...	mo·yuh buh·to·zhi·nuh ...
damaged	bola poškodená	bo·luh posh·ko·dye·na
lost	sa stratila	suh struh·tyi·luh
stolen	bola ukradnutá	bo·luh u·kruhd·nu·ta

getting around

Where does flight (number 333) arrive?
Kam prilieta let   kuhm pri·li·ye·tuh let
(číslo 333)?   (chees·lo tri·sto·tri·tsat'·tri)

Where does flight (number 333) depart?
Odkiaľ odlieta let   od·kyuhl od·li·ye·tuh let
(číslo 333)?   (chees·lo tri·sto·tri·tsat'·tri)

Where's (the) ...?	Kde je ...?	kdye ye ...
arrivals hall	príletová hala	pree·le·to·va huh·luh
departures hall	odletová hala	od·le·to·va huh·luh
duty-free shop	duty-free obchod	dyu·ti·free ob·khod
gate (12)	vchod (dvanásť)	vkhod (dvuh·nast')

Is this the ...	Je toto ...	ye to·to ...
to (Komárno)?	do (Komárna)?	do (ko·mar·nuh)?
boat	loď	lod'
bus	autobus	ow·to·bus
plane	lietadlo	li·ye·tuhd·lo
train	vlak	vluhk

What time's the ... bus?	Kedy príde ... autobus?	ke·di pree·dye ... ow·to·bus
first	prvý	pr·vee
last	posledný	po·sled·nee
next	nasledujúci	nuh·sle·du·yoo·tsi

At what time does it arrive/leave?
O koľkej prichádza/odchádza?   o kol'·key pri·kha·dzuh/od·kha·dzuh

How long will it be delayed?
Koľko je spozdenie?   kol'·ko ye spoz·dye·ni·ye

What station/stop is this?
Ktorá stanica/zastávka je toto?   kto·ra stuh·nyi·tsuh/zuhs·tav·kuh ye to·to

What's the next station/stop?
Ktorá je nasledujúca   kto·ra ye nuh·sle·du·yoo·tsuh
stanica/zastávka?   stuh·nyi·tsuh/zuhs·tav·kuh

Does it stop at (Štúrovo námestie)?
Stojí to na (Štúrovom námestí)? sto·yee to nuh (shtoo·ro·vom na·mes·tyee)

Please tell me when we get to (Hlavne námestie).
Môžete ma prosím upozorniť mwo·zhe·tye muh *pro*·seem u·po·zor·nyit'
keď budeme na … ked' *bu*·dye·me nuh …

How long do we stop here?
Ako dlho tu budeme stát'? uh·ko *dl*·ho tu *bu*·dye·me stat'

Is this seat available?
Je toto miesto voľné? ye *to*·to *mye*·sto *voľ*·nair

That's my seat.
Toto je moje miesto. *to*·to ye *mo*·ye *mye*·sto

I'd like a taxi …	*Chcel/Chcela by* m/f *som taxík na …*	khtsel/*khtse*·luh bi som *tuhk*·seek nuh …
at (9am)	*(deviatu ráno)*	(*dye*·vyuh·tu *ra*·no)
now	*teraz*	*te*·ruhz
tomorrow	*zajtra*	*zai*·truh

Is this taxi available?
Je tento taxík voľný? ye *ten*·to *tuhk*·seek *voľ*·nee

How much is it to …?
Koľko to bude stát' do …? *koľ*·ko to *bu*·dye stat' do …

Please put the meter on.
Zapnite taxameter, prosím. *zuhp*·nyi·tye *tuhk*·suh·me·ter *pro*·seem

Please take me to (this address).
Zavezte ma (na túto adresu), zuh·vez·tye muh (nuh *too*·to *uh*·dre·su)
prosím. *pro*·seem

Please …	*…, prosím.*	… *pro*·seem
slow down	*Spomaľte*	*spo*·muhľ·tye
stop here	*Zastavte tu*	*zuhs*·tuhv·tye tu
wait here	*Počkajte tu*	*poch*·kai·tye tu

car, motorbike & bicycle hire

I'd like to hire a …	*Chcel/Chcela by som si* m/f *prenajať …*	khtsel/*khtse*·luh bi som si *pre*·nuh·yuht' …
bicycle	*bicykel*	*bi*·tsi·kel
car	*auto*	*ow*·to
motorbike	*motorku*	*mo*·tor·ku

with ...	s ...	s ...
a driver	šoférom	sho·fair·rom
air conditioning	klimatizáciou	kli·muh·ti·za·tsi·oh
antifreeze	protimrazovou	pro·tyi·mruh·zo·voh
	zmesou	zme·soh
snow chains	snehovými	snye·ho·vee·mi
	reťazami	re·tyuh·zuh·mi
How much for	Koľko stojí	koľ·ko sto·yee
... hire?	prenájom na ...?	pre·na·yom nuh ...
hourly	hodinu	ho·dyi·nu
daily	deň	dyen'
weekly	týždeň	teezh·dyen'
air	stlačený vzduch m	stluh·che·nee vzdukh
oil	olej m	o·ley
petrol	benzín m	ben·zeen
tyres	pneumatiky f pl	pne·u·muh·ti·ki

I need a mechanic.
   Potrebujem automechanika.   *po·tre·bu·yem ow·to·me·khuh·ni·kuh*

I've run out of petrol.
   Minul sa mi benzín.   *mi·nul suh mi ben·zeen*

I have a flat tyre.
   Dostal/Dostala som defekt. m/f   *dos·tuhl/dos·tuh·luh som de·fekt*

directions

Where's the ...?	Kde je ...?	kdye ye ...
bank	banka	buhn·kuh
city centre	mestské centrum	mes·kair tsen·trum
hotel	hotel	ho·tel
market	trh	trh
police station	policajná stanica	po·li·tsai·na stuh·nyi·tsuh
post office	pošta	posh·tuh
public toilet	verejný záchod	ve·rey·nee za·khod
tourist office	turistická	tu·ris·tits·ka
	kancelária	kuhn·tse·la·ri·yuh

Is this the road to ...?   *Je toto cesta na ...?*   ye *to·to tses·tuh nuh ...*

Can you show me (on the map)?

Môžete mi ukázať   *mwo*·zhe·tye mi u·*kà·*zuñt
(na mape)?   (nuh *muh*·pe)

What's the address?

Aká je adresa?   *uh*·ka ye *uh*·dre·suh

How far is it?

Ako je to ďaleko?   *uh*·ko ye to *dyuh*·le·ko

How do I get there?

Ako sa tam dostanem?   *uh*·ko suh tuhm *dos*·tuh·nyem

Turn …	*Zabočte …*	*zuh*·boch·tye …
at the corner	*na rohu*	nuh *ro*·hu
at the traffic lights	*na svetelnej*	nuh *sve*·tyel·ney
	križovatke	*kri*·zho·vuht·ke
left	*doľava*	*do*·lyuh·vuh
right	*doprava*	*do*·pruh·vuh
It's …	*Je to …*	ye to …
behind …	*za …*	zuh …
far away	*ďaleko*	*dyuh*·le·ko
here	*tu*	tu
in front of …	*pred …*	pred …
left	*vľavo*	*vlyuh*·vo
near (to …)	*blízko (k …)*	*bleez*·ko (k …)
next to …	*vedľa …*	*ved*·lyuh …
on the corner	*na rohu*	nuh *ro*·hu
opposite …	*oproti …*	*o*·pro·tyi …
right	*vpravo*	*vpruh*·vo
straight ahead	*rovno*	*rov*·no
there	*tam*	tuhm
by bus	*autobusom*	*ow*·to·bu·som
by taxi	*taxíkom*	*tuhk*·see·kom
by train	*vlakom*	*vluh*·kom
on foot	*peši*	*pe*·shi
north	*sever*	*se*·ver
south	*juh*	yooh
east	*východ*	*vee*·khod
west	*západ*	*za*·puhd

signs

Vchod/Východ	vkhod/vee·khod	**Entrance/Exit**
Otvorené/Zatvorené	ot·vo·re·nair/zuht·vo·re·nair	**Open/Closed**
Ubytovanie	u·bi·to·vuh·ni·ye	**Rooms Available**
Plne obsadené	pl·nye ob·suh·dye·nair	**No Vacancies**
Informácie	in·for·ma·tsi·ye	**Information**
Policajná stanica	po·li·tsai·na stuh·nyi·tsuh	**Police Station**
Zakázané	zuh·ka·zuh·nair	**Prohibited**
Záchody/WC/Toalety	za·kho·di/vair·tsair/to·uh·le·ti	**Toilets**
Páni	pa·nyi	**Men**
Dámy	da·mi	**Women**
Horúca/Studená	ho·roo·tsuh/stu·dye·na	**Hot/Cold**

accommodation

finding accommodation

Where's a ...?	Kde je ...?	kdye ye ...
camping ground	táborisko	ta·bo·ris·ko
guesthouse	penzión	pen·zi·awn
hotel	hotel	ho·tel
youth hostel	nocľaháreň	nots·lyuh·ha·ren'
	pre mládež	pre mla·dyezh
Can you recommend somewhere ...?	Môžete odporučiť niečo ...?	mwo·zhe·tye od·po·ru·chit' ni·ye·cho ...
cheap	lacné	luhts·nair
good	dobré	dob·rair
nearby	nablízku	nuh·bleez·ku
I have a reservation.	Mám rezerváciu.	mam re·zer·va·tsi·yu
My name's ...	Volám sa ...	vo·lam suh ...
Do you have a twin room?	Máte dve oddelené postele?	ma·tye dve od·dye·le·nair pos·tye·le
Do you have a single room?	Máte jednoposteľovú izbu?	ma·tye yed·no·pos·tye·lyo·voo iz·bu
Do you have a double room?	Máte izbu s manželskou posteľou?	ma·tye iz·bu s muhn·zhels·koh pos·tye·lyoh

How much is it per ...?	Koľko to stojí na ...?	koľ·ko to sto·yee nuh ...
night	noc	nots
person	osobu	o·su·bu

Can I pay by ...?	Môžem platiť ...?	mwo·zhem pluh·tyiť ...
credit card	kreditnou kartou	kre·dit·noh kuhr·toh
travellers cheque	cestovnými šekmi	tses·tov·nee·mi shek·mi

I'd like to stay for (two) nights.

Chcel/Chcela by som	khtsel/khtse·luh bi som
zostať (dve) noci. m/f	zos·tuhť (dve) no·tsi

From (2 July) to (6 July).

Od (druhého júla)	od (dru·hair·ho yoo·luh)
do (šiesteho júla).	do (shyes·te·ho yoo·luh)

Can I see it?

Môžem to vidieť?	mwo·zhem to vi·di·yeť

Am I allowed to camp here?

Môžem tu stanovať?	mwo·zhem tu stuh·no·vuhť

Is there a camp site nearby?

Je tu nablízku táborisko?	ye tu nuh·blees·ku ta·bo·ris·ko

requests & queries

When/Where is breakfast served?

Kedy/Kde sa podávajú	ke·di/kdye suh po·da·vuh·yoo
raňajky?	ruh·nyai·ki

Please wake me at (seven).

Zobuďte ma o (siedmej), prosím.	zo·buď·tye muh o (syed·mey) pro·seem

Could I have my key, please?

Prosím si môj kľúč.	pro·seem si mwoy klyooch

Can I get another (blanket)?

Môžem dostať inú (prikrývku)?	mwo·zhem dos·tuhť i·noo (pri·kreev·ku)

Is there a/an ...?	Je tam ...?	ye tuhm ...
elevator	výťah	vee·tyah
safe	bezpečnostný trezor	bez·pech·nos·nee tre·zor

The room is too ...	Izba je príliš ...	iz·buh ye pree·lish ...
expensive	drahá	druh·ha
noisy	hlučná	hluch·na
small	malá	muh·la

The ... doesn't work.	... nefunguje.	... nye·fun·gu·ye
air conditioning	Klimatizácia	kli·muh·ti·za·tsi·yuh
fan	Ventilátor	ven·ti·la·tor
toilet	Toaleta	to·uh·le·tuh

This ... isn't clean.	Tento ... nie je čistý.	ten·to ... ni·ye ye chis·tee
pillow	vankúš	vuhn·koosh
towel	uterák	u·tye·rak

This sheet isn't clean.
Táto plachta nie je chistaa.　　ta·to pluhkh·tuh ni·ye ye chis·ta

checking out

What time is checkout?
O koľkej sa odhlasuje?　　o koľ'·key suh od·hluh·su·ye

Can I leave my luggage here?
Môžem si tu nechať batožinu?　　mwo·zhem si tu nye·khuhť buh·to·zhi·nu

Could I have my ...?	Poprosím vás o ...	po·pro·seem vas o ...
deposit	moju zálohu	mo·yu za·lo·hu
passport	môj cestovný pas	mwoy tses·tov·nee puhs
valuables	moje cennosti	mo·ye tsen·nos·tyi

communications & banking

the internet

Where's the local Internet café?
Kde je miestne internet café?　　kdye ye myes·ne in·ter·net kuh·fair

How much is it per hour?
Koľko stojí na hodinu?　　koľ'·ko sto·yee nuh ho·dyi·nu

I'd like to ...	Chcel/Chcela	khtsel/khtse·luh
	by som ... m/f	bi som ...
check my email	si skontrolovať email	si skon·tro·lo·vuhť ee·meyl
get Internet access	sa pripojiť na	suh pri·po·yiť nuh
	internet	in·ter·net
use a printer	použiť tlačiareň	po·u·zhiť tluh·chyuh·ren'
use a scanner	použiť scanner	po·u·zhiť ske·ner

mobile/cell phone

I'd like a . . .	*Chcel/Chcela*	khtsel/*khtse*·luh
	by som . . . m/f	bi som . . .
mobile/cell phone	*si prenajať*	si pre·nuh·yuht'
for hire	*mobilný telefón*	*mo*·bil·nee *te*·le·fawn
SIM card for your	*SIM kartu pre vašu*	sim *kuhr*·tu *pre vuh*·shu
network	*sieť*	syet'
What are the rates?	*Aké sú poplatky?*	uh·kair soo *pop*·luht·ki

telephone

What's your phone number?
Aké je vaše telefónne číslo?　　uh·kair ye *vuh*·she *te*·le·faw·ne *chees*·lo

The number is . . .
Číslo je . . .　　*chees*·lo ye . . .

Where's the nearest public phone?
Kde je najbližší verejný telefón?　　kdye ye *nai*·blizh·shee *ve*·rey·nee *te*·le·fawn

I'd like to buy a phonecard.
Chcel/Chcela by som si kúpiť　　khtsel/*khtse*·luh bi som si *koo*·pit'
telefónnu kartu. m/f　　*te*·le·faw·nu *kuhr*·tu

I want to . . .	*Chcem . . .*	khtsem . . .
call (Singapore)	*volať*	*vo*·luht'
	(do Singapúru)	(do *sin*·guh·poo·ru)
make a local call	*volať miestne číslo*	*vo*·luht' *myes*·ne *chees*·lo
reverse the	*hovor na účet*	*ho*·vor nuh *oo*·chet
charges	*volaného*	*vo*·luh·nair·ho

How much does . . . cost?	*Koľko . . . ?*	*koľ*·ko . . .
a (three)-minute	*stoja (tri) minúty*	*sto*·yuh (tri) *mi*·noo·ti
call	*volania*	*vo*·luh·ni·yuh
each extra	*stojí každá*	*sto*·yee *kuhzh*·da
minute	*ďalšia minúta*	*dyuhl*·shyuh *mi*·noo·tuh

(One) euro per minute.
(Jedno) euro za minútu.　　(*yed*·no) *e*·u·ro zuh *mi*·noo·tu

post office

I want to send a ...	Chcel/Chcela by som poslať ... m/f	khtsel/khtse·luh bi som pos·luht' ...
fax	fax	fuhks
letter	list	list
parcel	balík	buh·leek
postcard	pohľadnicu	po·hlyuhd·nyi·tsu
I want to buy a/an ...	Chcel/Chcela by som si kúpiť ... m/f	khtsel/ khtse·luh bi som si koo·pit' ...
envelope	obálku	o·bal·ku
stamp	známku	znam·ku
Please send it (to Australia) by ...	Prosím pošlite to (do Austrálie) ...	pro·seem posh·li·tye to (do ows·tra·li·ye) ...
airmail	leteckou poštou	le·tyets·koh posh·toh
express mail	expresne	eks·pres·nye
registered mail	doporučene	do·po·ru·che·nye
surface mail	obyčajnou poštou	o·bi·chai·noh posh·toh

Is there any mail for me?
Je tam nejaká pošta pre mňa?   ye tuhm nye·yuh·ka posh·tuh pre mnyuh

bank

Where's a/an ...?	Kde je ...?	kdye ye ...
ATM	nejaký bankomat	nye·yuh·kee buhn·ko·muht
foreign exchange office	nejaká zmenáreň	nye·yuh·ka zme·na·ren'
I'd like to ...	Chcel/Chcela by som ... m/f	khtsel/khtse·luh bi som ...
Where can I ...?	Kde môžem ...?	kdye mwo·zhem ...
arrange a transfer	zariadiť prevod	zuh·ryuh·dyit' pre·vod
cash a cheque	preplatiť šek	pre·pluh·tyit' shek
change a travellers cheque	zameniť cestovný šek	zuh·me·nyit' tses·tov·nee shek
change money	zameniť peniaze	zuh·me·nyit' pe·ni·yuh·ze
get a cash advance	dostať vopred hotovosť	dos·tuht' vo·pred ho·to·vost'
withdraw money	vybrať peniaze	vib·ruht' pe·ni·yuh·ze

What's the ...?	Aký je ...?	uh·kee ye ...
charge for that	za to poplatok	zuh tô pop·luh·tok
exchange rate	výmenný kurz	vee·men·nee kurz

It's ...	Je to ...	ye to ...
(12) euros	(dvanásť) euro	(dvuh·nast') e·u·ro
free	zadarmo	zuh·duhr·mo

What's the commission?
Aká je provízia? — uh·ka ye pro·vee·zi·yuh

What time does the bank open?
O koľkej otvára banka? — o koľ·key ot·va·ruh buhn·kuh

Has my money arrived yet?
Prišli už moje peniaze? — prish·li uzh mo·ye pe·ni·yuh·ze

sightseeing

getting in

What time does it open/close?
O koľkej otvárajú/ zatvárajú? — o koľ·key ot·va·ruh·yoo/ zuht·va·ruh·yoo

What's the admission charge?
Koľko je vstupné? — koľ·ko ye vstup·nair

Is there a discount for students/children?
Je nejaká zľava pre študentov/deti? — ye nye·yuh·ka zlyuh·vuh pre shtu·den·tov/dye·tyi

I'd like a ...	Chcel/Chcela by som ... m/f	khtsel/khtse·luh bi som ...
catalogue	katalóg	kuh·tuh·lawg
guide	sprievodcu	sprye·vod·tsu
local map	miestnu mapu	myest·nu muh·pu

I'd like to see ...	Rád/Rada by som videl/videla ... m/f	rad/ruh·duh bi som vi·dyel/vi·dye·luh ...
What's that?	Čo je to?	cho ye to
Can I take a photo?	Môžem fotografovať?	mwo·zhem fo·to·gruh·fo·vuht'

tours

When's the next ...?	Kedy je ďalší ...?	ke·di ye dyuhl·shee ...
day trip	celodenný výlet	tse·lo·den·nee vee·let
tour	zájazd	za·yuhzd

Is ... included?	Je zahrnuté ...?	ye zuh·hr·nu·tair ...
accommodation	ubytovanie	u·bi·to·vuh·ni·ye
the admission charge	vstupné	vstup·nair
food	jedlo	yed·lo

Is transport included?
Je zahrnutá doprava?   ye zuh·hr·nu·ta do·pruh·vuh

How long is the tour?
Koľko trvá zájazd?   koľ·ko tr·va za·yuhzd

What time should we be back?
O koľkej by sme mali byť späť?   o koľ·key bi sme muh·li biť späť

sightseeing

castle	zámok m	za·mok
cathedral	katedrála f	kuh·ted·ra·luh
church	kostol m	kos·tol
main square	hlavné námestie n	hluhv·nair na·mes·ti·ye
monastery	kláštor m	klash·tor
monument	pamätník m	puh·met·nyeek
museum	múzeum n	moo·ze·um
old city	staré mesto n	stuh·rair mes·to
palace	palác m	puh·lats
ruins	zrúcaniny pl	zroo·tsuh·nyi·ni
stadium	štadión m	shtuh·di·awn
statue	socha f	so·khuh

shopping

enquiries

Where's a ...?	Kde je ...?	kdye ye ...
bank	banka	buhn·kuh
bookshop	kníhkupectvo	knyeeh·ku·pets·tvo
camera shop	fotografický obchod	fo·to·gruh·fits·kee ob·khod
department store	obchodný dom	ob·khod·nee dom
grocery store	potraviny	po·truh·vi·ni
market	trh	trh
newsagency	predajňa novín	pre·dai·nyuh no·veen
supermarket	samoobsluha	suh·mo·ob·slu·huh

Where can I buy (a padlock)?
Kde si môžem kúpiť · kdye si mwo·zhem koo·pit'
(visiaci zámok)? · (vi·syuh·tsi za·mok)

I'm looking for ...
Hľadám ... · hlyuh·dam ...

Can I look at it?
Môžem sa na to pozrieť? · mwo·zhem suh nuh to poz·ryet'

Do you have any others?
Máte nejaké iné? · ma·tye nye·yuh·kair i·nair

Does it have a guarantee?
Je na to záruka? · ye nuh to za·ru·kuh

Can I have it sent abroad?
Môžem si to dať poslať do · mwo·zhem si to duht' pos·luht' do
zahraničia? · zuh·hruh·nyi·chyuh

Can I have my ... repaired?
Môžem si dať opraviť môj ...? · mwo·zhem si duht' o·pruh·vit' mwoy ...

It's faulty.
Je to pokazené. · ye to po·kuh·ze·nair

I'd like ..., please.
Poprosil/Poprosila · po·pro·sil/po·pro·si·luh
by som ... m/f · bi som ...

a bag	tašku	tuhsh·ku
a refund	vrátenie peňazi	vra·tye·ni·ye pe·nyuh·zee
to return this	toto vrátiť	to·to vra·tyit'

paying

How much is it?
Koľko to stojí? — koľ·ko to sto·yee

Can you write down the price?
Môžete napísať cenu? — mwo·zhe·tye nuh·pee·suhť tse·nu

That's too expensive.
To je príliš drahé. — to ye pree·lish druh·hair

What's your lowest price?
Aká je vaša najnižšia cena? — uh·ka ye vuh·shuh nai·nizh·shyuh tse·nuh

I'll give you (five) euros.
Dám vám (päť) euro. — dam vam (peť) e·u·ro

There's a mistake in the bill.
V účte je chyba. — v ooch·tye ye khi·buh

Do you accept ...?	*Príjmate ...?*	pree·muh·tye ...
credit cards	*kreditné karty*	kre·dit·nair kuhr·ti
debit cards	*debetné karty*	de·bet·nair kuhr·ti
travellers cheques	*cestovné šeky*	tses·tov·nair she·ki
I'd like ..., please.	*Prosím si ...*	pro·seem si ...
a receipt	*potvrdenie*	pot·vr·dye·ni·ye
my change	*môj výdavok*	mwoy vee·duh·vok

clothes & shoes

Can I try it on?	*Môžem si to vyskúšať?*	mwo·zhem si to vis·koo·shuhť
My size is (42).	*Moja veľkosť je (štyridsaťdva).*	mo·yuh veľ·kosť ye (shti·rid·suhť·dvuh)
It doesn't fit.	*Nesedí mi to.*	nye·se·dyee mi to
small	*malý*	muh·lee
medium	*stredný*	stred·nee
large	*veľký*	veľ·kee

books & music

I'd like a ...	Môžem dostať ...	mwo·zhem dos·tuht'...
newspaper	noviny	no·vi·ni
(in English)	(v angličtine)	(v uhn·glich·tyi·nye)
pen	pero	pe·ro

Is there an English-language bookshop?
Je tu anglické kníhkupectvo?   ye tu uhn·glits·kair kneeh·ku·pets·tvo

I'm looking for something by (Milan Lasica/Boris Filan).
Hľadám niečo od (Milana Lasicu/   hlyuh·dam ni·ye·cho od (mi·luh·nuh luh·si·tsu/
Borisa Filana).   bo·ri·suh fi·luh·nuh)

Can I listen to this?
Môžem si to vypočuť?   mwo·zhem si to vi·po·chut'

photography

Can you ...?	Mohli by ste ...?	mo·hli bi stye ...
burn a CD from	napáliť CD z	nuh·pa·lit' tsair·dair z
my memory card	mojej pamäťovej	mo·yey puh·me·tyo·vey
	karty	kuhr·ti
develop this film	vyvolať tento film	vi·vo·luht' ten·to film
load my film	zaviesť môj film	zuh·vyest' mwoy film

I need a/an ... film	Potrebujem ... film	po·tre·bu·yem ... film
for this camera.	do tohto fotoaparátu.	do to·hto fo·to·uh·puh·ra·tu
APS	APS	a pair es
B&W	čiernobiely	chyer·no·bye·li
colour	farebný	fuh·reb·nee
slide	navíjací	nuh·vee·yuh·tsee
(200) speed	(dvestovku) citlivosť	(dve·stov·ku) tsit·li·vost'

When will it be ready?   *Kedy to bude hotové?*   ke·di to bu·dye ho·to·vair

meeting people

greetings, goodbyes & introductions

Hello/Hi.	Dobrý deň/Ahoj.	*do·bree dyen'/uh·hoy*
Good night.	Dobrú noc.	*do·broo nots*
Goodbye/Bye.	Do videnia/Ahoj.	do *vi·dye·ni·yuh/uh·ho*

| Mr/Mrs | pán/pani | pan/*puh·*nyi |
| Miss | slečna | *slech·*nuh |

How are you?	Ako sa máte/máš? pol/inf	*uh·*ko suh *ma·*tye/mash
Fine, thanks.	Dobre, ďakujem.	*do·*bre *dyuh·*ku·yem
And you?	A vy/ty? pol/inf	uh vi/ti
What's your name?	Ako sa voláte/voláš? pol/inf	*uh·*ko suh *vo·*la·tye/*vo·*lash
My name is ...	Volám sa ...	*vo·*lam suh ...
I'm pleased to meet you.	Teší ma.	*tye·*shee muh

This is my ...	Toto je môj/moja ... m/f	*to·*to ye mwoy/*mo·*yuh ...
boyfriend	priateľ	*pryuh·*tyel'
brother	brat	bruht
daughter	dcéra	*tsair·*ruh
father	otec	*o·*tyets
friend	kamarát m	*kuh·*muh·rat
	kamarátka f	*kuh·*muh·rat·kuh
girlfriend	priateľka	*pryuh·*tyel'·kuh
husband	manžel	*muhn·*zhel
mother	matka	*muht·*kuh
partner (intimate)	partner/partnerka m/f	*part·*ner/*part·*ner·kuh
sister	sestra	*ses·*truh
son	syn	sin
wife	manželka	*muhn·*zhel·kuh

What's your ...?	Aká je vaša ...?	*uh·*ka ye *vuh·*shuh ...
address	adresa	*uhd·*re·suh
email address	emailová adresa	*ee·*mey·lo·va *uhd·*re·suh

Here's my ...	Tu je môj ...	tu ye mwoy ...
What's your ...?	Aké je vaše ...?	*uh·*kair ye *vuh·*she ...
fax number	faxové číslo	*fuhk·*so·vair chees·lo
phone number	telefónne číslo	te·le·fuhwn·ne chees·lo

occupations

What's your occupation?
Aké je vaše povolanie?   uh·kair ye *vuh*·she po·vo·luh·ni·ye

I'm a/an ...	Som ...	som ...
artist	umelec/umelkyňa m/f	u·me·lets/u·mel·ki·nyuh
businessperson	podnikateľ m	pod·nyi·kuh·tyel'
	podnikateľka f	pod·nyi·kuh·tyel'·kuh
farmer	pestovateľ m	pes·to·vuh·tyel'
	pestovateľka f	pes·to·vuh·tyel'·ka
manual worker	robotník m	ro·bot·nyeek
	robotníčka f	ro·bot·nyeech·kuh
office worker	úradník m	oo·ruhd·nyeek
	úradníčka f	oo·ruhd·nyeech·kuh
scientist	vedecký	ve·dyets·kee
	pracovník m	pruh·tsov·nyeek
	vedecká	ve·dets·ka
	pracovníčka f	pruh·tsov·nyeech·kuh
student	študent/študentka m/f	shtu·dent/shtu·dent·kuh
tradesperson	živnostník m	zhiv·nos·nyeek
	živnostníčka f	zhiv·nos·nyeech·kuh

background

Where are you from?	Odkiaľ ste?	od·kyuhľ stye
I'm from ...	Som z ...	som z ...
Australia	Austrálie	ows·tra·li·ye
Canada	Kanady	kuh·nuh·di
England	Anglicka	uhng·lits·kuh
New Zealand	Nového Zélandu	no·vair·ho zair·luhn·du
the USA	USA	oo·es·a
Are you married?	Ste ženatý/vydatá? m/f	stye zhe·nuh·tee/vi·duh·ta
I'm ...	Som ...	som ...
married	ženatý/vydatá m/f	zhe·nuh·tee/vi·duh·ta
single	slobodný m	slo·bod·nee
	slobodná f	slo·bod·na

age

How old ...?	*Koľko ... rokov?*	koľ·ko ... ro·kov
are you	*máte/máš* pol/inf	ma·tye/mash
is your daughter	*má vaša dcéra*	ma vuh·shuh tsair·ruh
is your son	*má váš syn*	ma vash sin

I'm ... years old.	*Ja mám ... rokov.*	yuh mam ... ro·kov
He/She is ... years old.	*On/Ona má ... rokov.*	on/onuh ma ... ro·kov

feelings

I'm (not) ...	*(Nie) Je mi ...*	(ni·ye) ye mi ...
Are you ...?	*Je vám ...?*	ye vam ...
cold	*zima*	zi·muh
hot	*teplo*	tye·plo

I'm (not) ...	*(Nie) Som ...*	(ni·ye) som ...
Are you ...?	*Ste ...?*	stye ...
happy	*šťastný/šťastná* m/f	shtyuhs·nee/shtyuhs·na
hungry	*hladný/hladná* m/f	hluhd·nee/hluhd·na
sad	*smutný/smutná* m/f	smut·nee/smut·na
thirsty	*smädný/smädná* m/f	smed·nee/smed·na

entertainment

going out

Where can I find ...?	*Kde nájdem ...?*	kdye nai·dyem ...
clubs	*kluby*	klu·bi
gay venues	*podniky pre homosexuálov*	pod·nyi·ki pre ho·mo·sek·su·a·lov
pubs	*krčmy*	krch·mi

I feel like going to a/the ...	*Mám chuť ísť ...*	mam khuť eesť ...
concert	*na koncert*	nuh kon·tsert
movies	*do kina*	do ki·nuh
restaurant	*do reštaurácie*	do resh·tow·ra·tsi·ye
theatre	*do divadla*	do dyi·vuhd·luh

interests

Do you like ...?	*Máte radi ...?*	*ma·tye ruh·di ...*
I like ...	*Mám rád/rada ...* m/f	mam rad/*ruh·duh* ...
I don't like ...	*Nemám rád/*	*nye·mam rad/*
	rada ... m/f	*ruh·duh ...*
art	*umenie*	*u·me·ni·ye*
cooking	*varenie*	*vuh·re·ni·ye*
movies	*filmy*	*fil·mi*
nightclubs	*nočné kluby*	*noch·nair klu·bi*
reading	*čítanie*	*chee·tuh·ni·ye*
shopping	*nakupovanie*	*nuh·ku·po·vuh·ni·ye*
sport	*šport*	shport
travelling	*cestovanie*	*tses·to·vuh·ni·ye*
Do you like to ...?	*Radi ...?*	*ruh·dyi ...*
dance	*tancujete*	*tuhn·tsu·ye·tye*
go to concerts	*chodíte na*	*kho·dyee·tye nuh*
	koncerty	*kon·tser·ti*
listen to music	*počúvate hudbu*	*po·choo·vuh·tye hud·bu*

food & drink

finding a place to eat

Can you	*Môžete mi*	*mwo·zhe·tye mi*
recommend a ...?	*odporučiť ...?*	*od·po·ru·chit' ...*
bar	*bar*	buhr
café	*kaviareň*	*kuh·vyuh·ren'*
restaurant	*reštauráciu*	*resh·tow·ra·tsi·yu*
I'd like ..., please.	*Chcel/Chcela by som*	khtsel/*khtse·*luh bi som
	..., prosím. m/f	*... pro·*seem
a table for (four)	*stôl pre (štyroch)*	stwol pre (*shti·*rokh)
the nonsmoking	*nefajčiarsku časť*	*nye·*fai·chyuhr·sku chuhst'
section		
the smoking section	*fajčiarsku časť*	*fai·*chyuhr·sku chuhst'

ordering food

breakfast	*raňajky* pl	*ruh*·nyai·ki
lunch	*obed* m	*o*·bed
dinner	*večera* f	*ve*·che·ruh
snack	*občerstvenie* n	*ob*·cherst·ve·ni·ye

What would you recommend?	*Čo by ste mi odporučili?*	cho bi stye mi *od*·po·ru·chi·li

I'd like (the) ..., please.	*Prosím si ...*	*pro*·seem si ...
bill	*účet*	*oo*·chet
drink list	*nápojový lístok*	*na*·po·yo·vee *lees*·tok
menu	*jedálny lístok*	*ye*·dal·ni *lees*·tok
that dish	*toto jedlo*	*to*·to *yed*·lo

drinks

(cup of) coffee/tea ...	*(šálka) kávy/čaju ...*	*(shal*·kuh) *ka*·vi/*chuh*·yu ...
with milk	*s mliekom*	s *mlye*·kom
without sugar	*bez cukru*	bez *tsuk*·ru

(orange) juice	*(pomarančový) džús* m	*(po*·muh·ruhn·cho·vee) dyoos
soft drink	*nealkoholický nápoj* m	*nye*·uhl·ko·ho·lits·kee *na*·poy
(boiled/mineral) water	*(prevarená/minerálna) voda* f	*(pre*·vuh·re·na/*mi*·ne·ral·nuh) *vo*·duh

in the bar

I'll have ...	*Dám si ...*	dam si ...
I'll buy you a drink.	*Kúpim ti/vám drink.* inf/pol	*koo*·pim tyi/vam drink
What would you like?	*Čo si dáš/dáte?* inf/pol	cho si dash/*da*·tye
Cheers!	*Nazdravie!*	*nuhz*·druh·vi·ye

| a shot of (whisky) | *štamperlík (whisky)* | *shtuhm*·per·leek (*vis*·ki) |
| a bottle/glass of beer | *fľaša/pohár piva* | *flyuh*·shuh/*po*·har *pi*·vuh |

a bottle/glass of ...wine	*fľaša/pohár ... vína*	*flyuh*·shuh/*po*·har ... *vee*·nuh
red	*červeného*	*cher*·ve·nair·ho
sparkling	*šumivého*	*shu*·mi·vair·ho
white	*bieleho*	*bye*·le·ho

self catering

What's the local speciality?
Čo je miestna špecialita?   cho ye *myes*·nuh *shpe*·tsyuh·li·tuh

What's that?
Čo je to?   cho ye to

How much is (a kilo of cheese)?
Koľko stojí (kilo syra)?   *koľ*·ko *sto*·yee (*ki*·lo *si*·ruh)

I'd like …	*Môžem dostať …*	mwo·zhem *dos*·tuht' …
(100) grams	*(sto) gramov*	(sto) *gruh*·mov
(two) kilos	*(dve) kilá*	(dve) *ki*·la
(three) pieces	*(tri) kusy*	(tri) *ku*·si
(six) slices	*(šesť) plátkov*	(shesť) *plat*·kov

Less.	*Menej.*	*me*·nyey
Enough.	*Stačí.*	*stuh*·chee
More.	*Viac.*	vyuhts

special diets & allergies

Is there a vegetarian restaurant near here?
Je tu nablízku vegetariánska   ye tu nuh·*bleez*·ku *ve*·ge·tuh·ri·yan·skuh
reštaurácia?   resh·tow·ra·tsi·yuh

Do you have vegetarian food?
Máte vegetariánske jedlá?   ma·tye *ve*·ge·tuh·ri·yan·ske *yed*·la

Could you prepare	*Mohli by ste pripraviť*	*mo*·hli bi stye *pri*·pruh·viť
a meal without …?	*jedlo bez …?*	*yed*·lo bez …
butter	*masla*	*muhs*·luh
eggs	*vajec*	*vuh*·yets
meat stock	*mäsového vývaru*	*me*·so·vair·ho *vee*·vuh·ru

I'm allergic to …	*Som alergický/*	som uh·*ler*·gits·kee/
	alergická na … m/f	uh·*ler*·gits·ka nuh …
dairy produce	*mliečne produkty*	*mlyech*·ne *pro*·duk·ti
gluten	*lepok*	*le*·pok
MSG	*zvýrazňovač*	*zvee*·ruhz·nyo·vuhch
	chute	*khu*·tye
nuts	*orechy*	*o*·re·khi
seafood	*dary mora*	*duh*·ri *mo*·ruh

menu decoder

balkánský šalát m	*buhl*-kan-ski *shuh*-lat	*lettuce, tomato, onion & cheese salad*
bravčové pečené s rascou n	*bruhv*-cho-vair *pe*-che-nair s *ruhs*-tsoh	*roast pork with caraway seeds*
držková polievka f	*drzh*-ko-va *po*-lyev-kuh	*sliced tripe soup*
dusené hovädzie na prírodno n	*du*-se-nair *ho*-ve-dzye nuh *pree*-rod-no	*braised beef slices in sauce*
guláš m	*gu*-lash	*thick, spicy beef & potato soup*
hovädzí guláš m	*ho*-ve-dzee *gu*-lash	*beef chunks in brown sauce*
hovädzí vývar m	*ho*-ve-dzee *vee*-vuhr	*beef in broth*
hrachová polievka f	*hruh*-kho-va *po*-lyev-kuh	*thick pea soup with bacon*
jablkový závin m	*yuh*-bl-ko-vee *za*-vin	*apple strudel*
kapor na víne m	*kuh*-por nuh *vee*-nye	*carp braised in wine*
koložvárska kapusta f	*ko*-lozh-var-skuh *kuh*-pus-tuh	*goulash with beef, pork, lamb & sauerkraut in a cream sauce*
krokety m pl	*kro*-ke-ti	*deep-fried mashed potato*
kuracia polievka f	*ku*-ruh-tsyuh *po*-lyev-kuh	*chicken soup*
kurací paprikáš m	*ku*-ruh-tsee *puhp*-ri-kash	*chicken braised in red (paprika) sauce*
kyslá uhorka f	*kis*-la *u*-hor-kuh	*dill pickle (gherkin)*
opékané zemiaky f pl	*o*-pe-kuh-nair *ze*-myuh-ki	*fried potatoes*
ovocné knedle f pl	*o* vots-nair *kned*-le	*fruit dumplings*
palacinky f pl	*puh*-luh-tsin-ki	*pancakes*
paradajková polievka s cibulkou f	*puh*-ruh-dai-ko-va *po*-lyev-kuh s *tsi*-bul'-koh	*tomato & onion soup*

pečené zemiaky i pl	pe·che·nuh ze·myuh·ki	roast potatoes
plnená paprika v paradajkovej omáčke f	pl·nye·na puhp·ri·kuh v puh·ruh·dai·ko·vey o·mach·ke	capsicum stuffed with minced meat & rice, served with tomato sauce
polievka z bažanta f	po·lyev·kuh z buh·zhuhn·tuh	pheasant soup
praženica f	pruh·zhe·nyi·tsuh	scrambled eggs
prírodný rezeň m	pree·rod·nee re·zen'	unbreaded pork or veal schnitzel
rizoto n	ri·zo·to	mixture of pork, onion, peas & rice
ruské vajcia n pl	rus·kair vai·tsyuh	hard-boiled egg, potato & salami, with mayonnaise
rybacia polievka f	ri·buh·tsyuh po·lyev·kuh	fish soup
ryžový nákyp m	ri·zho·vee na·kip	rice soufflé
salámový tanier s oblohou m	suh·la·mo·vee tuh·nyer s ob·lo·hoh	salami platter with fresh or pickled vegetables
sviečková na smotane f	svyech·ko·va nuh smo·tuh·nye	roast beef with sour cream sauce & spices
špenát m	shpe·nat	finely chopped spinach, cooked with onion, garlic & cream
šunka pečená s vajcom f	shun·kuh pe·che·na s vai·tsom	fried ham with egg
tatárska omáčka f	tuh·tar·skuh o·mach·kuh	creamy tartar sauce
tatársky biftek m	tuh·tar·ski bif·tek	raw steak
teľacie pečené n	tye·lyuh·tsye pe·che·nair	roast veal
tlačenka s octom a cibuľou f	tluh·chen·kuh s ots·tom uh tsi·bu·loh	jellied meat loaf with vinegar & onion
vyprážané rybacie filé n	vi·pra·zhuh·nair ri·buh·tsye fi·lair	fillet of fish fried in breadcrumbs

emergencies

basics

Help!	*Pomoc!*	*po*-mots
Stop!	*Stoj!*	stoy
Go away!	*Choďte preč!*	*khoď*-tye prech
Thief!	*Zlodej!*	*zlo*-dyey
Fire!	*Oheň!*	*o*-hen'
Watch out!	*Pozor!*	*po*-zor
Call a doctor!	*Zavolajte lekára!*	zuh-vo-lai-tye *le*-ka-ruh
Call an ambulance!	*Zavolajte záchranku!*	zuh-vo-lai-tye *zakh*-ruhn-ku
Call the police!	*Zavolajte políciu!*	zuh-vo-lai-tye *po*-lee-tsi-yu

It's an emergency!
Je to pohotovostný prípad!   ye to *po*-ho-to-vos-nee *pree*-puhd

Could you help me, please?
Môžete mi prosím pomôcť?   *mwo*-zhe-tye mi *pro*-seem po-mwotst'

I have to use the telephone.
Potrebujem telefón.   *po*-tre-bu-yem *te*-le-fawn

I'm lost.
Stratil/Stratila som sa. m/f   *struh*-tyil/*struh*-tyi-luh som suh

Where are the toilets?
Kde sú tu záchody?   kdye soo tu *za*-kho-di

police

Where's the police station?
Kde je policajná stanica?   kdye ye *po*-li-tsai-na *stuh*-nyi-tsuh

I want to report an offence. (serious/minor)
Chcem nahlásiť zločin/priestupok.   khtsem *nuh*-hla-sit' *zlo*-chin/*prye*-stu-pok

I've been ...	*Bol/Bola som ...* m/f	bol/*bo*-luh som ...
assaulted	*prepadnutý* m	*pre*-puhd-nu-tee
	prepadnutá f	*pre*-puhd-nu-ta
raped	*znásilnený* m	*zna*-sil-nye-nee
	znásilnená f	*zna*-sil-nye-na
robbed	*okradnutý* m	*o*-kruhd-nu-tee
	okradnutá f	*o*-kruhd-nu-ta

I've lost my ...	Stratil/Stratila som ... m/f	struh·tyil/struh·tyi·luh som ...
My ... was/were stolen.	Ukradli mi ...	u·kruhd·li mi ...
backpack	plecniak	plets·ni·yuhk
bags	batožinu	buh·to·zhi·nu
credit card	kreditnú kartu	kre·dit·noo kuhr·tu
handbag	kabelku	kuh·bel·ku
jewellery	šperky	shper·ki
money	peniaze	pe·nyuh·ze
passport	cestovný pas	tses·tov·nee puhs
travellers cheques	cestovné šeky	tses·tov·nair she·ki
wallet	peňaženku	pe·nyuh·zhen·ku
I want to contact my ...	Chcem sa spojiť s ...	khtsem suh spo·yit' s ...
consulate	mojím konzulátom	mo·yeem kon·zu·la·tom
embassy	mojou ambasádou	mo·yoh uhm·buh·sa·doh

health

medical needs

Where's the nearest ...?	Kde je najbližší/ najbližšia ...? m/f	kdye ye nai·blizh·shee/ nai·blizh·shyuh ...
dentist	zubár m	zu·bar
doctor	doktor m	dok·tor
hospital	nemocnica f	ne·mots·nyi·tsuh
(night) pharmacist	(pohotovostná) lekáreň f	(po·ho·to·vost·na) le·ka·ren'

I need a doctor (who speaks English).
Potrebujem lekára, — po·tre·bu·yem le·ka·ruh
(ktorý hovorí po anglicky). — (kto·ree ho·vo·ree po uhng·lits·ki)

Could I see a female doctor?
Mohla by som navštíviť — mo·hluh bi som nuhv·shtyee·vit'
ženského lekára? — zhen·skair·ho le·ka·ruh

I've run out of my medication.
Minuli sa mi lieky. — mi·nu·li suh mi li·ye·ki

symptoms, conditions & allergies

| I'm sick. | Som chorý/chorá. m/f | som kho·ree/kho·ra |
| It hurts here. | Tu ma to bolí. | tu muh to bo·lee |

I have (a) ...

asthma	Mám astmu.	mam uhst·mu
bronchitis	Mám zápal priedušiek.	mam za·puhl prye·du·shyek
constipation	Mám zápchu.	mam zap·khu
cough	Mám kašeľ.	mam kuh·shel
diarrhoea	Mám hnačku.	mam hnuhch·ku
fever	Mám horúčku.	mam ho·rooch·ku
headache	Bolí ma hlava.	bo·lee muh hluh·vuh
heart condition	Mám srdcovú príhodu.	mam srd·tso·voo pree·ho·du
nausea	Je mi nazvracanie.	ye mi nuhz·vruh·tsuh·ni·ye
pain	Mám bolesti.	mam bo·les·tyi
sore throat	Bolí ma hrdlo.	bo·lee muh hrd·lo
toothache	Bolí ma zub.	bo·lee muh zub

I'm allergic to ...	Som alergický/ alergická... m/f	som uh·ler·gits·kee/ uh·ler·gits·ka nuh ...
antibiotics	antibiotiká	uhn·ti·bi·o·ti·ka
anti-inflammatories	protizápalové lieky	pro·ti·za·puh·lo·vair lye·ki
aspirin	aspirín	uhs·pi·reen
bees	včely	fche·li
codeine	kodeín	ko·de·een
penicillin	penicilín	pe·ni·tsi·leen

antiseptic	antiseptikum n	uhn·ti·sep·ti·kum
bandage	obväz m	ob·vez
condoms	kondómy m pl	kon·daw·mi
contraceptives	antikoncepcia f	uhn·ti·kon·tsep·tsi·yuh
diarrhoea medicine	lieky proti hnačke m	li·ye·ki pro·tyi hnuhch·ke
insect repellent	repelent proti hmyzu m	re·pe·lent pro·tyi hmi·zu
laxatives	preháňadlá n pl	pre·ha·nyuhd·la
painkillers	analgetiká n pl	uh·nuhl·ge·ti·ka
rehydration salts	rehydratujúce soli f pl	re·hid·ruh·tu·yoo·tse so·li
sleeping tablets	tabletky na spanie f pl	tuhb·let·ki nuh spuh·ni·ye

english–slovak dictionary

Slovak nouns in this dictionary have their gender indicated by ⓜ (masculine), ⓕ (feminine) or ⓤ (neuter). If it's a plural noun, you'll also see pl. Adjectives are given in the masculine form only. Words are also marked as a (adjective), v (verb), sg (singular), pl (plural), inf (informal) or pol (polite) where necessary.

A

accident *nehoda* ⓕ *nye*-ho-duh
accommodation *ubytovanie* ⓤ *u*-bi-to-vuh-ni-ye
adaptor *rozvodka* ⓕ *roz*-vod-kuh
address *adresa* ⓕ *uh*-dre-suh
after *po* po
air-conditioned *klimatizovaný kli*-muh-ti-zo-vuh-nee
airplane *lietadlo* ⓤ *li*-ye-tuhd-lo
airport *letisko* ⓤ *le*-tis-ko
alcohol *alkohol* ⓜ *uhl*-ko-hol
all (everything) *všetko fshet*-ko
allergy *alergia* ⓕ *uh*-ler-gi-yuh
ambulance *ambulancia* ⓕ *uhm*-bu-luhn-tsi-yuh
and *a* uh
ankle *členok* ⓜ *chle*-nok
arm *rameno* ⓤ *ruh*-me-no
ashtray *popolník* ⓜ *po*-pol-nyeek
ATM *bankomat* ⓜ *buhn*-ko-muht

B

baby *dieťatko* ⓤ *di*-ye-tyuht-ko
back (body) *chrbát* ⓜ *khr*-baat
backpack *ruksak* ⓜ *ruk*-suhk
bad *zlý zlee*
bag *taška* ⓕ *tuhsh*-kuh
baggage claim *úložňa batožiiny* ⓕ *oo*-lozh-nyuh buh-to-zhi-ni
bank *banka* ⓕ *buhn*-kuh
bar *bar* ⓜ *buhr*
bathroom *kúpeľňa* ⓕ *koo*-peľ-nyuh
battery *batéria* ⓕ *buh*-tair-ri-yuh
beautiful *krásny kras*-ni
bed *posteľ* ⓕ *pos*-tyeľ
beer *pivo* ⓤ *pi*-vo
before *pred* pred
behind *za* zuh
bicycle *bicykel* ⓜ *bi*-tsi-kel
big *veľký veľ*-kee
bill *účet* ⓜ *oo*-chet
black *čierny chyer*-ni
blanket *prikrývka* ⓕ *pri*-kreev-kuh

blood group *krvná skupina* ⓕ *krv*-na *sku*-pi-nuh
blue *modrý mod*-ree
boat *loď* ⓕ *loď*
book (make a reservation) v *rezervovať re*-zer-vo-vuhť
bottle *fľaša* ⓕ *flyuh*-shuh
bottle opener *otvárač na fľašu* ⓜ *ot*-va-ruhch nuh *flyuh*-shu
boy *chlapec* ⓜ *khluh*-pets
brakes *brzdy* ⓕ pl *brz*-di
breakfast *raňajky* pl *ruh*-nyai-ki
broken (faulty) *pokazený po*-kuh-ze-nee
bus *autobus* ⓜ *ow*-to-bus
business *obchod* ⓜ *ob*-khod
buy *kúpiť koo*-piť

C

café *kaviareň* ⓕ *kuh*-vyuh-reň
camera *fotoaparát* ⓜ *fo*-to-uh-puh-rat
camp site *táborisko* ⓤ *ta*-bo-ris-ko
cancel *zrušiť zru*-shiť
can opener *otvárač na konzervu* ⓜ *ot*-va-ruhch nuh kon-zer-vu
car *auto* ⓤ *ow*-to
cash *hotovosť* ⓕ *ho*-to-vosť
cash (a cheque) v *preplatiť (šek)* prep-luh-tyiť (shek)
cell phone *mobil* ⓜ *mo*-bil
centre *centrum* ⓤ *tsen*-trum
change (money) v *zameniť (peniaze)* zuh-me-nyiť (pe-ni-yuh-ze)
cheap *lacný luhts*-nee
check (bill) *účet* ⓜ *oo*-chet
check-in *registrácia* ⓕ *re*-gis-tra-tsi-yuh
chest *hruď* ⓜ *hruď*
child *dieťa* ⓤ *di*-ye-tyuh
cigarette *cigareta* ⓕ *tsi*-guh-re-tuh
city *mesto* ⓤ *mes*-to
clean a *čistý chis*-tee
closed *zatvorený zuht*-vo-re-nee
coffee *káva* ⓕ *ka*-vuh
coins *mince* ⓕ pl *min*-tse
cold a *studený stu*-dye-nee

collect call *hovor na účet volaného* ⓜ
ho-vor nuh oo-chet vo-luh-nair-ho
come *prísť* preesť
computer *počítač* ⓜ po-chee-tuhch
condom *kondóm* ⓜ kon-duhwm
contact lenses *kontaktné šošovky* ⓕ pl
kon-tuhkt-nair sho-shov-ki
cook v *variť vuh-*riť
cost *cena* ⓕ tse-nuh
credit card *kreditná karta* ⓕ kre-dit-na kuhr-tuh
cup *šálka* ⓕ shaal-ka
currency exchange *výmena peňazí* ⓕ
vee-me-nuh pe-nyuh-zee
customs (immigration) *colnica* ⓕ tsol-nyi-tsuh

D

dangerous *nebezpečný* ne-bez-pech-nee
date (time) *dátum* ⓜ da-tum
day *deň* dyen'
delay *meškanie* ⓝ mesh-kuh-ni-ye
dentist *zubár* ⓜ zu-bar
depart *odchádzať* od-kha-dzať
diaper *plienka* ⓕ pli-yen-kuh
dictionary *slovník* ⓜ slov-nyeek
dinner *večera* ⓕ ve-che-ruh
direct a *priamy* pryuh-mi
dirty *špinavý* shpi-nuh-vee
disabled *postihnutý* pos-tyih-nu-tee
discount *zľava* ⓕ zlyuh-vuh
doctor *lekár* ⓜ le-kar
double bed *dvojitá posteľ* ⓕ dvo-yi-ta pos-tyel'
double room *dvojposteľová izba* ⓕ
dvoy-pos-tye-lyo-va iz-buh
drink *nápoj* ⓜ na-poy
drive v *riadiť ryuh-*dyiť
drivers licence *vodičský preukaz* ⓜ
vo-dyich-skee pre-u-kuhz
drug (illicit) *droga* ⓕ dro-guh
dummy (pacifier) *cumeľ* ⓜ tsu-mel'

E

ear *ucho* ⓝ u-kho
east *východ* vee-khod
eat *jesť* yesť
economy class *ekonomická trieda* ⓕ
e-ko-no-mits-ka trye-duh
electricity *elektrika* ⓕ e-lek-tri-kuh
elevator *výťah* ⓜ vee-tyah
email *email* ⓜ ee-meyl
embassy *veľvyslanectvo* ⓝ veľ-vis-luh-nyets-tvo
emergency *pohotovosť* ⓕ po-ho-to-vosť

English (language) *angličtina* ⓕ uhng-lich-tyi-nuh
entrance *vchod* ⓜ vkhod
evening *večer* ve-cher
exchange rate *výmenný kurz* ⓜ vee-men-nee kurz
exit *východ* ⓜ vee-khod
expensive *drahý* druh-hee
express mail *expresná pošta* ⓕ eks-pres-na posh-tuh
eye *oko* ⓝ o-ko

F

far *ďaleko* dyuh-le-ko
fast *rýchly* reekh-li
father *otec* ⓜ o-tyets
film (camera) *film* ⓜ film
finger *prst* ⓜ prst
first-aid kit *lekárnička* ⓕ le-kar-nyich-kuh
first class *prvá trieda* ⓕ pr-va trye-duh
fish *ryba* ⓕ ri-buh
food *jedlo* ⓝ yed-lo
foot *noha* ⓕ no-huh
fork *vidlička* ⓕ vid-lich-kuh
free (of charge) *zadarmo* zuh-duhr-mo
friend *priateľ/priateľka* ⓜ/ⓕ pryuh-teľ/prya-tyeľ-ka
fruit *ovocie* ⓝ o-vo-tsye
full *plný* pl-nee
funny *smiešny* smyesh-ni

G

gift *dar* ⓜ duhr
girl *dievča* ⓝ di-yev-chuh
glass (drinking) *pohár* ⓜ po-har
glasses *okuliare* pl o-ku-lyuh-re
go *ísť* eesť
good *dobrý* dob-ree
green *zelený* ze-le-nee
guide *sprievodca* ⓜ sprye-vod-tsuh

H

half *polovica* ⓕ po-lo-vi-tsuh
hand *ruka* ⓕ ru-kuh
handbag *kabelka* ⓕ kuh-bel-kuh
happy *šťastný* shtyuhs-nee
have *mať muhť*
he on on
head *hlava* ⓕ hluh-vuh
heart *srdce* ⓝ srd-tse
heat *teplo* ⓝ tyep-lo
heavy *ťažký* tyuhzh-kee
help v *pomôcť* pom-wotsť

here *tu* tu
high *vysoký* vi-so-kee
highway *diaľnica* ① di-*yuhl*-nyi-tsuh
hike v *ísť na turistiku* eesť nuh *tu*-ris-ti-ku
holiday *dovolenka* ① *do*-vo-len-kuh
homosexual *homosexuál* ⓜ *ho*-mo-sek-su-al
hospital *nemocnica* ① *ne*-mots-nyi-tsuh
hot *horúci* ho-roo-tsi
hotel *hotel* ⓜ *ho*-tel
hungry *hladný* hluhd-nee
husband *manžel* ⓜ *muhn*-zhel

I

I *ja* yuh
identification (card) *občiansky preukaz* ⓜ
  ob-chyuhns-ki *pre*-u-kuhz
ill *chorý* kho-ree
important *dôležitý* dwo-le-zhi-tee
included *zahrnutý* zuh-hr-nu-tee
injury *poranenie* ⓝ po-ruh-nye-ni-ye
insurance *poistenie* ⓝ po-is-tye-ni-ye
Internet *internet* ⓜ *in*-ter-net
interpreter *tlmočník* ⓜ *tl*-moch-nyeek

J

jewellery *šperky* ⓝ pl *shper*-ki
job *zamestnanie* ⓝ *zuh*-mest-nuh-ni-ye

K

key *kľúč* ⓜ kľooch
kilogram *kilogram* ⓜ *ki*-log-ruhm
kitchen *kuchyňa* ① *ku*-khi-nyuh
knife *nôž* ⓜ nwozh

L

laundry (place) *práčovňa* ① *pra*-chov-nyuh
lawyer *právnik* ⓜ *prav*-nyik
left (direction) *vľavo* vluh-vo
left-luggage office *úschovňa batožiny* ①
  oos-khov-nyuh buh-to-zhi-ni
leg *noha* ① *no*-huh
lesbian *lesbia* ① *les*-bi-yuh
less *menej* me-nyey
letter (mail) *list* ⓜ list
lift (elevator) *výťah* ⓜ *vee*-tyah
light *svetlo* ⓝ *svet*-lo
like v *mať rád* muhť rad

lock *zámok* ⓜ *za*-mok
long *dlhý* dľhoo
lost *stratený* struh-tye-nee
lost-property office *straty a nálezy* ①
  struh-ti uh na-le-zi
love v *ľúbiť* ℓyoo-biť
luggage *batožina* ① *buh*-to-zhi-nuh
lunch *obed* ⓜ *o*-bed

M

mail *pošta* ① *posh*-tuh
man *muž* ⓜ muzh
map *mapa* ① *muh*-puh
market *trh* ⓜ trh
matches *zápalky* ① pl *za*-puhl-ki
meat *mäso* ⓝ *me*-so
medicine *liek* ⓜ li-yek
menu *jedálny lístok* ① ye-dal-ni lees-tok
message *správa* ① *spra*-vuh
milk *mlieko* ⓝ mli-ye-ko
minute *minúta* ① mi-noo-tuh
mobile (phone) *mobil* ⓜ *mo*-bil
money *peniaze* ⓝ pl *pe*-ni-yuh-ze
month *mesiac* ⓜ *me*-syuhts
morning *ráno* ⓝ *ra*-no
mother *matka* ① *muht*-kuh
motorcycle *motorka* ① *mo*-tor-kuh
motorway *hlavná cesta* ① *hluhv*-na *tses*-tuh
mouth *ústa* pl *oos*-tuh
music *hudba* ① *hud*-buh

N

name *meno* ⓝ *me*-no
napkin *obrúsok* ⓜ *ob*-roo-sok
nappy *plienka* ① *plyen*-kuh
near *blízko* bleez-ko
neck *krk* ⓜ krk
new *nový* no-vee
news *správy* ① pl *spra*-vi
newspaper *noviny* pl *no*-vi-ni
night *noc* ① nots
no *nie* ni-ye
noisy *hlučný* hluch-nee
nonsmoking *nefajčiarsky* ne-fai-chyuhr-ski
north *sever* se-ver
nose *nos* ⓜ nos
now *teraz* te-ruhz
number *číslo* ⓝ *chees*-lo

O

oil (engine) olej ⓜ o-ley
old starý stuh-ree
one-way ticket jednosmerný lístok ⓜ
  yed-no-smer-nee lees-tok
open a otvorený ot-vo-re-nee
outside vonku von-ku

P

package balík ⓜ buh-leek
paper papier ⓜ puh-pyer
park (car) v zaparkovať zuh-puhr-ko-vuhť
passport cestovný pas ⓜ tses-tov-nee puhs
pay platiť pluh-tyiť
pen pero ⓝ pe-ro
petrol benzín ⓜ ben-zeen
pharmacy lekáreň ⓕ le-ka-reň'
phonecard telefónna karta ⓕ
  te-le-fuhwn-nuh kuhr-tuh
photo fotografia ⓕ fo-to-gruh-fi-yuh
plate tanier ⓜ tuh-ni-yer
police polícia ⓕ po-lee-tsi-yuh
postcard pohľadnica ⓕ poh-lyuhd-nyi-tsuh
post office pošta ⓕ posh-tuh
pregnant tehotná tye-hot-na
price cena ⓕ tse-nuh

Q

quiet tichý tyi-khee

R

rain dážď ⓜ dazhď
razor žiletka ⓕ zhi-let-kuh
receipt potvrdenie ⓝ pot-vr-dye-ni-ye
refund vrátenie peňazí ⓝ
  vra-tye-ni-ye pe-nyuh-zee
registered mail doporučená pošta ⓕ
  do-po-ru-che-na posh-tuh
rent v prenajať pre-nuh-yuhť
repair v opraviť o-pruh-viť
reservation rezervácia ⓕ re-zer-va-tsi-yuh
restaurant reštaurácia ⓕ resh-tow-ra-tsi-yuh
return v vrátiť vra-tyiť
return ticket spiatočný lístok ⓜ
  spyuh-toch-nee lees-tok
right (direction) vpravo vpruh-vo

S

road cesta ⓕ tses-tuh
room izba ⓕ iz-buh

safe a bezpečný bez-pech-nee
sanitary napkin dámska vložka ⓕ dams-kuh
  vlozh-kuh
seat sedadlo ⓝ se-duhd-lo
send poslať pos-luhť
service station benzínová stanica ⓕ
  ben-zee-no-va stuh-nyi-tsuh
sex sex ⓜ seks
shampoo šampón ⓜ shuhm-puhwn
share (a dorm) deliť sa (o izbu)
  dye-liť suh (o iz-bu)
shaving cream krém na holenie ⓜ
  krairm nuh ho-le-ni-ye
she ona o-nuh
sheet (bed) plachta ⓕ pluhkh-tuh
shirt košeľa ⓕ ko-she-lyuh
shoes topánky ⓕ pl to-pan-ki
shop obchod ⓜ ob-khod
short krátky krat-ki
shower sprcha ⓕ spr-khuh
single room jednoposteľová izba ⓕ
  yed-no-pos-tye-lyo-va iz-buh
skin koža ⓕ ko-zhuh
skirt sukňa ⓕ suk-nyuh
sleep v spať spuhť
Slovakia Slovensko ⓝ slo-vens-ko
Slovak (language) slovenčina ⓕ slo-ven-chi-na
Slovak a slovenský slo-vens-kee
slowly pomaly po-muh-li
small malý muh-lee
smoke (cigarettes) v fajčiť fai-chiť
soap mydlo ⓝ mid-lo
some nejaký nye-yuh-kee
soon skoro sko-ro
south juh yooh
souvenir shop obchod so suvenírmi ⓜ
  ob-khod zo su-ve-neer-mi
speak hovoriť ho-vo-riť
spoon lyžica ⓕ li-zhi-tsuh
stamp známka ⓕ znam-kuh
stand-by ticket lístok na čakacom zozname ⓜ
  lees-tok nuh chuh-kuh-tsom zoz-nuh-me
station (train) železničná stanica ⓕ
  zhe-lez-nich-na stuh-ni-tsuh
stomach žalúdok ⓜ zhuh-loo-dok
stop v stáť stať

stop (bus) *autobusová zastávka* ⓕ ow-to-bu-so-va *zuhs*-tăv-*kuh*

street *ulica* ⓕ u-*li*-tsah

student *študent/študentka* ⓜ/ⓕ *shtu*-dent/*shtu*-dent-ka

sun *slnko* ⓝ *sln*-ko

sunscreen *ochranný faktor* ⓜ o-khruhn-nee *fuhk*-tor

swim v *plávať pla*-vuhť

T

tampons *tampóny* ⓜ pl *tuhm*-puhw-ni

taxi *taxík* ⓜ *tuhk*-seek

teaspoon *lyžička* ⓕ *li*-zhich-ku

teeth *zuby* ⓜ pl *zu*-bi

telephone *telefón* ⓜ *te*-le-fuhwn

television *televízia* ⓕ *te*-le-vee-zi-yuh

temperature (weather) *teplota* ⓕ *tep*-lo-tuh

tent *stan* ⓜ stuhn

that (one) *to* to

they *oni* o-nyi

thirsty *smädný smed*-nee

this (one) *toto* to-to

throat *hrdlo* ⓝ *hrd*-lo

ticket *lístok* ⓜ *lees*-tok

time *čas* ⓜ chuhs

tired *unavený* u-nuh-ve-nee

tissues *servítky* ⓕ pl *ser*-veet-ki

today *dnes* dnyes

toilet *záchod* ⓜ *za*-khod

tomorrow *zajtra zai*-truh

tonight *dnes večer* dnyes *ve*-cher

toothbrush *zubná kefka* ⓕ *zub*-na *kef*-kuh

toothpaste *zubná pasta* ⓕ *zub*-na *puhs*-tuh

torch (flashlight) *baterka* ⓕ *buh*-ter-kuh

tour *zájazd* ⓜ *za*-yuhzd

tourist office *turistická kancelária* ⓕ tu-ris-tits-ka *kuhn*-tse-la-ri-yuh

towel *uterák* ⓜ u-tye-rak

train *vlak* ⓜ vluhk

translate *prekladať pre*-kluh-duhť

travel agency *cestovná kancelária* ⓕ *tses*-tov-na *kuhn*-tse-la-ri-yuh

travellers cheque *cestovný šek* ⓜ *tses*-tov-nee shek

trousers *nohavice* pl *no*-huh-vi-tse

twin beds *dve oddelené postele* ⓕ pl dve *od*-dye-le-nair *pos*-tye-le

tyre *pneumatika* ⓕ *pne*-u-muh-ti-kuh

U

underwear *spodné prádlo* ⓝ *spod*-nair *prad*-lo

urgent *súrny soor*-ni

V

vacant *voľný voly*-nee

vacation *dovolenka* ⓕ *do*-vo-len-kuh

vegetable *zelenina* ⓕ *ze*-le-nyi-nuh

vegetarian a *vegetariánsky ve*-ge-tuh-ri-yans-ki

visa *vízum* ⓝ *vee*-zum

W

waiter *čašník* ⓜ *chuhsh*-nyeek

walk v *kráčať kra*-chuhť

wallet *peňaženka* ⓕ *pe*-nyuh-zhen-kuh

warm a *teplý tep*-lee

wash (something) *umývať u*-mee-vuhť

watch *hodinky* pl *ho*-dyin-ki

water *voda* ⓕ *vo*-duh

we *my* mi

weekend *víkend* ⓜ *vee*-kend

west *západ za*-puhd

wheelchair *invalidný vozík* ⓜ *in*-vuh-lid-nee *vo*-zeek

when *kedy ke*-di

where *kde* kdye

white *biely bye*-li

who *kto* kto

why *prečo pre*-cho

wife *manželka* ⓕ *muhn*-zhel-kuh

window *okno* ⓝ *ok*-no

wine *víno* ⓝ *vee*-no

with s s

without *bez* bez

woman *žena* ⓕ *zhe*-nuh

write *písať pee*-suhť

Y

yellow *žltý zhl*-tee

yes *áno a*-no

yesterday *včera vche*-ruh

you sg inf *ty* ti

you sg pol & pl *vy* vi

Slovene

A a a	D d buh	C c tsuh	Č č chuh	D d duh
E e e	F f fuh	G g guh	H h huh	I i ee
J j yuh	K k kuh	L l luh	M m muh	N n nuh
O o o	P p puh	R r ruh	S s suh	Š š shuh
T t tuh	U u oo	V v vuh	Z z zuh	Ž ž zhuh

■ slovene

SLOVENŠČINA

introduction

The language spoken by about 2 million people 'on the sunny side of the Alps', Slovene (*slovenščina* slo·*vensh*·chee·na) is sandwiched between German, Italian and Hungarian, against the backdrop of its wider South Slavic family. Its distinctive geographical position parallels its unique evolution, beginning with Slav settlement in this corner of Europe back in the 6th century, then becoming the official language of Slovenia – first as a part of Yugoslavia and since 1991 an independent republic.

Although Croatian and Serbian are its closest relatives within the South Slavic group, Slovene is nevertheless much closer to Croatia's northwestern and coastal dialects. It also shares some features with the more distant West Slavic languages (through contact with a dialect of Slovak, from which it was later separated by the arrival of the Hungarians to Central Europe in the 9th century). Unlike any other modern Slavic language, it has preserved the archaic Indo-European dual grammatical form, which means, for example, that instead of *pivo* pee·vo (a beer) or *piva* pee·va (beers), you and a friend could simply order *pivi* pee·vee (two beers).

German, Italian and Hungarian words entered Slovene during the centuries of foreign rule (in the Austro-Hungarian Empire or under the control of Venice), as these were the languages of the elite when all three countries coexisted, while the common people spoke one of the Slovene dialects. Croatian and Serbian influence on Slovene was particularly significant during the 20th century within the Yugoslav state.

For a language with a relatively small number of speakers, Slovene abounds in regional variations – eight major dialect groups have been identified, which are further divided into fifty or so regional dialects. Some of these cover the neighbouring areas of Austria, Italy and Hungary. The modern literary language is based largely on the central dialects and was shaped through a gradual process that lasted from the 16th to the 19th century.

Slovenia has been called 'a nation of poets', and what better way to get immersed in that spirit than to plunge into this beautiful language first? While you're soaking up the atmosphere of the capital, Ljubljana (whose central square is graced with a monument in honour of the nation's greatest poet, France Prešeren), remember that its name almost equals 'beloved' (*ljubljena* lyoob·lye·na) in Slovene!

pronunciation

vowel sounds

The vowels in Slovene can be pronounced differently, depending on whether they're stressed or unstressed, long or short. Don't worry about these distinctions though, as you shouldn't have too much trouble being understood if you follow our coloured pronunciation guide. Note that we've used the symbols oh and ow to help you pronounce vowels followed by the letters *l* and *v* in written Slovene – when they appear at the end of a syllable, these combinations sometimes produce a sound similar to the 'w' in English.

symbol	english equivalent	slovene example	transliteration
a	father	*dan*	dan
ai	aisle	*srajca*	*srai*·tsa
e	bet	*center*	*tsen*·ter
ee	see	*riba*	*ree*·ba
o	pot	*oče*	*o*·che
oh	oh	*pol, nov*	poh, noh
oo	zoo	*jug*	yoog
ow	how	*ostal, prav*	os·*tow*, prow
uh	ago	*pes*	puhs

word stress

Slovene has free stress, which means there's no general rule regarding which syllable the stress falls on – it simply has to be learned. You'll be fine if you just follow our coloured pronunciation guides, in which the stressed syllable is always in italics.

consonant sounds

Most Slovene consonant sounds are pronounced more or less as they are in English. Don't be intimidated by the vowel-less words such as *trg* tuhrg (square) or *vrt* vuhrt (garden) – we've put a slight 'uh' sound before the *r*, which serves as a semi-vowel between the two other consonants.

symbol	english equivalent	slovene example	transliteration
b	bed	*brat*	brat
ch	cheat	*hči*	hchee
d	dog	*datum*	da·toom
f	fat	*telefon*	te·le·fon
g	go	*grad*	grad
h	hat	*hvala*	hva·la
k	kit	*karta*	kar·ta
l	lot	*ulica*	oo·lee·tsa
m	man	*mož*	mozh
n	not	*naslov*	nas·loh
p	pet	*pošta*	po·shta
r	run (rolled)	*brez*	brez
s	sun	*sin*	seen
sh	shot	*tuš*	toosh
t	top	*sto*	sto
ts	hats	*cesta*	tse·sta
v	very	*vlak*	vlak
y	yes	*jesen*	ye·sen
z	zero	*zima*	zee·ma
zh	pleasure	*žena*	zhe·na
'	a slight y sound	*kašelj, manj*	ka·shel', man'

basics

language difficulties

Do you speak English?
Ali govorite angleško?
a·lee go·vo·ree·te ang·lesh·ko

Do you understand?
Ali razumete?
a·lee ra·zoo·me·te

I (don't) understand.
(Ne) Razumem.
(ne) ra·zoo·mem

What does (danes) mean?
Kaj pomeni (danes)?
kai po·me·nee (da·nes)

Could you repeat that?
Lahko ponovite?
lah·ko po·no·vee·te

How do you ...?   *Kako se ...?*   ka·ko se ...
  pronounce this word   *izgovori to besedo*   eez·go·vo·ree to be·se·do
  write (hvala)   *napiše (hvala)*   na·pee·she (hva·la)

Could you please ...?   *Prosim ...*   pro·seem ...
  speak more slowly   *govorite počasneje*   go·vo·ree·te po·cha·sne·ye
  write it down   *napišite*   na·pee·shee·te

essentials

Yes.	*Da.*	da
No.	*Ne.*	ne
Please.	*Prosim.*	pro·seem
Thank you (very much).	*Hvala (lepa).*	hva·la (le·pa)
You're welcome.	*Ni za kaj.*	nee za kai
Excuse me.	*Dovolite.*	do·vo·lee·te
Sorry.	*Oprostite.*	op·ros·tee·te

numbers

0	*nula*	noo-la	16	*šestnajst*	shest-naist
1	*en/ena* m/f	en/e-na	17	*sedemnajst*	se-dem-naist
2	*dva/dve* m/f	dva/dve	18	*osemnajst*	o-sem-naist
3	*trije/tri* m/f	tree-ye/tree	19	*devetnajst*	de-vet-naist
4	*štirje* m	shtee-rye	20	*dvajset*	dvai-set
	štiri f	shtee-ree	21	*enaindvajset*	e-na-een-dvai-set
5	*pet*	pet	22	*dvaindvajset*	dva-een-dvai-set
6	*šest*	shest			
7	*sedem*	se-dem	30	*trideset*	tree-de-set
8	*osem*	o-sem	40	*štirideset*	shtee-ree-de-set
9	*devet*	de-vet	50	*petdeset*	pet-de-set
10	*deset*	de-set	60	*šestdeset*	shest-de-set
11	*enajst*	e-naist	70	*sedemdeset*	se-dem-de-set
12	*dvanajst*	dva-naist	80	*osemdeset*	o-sem-de-set
13	*trinajst*	tree-naist	90	*devetdeset*	de-vet-de-set
14	*štirinajst*	shtee-ree-naist	100	*sto*	sto
15	*petnajst*	pet-naist	1000	*tisoč*	tee-soch

time & dates

What time is it?	*Koliko je ura?*	ko-lee-ko ye oo-ra
It's one o'clock.	*Ura je ena.*	oo-ra ye e-na
It's (10) o'clock.	*Ura je (deset).*	oo-ra ye (de-set)
Quarter past (one).	*Četrt čez (ena).*	che-tuhrt chez (e-na)
Half past (one).	*Pol (dveh).* (lit: half two)	pol (dveh)
Quarter to (one).	*Petnajst do (enih).*	pet-naist do (e-neeh)
At what time ...?	*Ob kateri uri ...?*	ob ka-te-ree oo-ree ...
At ...	*Ob ...*	ob ...
am	*dopoldne*	do-poh-dne
pm	*popoldne*	po-poh-dne
Monday	*ponedeljek*	po-ne-del-yek
Tuesday	*torek*	to-rek
Wednesday	*sreda*	sre-da
Thursday	*četrtek*	che-tuhr-tek
Friday	*petek*	pe-tek
Saturday	*sobota*	so-bo-ta
Sunday	*nedelja*	ne-del-ya

January	januar	ya·noo·ar
February	februar	feb·roo·ar
March	marec	ma·rets
April	april	ap·reel
May	maj	mai
June	junij	yoo·neey
July	julij	yoo·leey
August	avgust	av·goost
September	september	sep·tem·ber
October	oktober	ok·to·ber
November	november	no·vem·ber
December	december	de·tsem·ber

What date is it today?
    Katerega smo danes?   ka·*te*·re·ga smo *da*·nes

It's (18 October).
    Smo (osemnajstega oktobra).   smo (o·sem·*nai*·ste·ga) ok·*tob*·ra

since (May)	od (maja)	od (ma·ya)
until (June)	do (junija)	do (yoo·nee·ya)

last ...
night	prejšnji večer	preysh·nyee ve·cher
week	prejšnji teden	preysh·nyee te·den
month	prejšnji mesec	preysh·nyee me·sets
year	prejšnje leto	preysh·nye le·to

next ...
week	naslednji teden	nas·led·nyee te·den
month	naslednji mesec	nas·led·nyee me·sets
year	naslednje leto	nas·led·nye le·to

yesterday/tomorrow ...
	včeraj/jutri ...	vche·rai/yoot·ree ...
morning	zjutraj	zyoot·rai
afternoon	popoldne	po·poh·dne
evening	zvečer	zve·cher

weather

What's the weather like?	Kakšno je vreme?	*kak*·shno ye *vre*·me
It's raining/snowing.	Dežuje/Sneži.	de·*zhoo*·ye/sne·*zhee*

It's	... je.	... ye
cloudy	Oblačno	ob·*lach*·no
cold	Mrzlo	*muhr*·zlo
hot	Vroče	*vro*·che
sunny	Sončno	*sonch*·no
warm	Toplo	*top*·lo
windy	Vetrovno	vet·*roh*·no

spring	pomlad f	pom·*lad*
summer	poletje n	po·*let*·ye
autumn	jesen f	ye·*sen*
winter	zima f	*zee*·ma

border crossing

I'm here ...	Tu sem ...	too sem ...
on business	poslovno	pos·*lov*·no
on holiday	na počitnicah	na po·*cheet*·nee·tsah

I'm here for ...	Ostanem ...	os·*ta*·nem ...
(10) days	(deset) dni	(de·*set*) dnee
(two) months	(dva) meseca	(dva) *me*·se·tsa
(three) weeks	(tri) tedne	(tree) *ted*·ne

I'm going to ...
Namenjen/Namenjena sem v ... m/f   na·*men*·yen/na·*men*·ye·na sem v ...

I'm staying at the (Slon).
Stanujem v (Slonu).   sta·*noo*·yem v (*slo*·noo)

I have nothing to declare.
Ničesar nimam za prijaviti.   nee·*che*·sar *nee*·mam za pree·*ya*·vee·tee

I have something to declare.
Nekaj imam za prijaviti.   *ne*·kai ee·*mam* za pree·*ya*·vee·tee

That's mine.
To je moje.   to ye *mo*·ye

That's not mine.
To ni moje.   to nee *mo*·ye

transport

tickets & luggage

Where can I buy a ticket?
Kje lahko kupim vozovnico?　　　kye lah·*ko* koo·peem vo·*zov*·nee·tso

Do I need to book a seat?
Ali moram rezervirati sedež?　　a·lee *mo*·ram re·zer·*vee*·ra·tee se·dezh

One ... ticket to (Koper), please.	... vozovnico do (Kopra), prosim.	... vo·*zov*·nee·tso do (*ko*·pra) *pro*·seem
one-way	Enosmerno	e·no·*smer*·no
return	Povratno	pov·*rat*·no

I'd like to ... my ticket, please.	Želim ... vozovnico, prosim.	zhe·*leem* ... vo·*zov*·nee·tso *pro*·seem
cancel	preklicati	prek·*lee*·tsa·tee
change	zamenjati	za·*men*·ya·tee
collect	dvigniti	*dveeg*·nee·tee
confirm	potrditi	po·tuhr·*dee*·tee

I'd like a ... seat, please.	Želim ... sedež, prosim.	zhe·*leem* ... se·dezh *pro*·seem
nonsmoking	nekadilski	ne·ka·*deel*·skee
smoking	kadilski	ka·*deel*·skee

How much is it?
Koliko stane?　　　*ko*·lee·ko *sta*·ne

Is there air conditioning?
Ali ima klimo?　　　a·lee ee·*ma* klee·mo

Is there a toilet?
Ali ima stranišče?　　　a·lee ee·*ma* stra·*neesh*·che

How long does the trip take?
Kako dolgo traja potovanje?　　　ka·*ko* dol·go *tra*·ya po·to·*van*·ye

Is it a direct route?
Je to direktna proga?　　　ye to dee·*rekt*·na *pro*·ga

I'd like a luggage locker.
Želim garderobno omarico.　　　zhe·*leem* gar·de·*rob*·no o·*ma*·ree·tso

My luggage has been ...   *Moja prtljaga je ...*   mo·ya puhrt·*lya*·ga ye ...
  damaged   *poškodovana*   posh·ko·do·*va*·na
  lost   *izgubljena*   eez·goob·*lye*·na
  stolen   *ukradena*   oo·*kra*·de·na

getting around

Where does flight (AF 46) arrive/depart?
  Kje pristane/odleti let   kye pree·*sta*·ne/od·le·*tee* let
  številka (AF 46)?   shte·*veel*·ka (a fuh *shtee*·ree shest)

Where's (the) ...?   *Kje je/so ...?* sg/pl   kye ye/so ...
  arrivals hall   *prihodi* pl   pree·*ho*·dee
  departures hall   *odhodi* pl   od·*ho*·dee
  duty-free shop   *brezcarinska*   brez·tsa·*reen*·ska
     trgovina sg   tuhr·go·*vee*·na
  gate (12)   *izhod (dvanajst)* sg   eez·*hod* (*dva*·naist)

Is this the ... to (Venice)?   *Je to ... za (Benetke)?*   ye to ... za (be·*net*·ke)
  boat   *ladja*   *lad*·ya
  bus   *avtobus*   *av*·to·boos
  plane   *letalo*   le·*ta*·lo
  train   *vlak*   vlak

What time's the ... bus?   *Kdaj odpelje ... avtobus?*   kdai od·*pel*·ye ... *av*·to·boos
  first   *prvi*   *puhr*·vee
  last   *zadnji*   *zad*·nyee
  next   *naslednji*   nas·*led*·nyee

At what time does it arrive/leave?
  Kdaj prispe/odpelje?   kdai prees·*pe*/od·*pel*·ye

How long will it be delayed?
  Koliko je zamujen?   ko·lee·ko ye za·moo·*yen*

What station is this?
  Katera postaja je to?   ka·*te*·ra pos·*ta*·ya ye to

What stop Is this?
  Katero postajališče je to?   ka·*te*·ro pos·ta·ya·*leesh*·che ye to

What's the next station?
  Katera je naslednja postaja?   ka·*te*·ra ye nas·*led*·nya pos·*ta*·ya

What's the next stop?
  Katero je naslednje postajališče?   ka·*te*·ro ye nas·*led*·nye pos·ta·ya·*leesh*·che

Does it stop at (Postojna)?
Ali ustavi v (Postojni)?　　　　　　　　*a·lee oos·ta·vee v (pos·toy·nee)*

Please tell me when we get to (Kranj).
Prosim povejte mi,　　　　　*pro·seem po·vey·te mee*
ko prispemo v (Kranj).　　　　*ko prees·pe·mo v (kran)*

How long do we stop here?
Kako dolgo stojimo tu?　　　　*ka·ko dol·go sto·yee·mo too*

Is this seat available?
Je ta sedež prost?　　　　*ye ta se·dezh prost*

That's my seat.
To je moj sedež.　　　　*to ye moy se·dezh*

I'd like a taxi ...　　*Želim taksi ...*　　*zhe·leem tak·see ...*
　　at (9am)　　　　　　*ob (devetih*　　　　ob (de·ve·teeh
　　　　　　　　　　　　dopoldne)　　　　　do·poh·dne)
　　now　　　　　　　　*zdaj*　　　　　　　zdai
　　tomorrow　　　　　　*jutri*　　　　　　　yoot·ree

Is this taxi available?
Je ta taksi prost?　　　　*ye ta tak·see prost*

How much is it to ...?
Koliko stane do ...?　　　*ko·lee·ko sta·ne do ...*

Please put the meter on.
Prosim, vključite taksimeter.　　*pro·seem vklyoo·chee·te tak·see·me·ter*

Please take me to (this address).
Prosim, peljite me na (ta naslov).　　*pro·seem pel·yee·te me na (ta nas·loh)*

Please ...　　　　*Prosim ...*　　　　*pro·seem ...*
　　slow down　　　*vozite počasneje*　　vo·zee·te po·chas·ne·ye
　　stop here　　　　*ustavite tukaj*　　　oos·ta·vee·te too·kai
　　wait here　　　　*počakajte tukaj*　　po·cha·kai·te too·kai

car, motorbike & bicycle hire

I'd like to hire a ...　　*Želim najeti ...*　　*zhe·leem na·ye·tee ...*
　　bicycle　　　　　　*kolo*　　　　　　　ko·lo
　　car　　　　　　　　*avto*　　　　　　　av·to
　　motorbike　　　　　*motor*　　　　　　mo·tor

with ...	s ...	s ...
a driver	šoferjem	sho-*fer*-yem
air conditioning	klimo	*klee*-mo
antifreeze	sredstvom proti	*sreds*-tvom *pro*-tee
	zmrzovanju	zmuhr-zo-*van*-yoo
snow chains	snežnimi	*snezh*-nee-mee
	verigami	ve-*ree*-ga-mee

How much for	Koliko stane najem	ko-lee-ko *sta*-ne na-*yem*
... hire?	na ...?	na ...
hourly	uro	*oo*-ro
daily	dan	dan
weekly	teden	*te*-den

air	zrak m	zrak
oil	olje n	*ol*-ye
petrol	bencin m	ben-*tseen*
tyres	gume f	*goo*-me

I need a mechanic.
Potrebujem mehanika. pot-re-*boo*-yem me-*ha*-nee-ka

I've run out of petrol.
Zmanjkalo mi je bencina. zman'-ka-lo mee ye ben-*tsee*-na

I have a flat tyre.
Počila mi je guma. po-*chee*-la mee ye *goo*-ma

directions

Where's the ...?	Kje je ...?	kye ye ...
bank	banka	*ban*-ka
city centre	center mesta	*tsen*-ter *mes*-ta
hotel	hotel	ho-*tel*
market	tržnica	*tuhrzh*-nee-tsa
police station	policijska	po-lee-*tseey*-ska
	postaja	pos-*ta*-ya
post office	pošta	*posh*-ta
public toilet	javno stranišče	*yav*-no stra-*neesh*-che
tourist office	turistični	too-rees-*teech*-nee
	urad	oo-*rad*

Is this the road to (Ptuj)?
Pelje ta cesta do (Ptuja)?   pel·ye ta tses·ta do (ptoo·ya)

Can you show me (on the map)?
Mi lahko pokažete   mee lah·ko po·ka·zhe·te
(na zemljevidu)?   (na zem·lye·vee·doo)

What's the address?
Na katerem naslovu je?   na ka·te·rem nas·lo·voo ye

How far is it?
Kako daleč je?   ka·ko da·lech ye

How do I get there?
Kako pridem tja?   ka·ko pree·dem tya

Turn ...	*Zavijte ...*	za·veey·te ...
at the corner	*na vogalu*	na vo·ga·loo
at the traffic lights	*pri semaforju*	pree se·ma·for·yoo
left/right	*levo/desno*	le·vo/des·no

It's ...		
behind ...	*Za ...*	za ...
far away	*Daleč.*	da·lech
here	*Tukaj.*	too·kai
in front of ...	*Pred ...*	pred ...
left	*Levo.*	le·vo
near (to ...)	*Blizu ...*	blee·zoo ...
next to ...	*Poleg ...*	po·leg ...
on the corner	*Na vogalu.*	na vo·ga·loo
opposite ...	*Nasproti ...*	nas·pro·tee ...
right	*Desno.*	des·no
straight ahead	*Naravnost naprej.*	na·rav·nost na·prey
there	*Tam.*	tam

by bus	*z avtobusom*	z av·to·boo·som
by taxi	*s taksijem*	s tak·see·yem
by train	*z vlakom*	z vla·kom
on foot	*peš*	pesh

north	*sever*	se·ver
south	*jug*	yoog
east	*vzhod*	vzhod
west	*zahod*	za·hod

Vhod/Izhod	vhod/eez·hod	Entrance/Exit
Odprto/Zaprto	od·puhr·to/za·puhr·to	Open/Closed
Proste sobe	pros·te so·be	Rooms Available
Ni prostih mest	nee pros·teeh mest	No Vacancies
Informacije	een·for·ma·tsee·ye	Information
Policijska postaja	po·lee·tseey·ska pos·ta·ya	Police Station
Prepovedano	pre·po·ve·da·no	Prohibited
Stranišče	stra·neesh·che	Toilets
Moški	mosh·kee	Men
Ženske	zhen·ske	Women
Vroče/Mrzlo	vro·che/muhr·zlo	Hot/Cold

accommodation

finding accommodation

Where's a ...?	Kje je ... ?	kye ye ...
camping ground	kamp	kamp
guesthouse	gostišče	gos·teesh·che
hotel	hotel	ho·tel
youth hostel	mladinski hotel	mla·deen·skee ho·tel
Can you recommend a ... hotel?	Mi lahko priporočite ... hotel?	mee lah·ko pree·po·ro·chee·te ... ho·tel
cheap	poceni	po·tse·nee
good	dober	do·ber

Can you recommend a hotel nearby?
Mi lahko priporočite hotel v bližini?
mee lah·ko pree·po·ro·chee·te ho·tel oo blee·zhee·nee

I'd like to book a room, please.
Želim rezervirati sobo, prosim.
zhe·leem re·zer·vee·ra·tee so·bo pro·seem

I have a reservation.
Imam rezervacijo.
ee·mam re·zer·va·tsee·yo

My name's ...
Ime mi je ...
ee·me mee ye ...

Do you have a twin room?
Imate sobo z ločenima posteljama?   ee·ma·te so·bo z lo·che·nee·ma pos·tel·va·ma

Do you have a ... room?	*Ali imate ... sobo?*	a·lee ee·ma·te ... so·bo
single	*enoposteljno*	e·no·pos·tel'·no
double	*dvoposteljno*	dvo·pos·tel'·no

How much is it per ...?	*Koliko stane na ...?*	ko·lee·ko sta·ne na ...
night	*noč*	noch
person	*osebo*	o·se·bo

Can I pay by ...?	*Lahko plačam s ...?*	lah·ko pla·cham s ...
credit card	*kreditno kartico*	kre·deet·no kar·tee·tso
travellers cheque	*potovalnim čekom*	po·to·val·neem che·kom

I'd like to stay for (three) nights.
Rad bi ostal (tri) noči. m   rada bee os·tow (tree) no·chee
Rada bi ostala (tri) noči. f   ra·da bee os·ta·la (tree) no·chee

From (2 July) to (6 July).
Od (drugega julija)   od (droo·ge·ga yoo·lee·ya)
do (šestega julija).   do (shes·te·ga yoo·lee·ya)

Can I see the room?
Lahko vidim sobo?   lah·ko vee·deem so·bo

Am I allowed to camp here?
Smem tu kampirati?   smem too kam·pee·ra·tee

Is there a camp site nearby?
Je v bližini kakšen kamp?   ye v blee·zhee·nee kak·shen kamp

requests & queries

When/Where is breakfast served?
Kdaj/Kje strežete zajtrk?   kdai/kye stre·zhe·te zai·tuhrk

Please wake me at (seven).
Prosim, zbudite me ob (sedmih).   pro·seem zboo·dee·te me ob (sed·meeh)

Could I have my key, please?
Lahko prosim dobim ključ?   lah·ko pro·sim do·beem klyooch

Can I get another (blanket)?
Lahko dobim drugo (odejo)?   lah·ko do·beem droo·go (o·de·yo)

Is there an elevator/a safe?
Imate dvigalo/sef?   ee·ma·te dvee·ga·lo/sef

The room is too...	Soba je ...	so·ba ye ...
expensive	predraga	pre·dra·ga
noisy	prehrupna	pre·hroop·na
small	premajhna	pre·mai·hna

This ... isn't clean.	Ta ... ni čista.	ta ... nee chees·ta
pillow	blazina	bla·zee·na
sheet	rjuha	ryoo·ha
towel	brisača	bree·sa·cha

The fan doesn't work.
Ventilator je pokvarjen.   ven·tee·la·tor ye pok·var·yen

The air conditioning doesn't work.
Klima je pokvarjena.   klee·ma ye pok·var·ye·na

The toilet doesn't work.
Stranišče je pokvarjeno.   stra·neesh·che ye pok·var·ye·no

checking out

What time is checkout?
Kdaj se moram odjaviti?   kdai se mo·ram od·ya·vee·tee

Can I leave my luggage here?
Lahko pustim prtljago tu?   lah·ko poos·teem puhrt·lya·go too

Could I have my ..., please?	Lahko prosim dobim ...?	lah·ko pro·seem do·beem ...
deposit	moj polog	moy po·log
passport	moj potni list	moy pot·nee leest
valuables	moje dragocenosti	mo·ye dra·go·tse·nos·tee

communications & banking

the internet

Where's the local Internet café?
Kje je najbližja internetna kavarna?   kye ye nai·bleezh·ya een·ter·net·na ka·var·na

How much is it per hour?
Koliko stane ena ura?   ko·lee·ko sta·ne e·na oo·ra

I'd like to ...	Želim ...	zhe·leem ...
check my email	preveriti	pre·ve·ree·tee
	elektronsko pošto	e·lek·tron·sko posh·to
get Internet access	dostop do interneta	dos·top do een·ter·ne·ta
use a printer	uporabiti tiskalnik	oo·po·ra·bee·tee tees·kal·neek
use a scanner	uporabiti optični	oo·po·ra·bee·tee op·teech·nee
	čitalnik	chee·tal·neek

mobile/cell phone

I'd like a ...	Želim ...	zhe·leem ...
mobile/cell phone for hire	najeti mobilni telefon	na·ye·tee mo·beel·nee te·le·fon
SIM card for your network	SIM kartico za vaše omrežje	seem kar·tee·tso za va·she om·rezh·ye
What are the rates?	Kakšne so cene?	kak·shne so tse·ne

telephone

What's your phone number?
Lahko izvem vašo telefonsko   lah·ko eez·vem va·sho te·le·fon·sko
številko?   shte·veel·ko

The number is ...
Številka je ...   shte·veel·ka ye ...

Where's the nearest public phone?
Kje je najbližja govorilnica?   kye ye nai·bleezh·ya go·vo·reel·nee·tsa

I'd like to buy a phonecard.
Želim kupiti telefonsko kartico.   zhe·leem koo·pee·tee te·le·fon·sko kar·tee·tso

I want to ...	Želim ...	zhe·leem ...
call (Singapore)	poklicati (Singapur)	pok·lee·tsa·tee (seen·ga·poor)
make a local call	klicati lokalno	klee·tsa·tee lo·kal·no
reverse the charges	klicati na stroške klicanega	klee·tsa·tee na strosh·ke klee·tsa·ne·ga

How much does ... cost?	Koliko stane ...?	ko·lee·ko sta·ne ...
a (three)-minute call	(tri)minutni klic	(tree·)mee·noot·nee kleets
each extra minute	vsaka dodatna minuta	vsa·ka do·dat·na mee·noo·ta

post office

I want to send a ...	Želim poslati ...	zhe·leem pos·la·tee ...
letter	pismo	pees·mo
parcel	paket	pa·ket
postcard	razglednico	raz·gled·nee·tso
I want to buy a/an ...	Želim kupiti ...	zhe·leem koo·pee·tee ...
envelope	kuverto	koo·ver·to
stamp	znamko	znam·ko
Please send it by ...	Prosim, pošljite ...	pro·seem posh·lyee·te ...
airmail	z letalsko pošto	z le·tal·sko posh·to
express mail	s hitro pošto	s heet·ro posh·to
registered mail	s priporočeno pošto	s pree·po·ro·che·no posh·to
surface mail	z navadno pošto	z na·vad·no posh·to

bank

Where's a/an ...?	Kje je ...?	kye ye ...
ATM	bankomat	ban·ko·mat
foreign exchange office	menjalnica	men·yal·nee·tsa
I'd like to ...	Želim ...	zhe·leem ...
Where can I ...?	Kje je mogoče ...?	kye ye mo·go·che ...
cash a cheque	unovčiti ček	oo·nov·chee·tee chek
change a travellers cheque	zamenjati potovalni ček	za·men·ya·tee po·to·val·nee chek
change money	zamenjati denar	za·men·ya·te de·nar
withdraw money	dvigniti denar	dveeg·nee·tee de·nar
What's the ...?	Kakšen/Kakšna je ...? m/f	kak·shen/kak·shna ye ...
commission	provizija f	pro·vee·zee·ya
exchange rate	menjalni tečaj m	men·yal·nee te·chai

Can I arrange a transfer of money?
Lahko uredim prenos denarja?   lah·ko oo·re·deem pre·nos de·nar·ya

What time does the bank open?
Kdaj se banka odpre?   kdai se ban·ka od·pre

Has my money arrived yet?
Je moj denar že prispel?   ye moy de·nar zhe prees·pe·oo

sightseeing

getting in

What time does it open/close?
Kdaj se odpre/zapre?
kdai se od·*pre*/za·*pre*

What's the admission charge?
Koliko stane vstopnica?
ko·lee·ko *sta*·ne *vstop*·nee·tsa

Is there a discount for students/children?
Imate popust za
ee·*ma*·te po·*poost* za
študente/otroke?
shtoo·*den*·te/ot·*ro*·ke

I'd like a ...	*Želim ...*	zhe·*leem* ...
catalogue	*katalog*	ka·ta·*log*
guide	*vodnik*	vod·*neek*
local map	*zemljevid kraja*	zem·lye·*veed kra*·ya

I'd like to see ...	*Želim videti ...*	zhe·*leem* vee·de·tee ...
What's that?	*Kaj je to?*	kai ye to
Can I take a photo?	*Ali lahko fotografiram?*	a·lee lah·*ko* fo·to·gra·*fee*·ram

tours

When's the next ...?	*Kdaj je naslednji ...?*	kdai ye nas·*led*·nyee ...
boat trip	*izlet s čolnom*	eez·*let* s *choh*·nom
day trip	*dnevni izlet*	*dnev*·nee eez·*let*
tour	*izlet*	eez·*let*

Is ... included?	*Je ... vključena?*	ye ... *vklyoo*·che·na
accommodation	*nastanitev*	nas·ta·*nee*·tev
the admission charge	*vstopnina*	vstop·*nee*·na
food	*hrana*	*hra*·na

Is transport included?
Je prevoz vključen?
ye pre·*voz* vklyoo·chen

How long is the tour?
Koliko časa traja izlet?
ko·lee·ko *cha*·sa *tra*·ya eez·*let*

What time should we be back?
Kdaj naj se vrnemo?
kdai nai se *vuhr*·ne·mo

sightseeing

castle	*grad* m	grad
cathedral	*stolnica* f	*stol*·nee·tsa
church	*cerkev* f	*tser*·kev
main square	*glavni trg* m	*glav*·nee tuhrg
monastery	*samostan* m	sa·mos·*tan*
monument	*spomenik* m	spo·me·*neek*
museum	*muzej* m	moo·*zey*
old city	*staro mesto* n	*sta*·ro *mes*·to
palace	*palača* f	pa·*la*·cha
ruins	*ruševine* f	roo·she·*vee*·ne
stadium	*stadion* m	*sta*·dee·on
statue	*kip* m	keep

shopping

enquiries

Where's a …?	*Kje je …?*	kye ye …
bank	*banka*	*ban*·ka
bookshop	*knjigarna*	knyee·*gar*·na
camera shop	*trgovina s*	tuhr·go·*vee*·na s
	fotografsko opremo	fo·to·*graf*·sko op·*re*·mo
department store	*blagovnica*	bla·*gov*·nee·tsa
grocery store	*trgovina s*	tuhr·go·*vee*·na s
	špecerijo	shpe·tse·*ree*·yo
market	*tržnica*	*tuhrzh*·nee·tsa
newsagency	*kiosk*	*kee*·osk
supermarket	*trgovina*	tuhr·go·*vee*·na

Where can I buy (a padlock)?
Kje lahko kupim (ključavnico)?   kye lah·*ko koo*·peem (klyoo·*chav*·nee·tso)

I'm looking for …
Iščem …   *eesh*·chem …

Can I look at it?
Lahko pogledam?   lah·*ko* pog·*le*·dam

Do you have any others?
Imate še kakšnega/kakšno? m/f
ee-*ma*-te she *kak*-shne-ga/*kak*-shno

Does it have a guarantee?
Ali ima garancijo?
a-lee ee-*ma* ga-ran-*tsee*-yo

Can I have it sent abroad?
Mi lahko pošljete v tujino?
mee lah-*ko posh*-lye-te v too-*yee*-no

Can I have my ... repaired?
Mi lahko popravite ...?
mee lah-*ko* po-*pra*-vee-te ...

It's faulty.
Ne deluje.
ne de-*loo*-ye

I'd like ..., please.	*Želim ..., prosim.*	zhe-*leem* ... *pro*-seem
a bag	*vrečko*	*vrech*-ko
a refund	*vračilo denarja*	vra-*chee*-lo de-*nar*-ya
to return this	*vrniti tole*	vr-*nee*-te *to*-le

paying

How much is this?
Koliko stane?
ko-lee-ko *sta*-ne

Can you write down the price?
Lahko napišete ceno?
lah-*ko* na-*pee*-she-te *tse*-no

That's too expensive.
To je predrago.
to ye pre-dra-*go*

What's your lowest price?
Povejte vašo najnižjo ceno.
po-*vey*-te *va*-sho nai-*neezh*-yo *tse*-no

I'll give you (five) euros.
Dam vam (pet) evrov.
dam vam (pet) *ev*-roh

There's a mistake in the bill.
Na računu je napaka.
na ra-*choo*-noo ye na-*pa*-ka

Do you accept ...?	*Ali sprejemate ...?*	*a*-lee spre-ye-*ma*-te ...
credit cards	*kreditne kartice*	kre-*deet*-ne *kar*-tee-tse
debit cards	*debetne kartice*	de-*bet*-ne *kar*-tee-tse
travellers cheques	*potovalne čeke*	po-to-*val*-ne *che*-ke

I'd like ..., please.	*Želim ..., prosim.*	zhe-*leem* ... *pro*-seem
a receipt	*račun*	ra-*choon*
my change	*drobiž*	dro-*beezh*

clothes & shoes

Can I try it on?	*Lahko pomerim?*	lah·ko po·me·reem
My size is (42).	*Nosim številko*	no·seem shte·veel·ko
	(dvaištirideset).	(dva·een·shtee·ree·de·set)
It doesn't fit.	*Ni mi prav.*	nee mee prow
... size	*... številka*	... shte·veel·ka
small	*majhna*	mai·hna
medium	*srednja*	sred·nya
large	*velika*	ve·lee·ka

books & music

I'd like a ...	*Želim ...*	zhe·leem ...
newspaper	*časopis*	cha·so·pees
(in English)	*(v angleščini)*	(v ang·lesh·chee·nee)
pen	*pisalo*	pee·sa·lo

I'm looking for an English-language bookshop.
Iščem angleško knjigarno.   eesh·chem ang·lesh·ko knyee·gar·no

I'm looking for a book/music by (Miha Mazzini/Zoran Predin).
Iščem knjigo/glasbo   eesh·chem knyee·go/glaz·bo
(Mihe Mazzinija/Zorana Predina).   (mee·he ma·tsee·nee·ya/zo·ra·na pre·dee·na)

Can I listen to this?
Lahko tole poslušam?   lah·ko to·le pos·loo·sham

photography

Can you ...?	*Lahko ...?*	lah·ko ...
burn a CD from	*zapečete CD z moje*	za·pe·che·te tse·de z mo·ye
my memory card	*spominske kartice*	spo·meen·ske kar·tee·tse
develop this film	*razvijete ta film*	raz·vee·ye·te ta feelm
load this film	*vstavite ta film*	vsta·vee·te ta feelm
I need a/an ... film	*Potrebujem ... film*	pot·re·boo·yem ... feelm
for this camera.	*za ta fotoaparat.*	za ta fo·to·a·pa·rat
APS	*APS*	a pe es
B&W	*črno-bel*	chuhr·no·be·oo
colour	*barvni*	barv·nee
(200) speed	*(dvesto) ASA*	(dve·sto) a·sa

I need a slide film for this camera.
> *Potrebujem film za diapozitive* — pot·re·*boo*·yem feelm za dee·a·po·zee·*tee*·ve
> *za ta fotoaparat.* — za ta fo·to·a·pa·*rat*

When will it be ready?
> *Kdaj bo gotovo?* — kdai bo go·*to*·vo

meeting people

greetings, goodbyes & introductions

Hello/Hi.	*Zdravo.*	*zdra*·vo
Good night.	*Lahko noč.*	*lah*·ko noch
Goodbye/Bye.	*Na svidenje/Adijo.*	na *svee*·den·ye/a·*dee*·yo
See you later.	*Se vidiva.*	se *vee*·dee·va
Mr/Mrs	*gospod/gospa*	gos·*pod*/gos·*pa*
Miss	*gospodična*	gos·po·*deech*·na
How are you?	*Kako ste/si?* pol/inf	ka·*ko* ste/see
Fine, thanks.	*Dobro, hvala.*	*dob*·ro *hva*·la
And you?	*Pa vi/ti?* pol/inf	pa vee/tee
What's your name?	*Kako vam/ti je ime?* pol/inf	ka·*ko* vam/tee ye ee·*me*
My name is ...	*Ime mi je ...*	ee·*me* mee ye ...
I'm pleased to meet you.	*Veseli me, da sem vas spoznal/spoznala.* m/f	ve·se·*lee* me da sem vas spoz·*now*/spoz·*na*·la
This is my ...	*To je moj/moja ...* m/f	to ye moy/*mo*·ya ...
boyfriend	*fant*	fant
brother	*brat*	brat
daughter	*hči*	hchee
father	*oče*	*o*·che
friend	*prijatelj* m	pree·*ya*·tel'
	prijateljica f	pree·*ya*·tel·yee·tsa
girlfriend	*punca*	*poon*·tsa
husband	*mož*	mozh
mother	*mama*	*ma*·ma
partner (intimate)	*partner/partnerka* m/f	*part*·ner/*part*·ner·ka
sister	*sestra*	*ses*·tra
son	*sin*	seen
wife	*žena*	*zhe*·na

Here's my phone number.
Tu je moja telefonska številka. too ye *mo*·ya te·le·*fon*·ska shte·*veel*·ka

What's your phone number?
Mi poveste vašo telefonsko številko? mee po·*ves*·te *va*·sho te·le·*fon*·sko shte·*veel*·ko

Here's my ...	*Tu je moj/moja ...* m/f	too ye moy/*mo*·ya ...
What's your ...?	*Kakšen je vaš ...?* m	*kak*·shen ye vash ...
	Kakšna je vaša ...? f	*kak*·shna ye *va*·sha ...
(email) address	*(elektronski) naslov* m	(e·lek·*tron*·skee) nas·*loh*
fax number	*številka faksa* f	shte·*veel*·ka *fak*·sa

occupations

What's your occupation?	*Kaj ste po poklicu?*	kai ste po pok·*lee*·tsoo
I'm a/an ...	*... sem.*	... sem
artist	*Umetnik* m	oo·*met*·neek
	Umetnica f	oo·*met*·nee·tsa
farmer	*Kmet/Kmetica* m/f	kmet/kme·*tee*·tsa
office worker	*Uradnik* m	oo·*rad*·neek
	Uradnica f	oo·*rad*·nee·tsa
scientist	*Znanstvenik* m	znans·*tve*·neek
	Znanstvenica f	znans·*tve*·nee·tsa
student	*Študent/Študentka* m/f	shtoo·*dent*/shtoo·*dent*·ka
tradesperson	*Trgovec/Trgovka* m/f	tuhr·*go*·vets/ tuhr·*gov*·ka

background

Where are you from?	*Od kod ste?*	od kod ste
I'm from ...	*Iz ... sem.*	eez ... sem
Australia	*Avstralije*	av·*stra*·lee·ye
Canada	*Kanade*	*ka*·na·de
England	*Anglije*	an·*glee*·ye
New Zealand	*Nove Zelandije*	*no*·ve ze·*lan*·dee·ye
the USA	*Združenih držav*	zdroo·zhe·neeh dr·*zhav*
Are you married?	*Ste poročeni?*	ste po·ro·*che*·nee
I'm married.	*Poročen/Poročena*	po·ro·*chen*/po·ro·*che*·na
	sem. m/f	sem
I'm single.	*Samski/Samska sem.* m/f	*sam*·skee/*sam*·ska sem

How old ...?	Koliko ...?	ko·lee·ko ...
are you	si star/stara m/f inf	see star/sta·ra
are you	ste stari m&f pol	ste sta·ree
is your daughter	je stara vaša hči	ye sta·ra va·sha hchee
is your son	je star vaš sin	ye star vash seen
I'm ... years old.	Imam ... let.	ee·mam ... let
He/She is ... years old.	... let ima.	... let ee·ma

feelings

I'm ...	... sem.	... sem
hungry	Lačen/Lačna m/f	la·chen/lach·na
thirsty	Žejen/Žejna m/f	zhe·yen/zhey·na
tired	Utrujen m	oot·roo·yen
	Utrujena f	oot·roo·ye·na
I'm not ...	Nisem ...	nee·sem ...
hungry	lačen/lačna m/f	la·chen/lach·na
thirsty	žejen/žejna m/f	zhe·yen/zhey·na
tired	utrujen/utrujena m/f	oot·roo·yen/oot·roo·ye·na
Are you ... ?	Ste ... ?	ste ...
hungry	lačni	lach·nee
thirsty	žejni	zhey·nee
tired	utrujeni	oot·roo·ye·nee
I'm ...	... mi je.	... mee ye
hot	Vroče	vro·che
well	Dobro	dob·ro
I'm not ...	Ni mi ...	nee mee ...
Are you ...?	Vam je ...?	vam ye ...
hot	vroče	vro·che
well	dobro	dob·ro
I'm (not) cold.	(Ne) Zebe me.	ne ze·be me
Are you cold?	Vas zebe?	vas ze·be

entertainment

going out

Where can I find ...?	Kje je kakšen ...?	kye ye *kak*·shen ...
clubs	klub	kloob
gay venues	homoseksualski bar	ho·mo·sek·soo·*al*·skee bar
pubs	bar	bar
I feel like going to a/the ...	Želim iti	zhe·*leem* ee·tee ...
concert	na koncert	na kon·*tsert*
movies	v kino	oo *kee*·no
party	na zabavo	na za·*ba*·vo
restaurant	v restavracijo	oo res·tav·*ra*·tsee·yo
theatre	v gledališče	oo gle·da·*leesh*·che

interests

Do you like ...?	Vam je všeč ...?	vam ye vshech ...
I like ...	Všeč mi je ...	vshech mee ye ...
I don't like ...	Ni mi všeč ...	nee mee vshech ...
art	umetnost	oo·*met*·nost
cooking	kuhanje	*koo*·han·ye
reading	branje	*bran*·ye
shopping	nakupovanje	na·koo·po·*van*·ye
sport	šport	shport
Do you like ...?	So vam všeč ...?	so vam vshech ...
I like ...	Všeč so mi ...	vshech so mee ...
I don't like ...	Niso mi všeč ...	*nee*·so mee vshech ...
movies	filmi	*feel*·mee
nightclubs	nočni bari	*noch*·nee *ba*·ree
travelling	potovanja	po·to·*van*·ya
Do you like to ...?	Ali radi ...?	*a*·lee *ra*·dee ...
dance	plešete	*ple*·she·te
go to concerts	hodite na koncerte	*ho*·dee·te na kon·*tser*·te
listen to music	poslušate glasbo	pos·*loo*·sha·te *glas*·bo

food & drink

finding a place to eat

Can you recommend a ...?	*Mi lahko priporočite ...?*	mee lah·*ko* pree·po·ro·*chee*·te ...
bar	*bar*	bar
café	*kavarno*	ka·*var*·no
restaurant	*restavracijo*	res·tav·*ra*·tsee·yo
I'd like ..., please.	*Želim ..., prosim.*	zhe·*leem* ... *pro*·seem
a table for (five)	*mizo za (pet)*	*mee*·zo za (pet)
the (non)smoking section	*prostor za (ne)kadilce*	*pros*·tor za (ne·)ka·*deel*·tse

ordering food

breakfast	*zajtrk* m	*zai*·tuhrk
lunch	*kosilo* n	ko·*see*·lo
dinner	*večerja* f	ve·*cher*·ya
snack	*malica* f	*ma*·lee·tsa
today's special	*danes nudimo*	*da*·nes *noo*·dee·mo
What would you recommend?	*Kaj priporočate?*	kai pree·po·*ro*·cha·te
I'd like (the) ..., please.	*Želim ..., prosim.*	zhe·*leem* ... *pro*·seem
bill	*račun*	ra·*choon*
drink list	*meni pijač*	me·*nee* pee·*yach*
menu	*jedilni list*	ye·*deel*·nee leest
that dish	*to jed*	to yed

drinks

cup of coffee ...	*skodelica kave ...*	sko·*de*·lee·tsa *ka*·ve ...
cup of tea ...	*skodelica čaja ...*	sko·*de*·lee·tsa *cha*·ya ...
with milk	*z mlekom*	z *mle*·kom
without sugar	*brez sladkorja*	brez slad·*kor*·ya

(orange) juice	(pomarančni) sok m	(po·ma·ranch·nee) sok
soft drink	brezalkoholna	brez·al·ko·hol·na
	pijača f	pee·ya·cha
... water	... voda	... vo·da
boiled	prekuhana	pre·koo·ha·na
(sparkling)	mineralna	mee·ne·ral·na
mineral	(gazirana)	(ga·zee·ra·na)

in the bar

I'll have ...
Jaz bom ...   yaz bom ...

I'll buy you a drink.
Povabim te na pijačo. inf   po·va·beem te na pee·ya·cho

What would you like?
Kaj boš? inf   kai bosh

Cheers!
Na zdravje!   na zdrav·ye

brandy	vinjak m	veen·yak
champagne	šampanjec m	sham·pan·yets
cocktail	koktajl m	kok·tail
cognac	konjak m	kon·yak
a shot of (whisky)	kozarček (viskija)	ko·zar·chek (vees·kee·ya)
a ... of beer	... piva	... pee·va
glass	kozarec	ko·za·rets
jug	vrč	vuhrch
pint	vrček	vuhr·chek
a bottle/glass	steklenica/kozarec	stek·le·nee·tsa/ko·za·rets
of ... wine	... vina	... vee·na
red	rdečega	rde·che·ga
sparkling	penečega	pe·ne·che·ga
white	belega	be·le·ga

self-catering

What's the local speciality?
Kaj je lokalna specialiteta?   kai ye lo·*kal*·na spe·tsee·a·lee·*te*·ta

What's that?
Kaj je to?   kai ye to

How much is (a kilo of cheese)?
Koliko stane (kila sira)?   ko·lee·ko *sta*·ne (*kee*·la *see*·ra)

I'd like ...	*Želim ...*	zhe·*leem* ...
(200) grams	*(dvesto) gramov*	(*dve*·sto) *gra*·mov
(two) kilos	*(dva) kilograma*	(dva) kee·lo·*gra*·ma
(three) pieces	*(tri) kose*	(tree) *ko*·se
(six) slices	*(šest) rezin*	(shest) re·*zeen*

Less.	*Manj.*	man'
Enough.	*Dovolj.*	do·*vol*
More.	*Več.*	vech

special diets & allergies

Is there a vegetarian restaurant near here?
Je tu blizu vegetarijanska   ye too *blee*·zoo ve·ge·ta·ree·*yan*·ska
restavracija?   res·tav·*ra*·tsee·ya

Do you have vegetarian food?
Ali imate vegetarijansko hrano?   a·lee ee·*ma*·te ve·ge·ta·ree·*yan*·sko *hra*·no

Could you prepare	*Lahko pripravite*	lah·ko pree·*pra*·vee·te
a meal without ...?	*obed brez ...?*	o·*bed* brez ...
butter	*masla*	*mas*·la
eggs	*jajc*	yaits
meat stock	*mesne osnove*	*mes*·ne os·*no*·ve

I'm allergic to ...	*Alergičen/Alergična*	a·*ler*·gee·chen/a·*ler*·geech·na
	sem na ... m/f	sem na ...
dairy produce	*mlečne izdelke*	*mlech*·ne eez·*del*·ke
gluten	*gluten*	gloo·*ten*
MSG	*MSG*	em es ge
nuts	*oreške*	o·*resh*·ke
seafood	*morsko hrano*	*mor*·sko *hra*·no

menu decoder

bograč m	bog-rach	beef goulash
brancin na maslu m	bran-tseen na mas-loo	sea bass in butter
čebulna bržola f	che-bool-na br-zho-la	braised beef with onions
čevapčiči m	che-vap-chee-chee	spicy beef or pork meatballs
drobnjakovi štruklji m	drob-nya-ko-vee shtrook-lyee	dumplings of cottage cheese & chives
dunajski zrezek m	doo-nai-skee zre-zek	breaded veal or pork cutlet
francoska solata f	fran-tsos-ka so-la-ta	diced potatoes & vegetables with mayonnaise
gobova kremna juha f	go-bo-va krem-na yoo-ha	creamed mushroom soup
goveja juha z rezanci f	go-ve-ya yoo-ha z re-zan-tsee	beef broth with little egg noodles
jota f	yo-ta	beans, sauerkraut & potatoes or barley cooked with pork
kisle kumarice f	kees-le koo-ma-ree-tse	pickled cucumbers
kmečka pojedina f	kmech-ka po-ye-dee-na	smoked meats with sauerkraut
kranjska klobasa z gorčico f	kran'-ska klo-ba-sa z gor-chee-tso	sausage with mustard
kraški pršut z olivami m	krash-kee puhr-shoot z o-lee-va-mee	air-dried ham with black olives
krofi m	kro-fee	jam-filled doughnuts
kuhana govedina s hrenom f	koo-ha-na go-ve-dee-na s hre-nom	boiled beef with horseradish
kuhana postrv f	koo-ha-na pos-tuhrv	boiled trout
kumarična solata f	koo-ma-reech-na so-la-ta	cucumber salad
ljubljanski zrezek m	lyoob-lyan-skee zre-zek	breaded cutlet with cheese

mešano meso na žaru	me·sha·no me·so na zhu·roo	mixed grill
ocvrt oslič m	ots·vuhrt os·leech	fried cod
ocvrt piščanec m	ots·vuhrt peesh·cha·nets	fried chicken
orada na žaru f	o·ra·da na zha·roo	grilled sea bream
palačinke f	pa·la·cheen·ke	thin pancakes with marmalade, nuts or chocolate
pečena postrv f	pe·che·na pos·tuhrv	grilled trout
pečene sardele f	pe·che·ne sar·de·le	grilled sardines
pleskavica f	ples·ka·vee·tsa	spicy meat patties
pariški zrezek m	pa·reesh·kee zre·zek	cutlet fried in egg batter
puranov zrezek s šampinjoni m	poo·ra·nov zre·zek s sham·peen·yo·nee	turkey steak with white mushrooms
ražnjiči m	razh·nyee·chee	shish kebab
riba v marinadi f	ree·ba v ma·ree·na·dee	marinated fish
ričet m	ree·chet	barley stew with smoked pork ribs
rižota z gobami f	ree·zho·ta z go·ba·mee	risotto with mushrooms
sadna kupa f	sad·na koo·pa	fruit salad with whipped cream
srbska solata f	suhrb·ska so·la·ta	salad of tomatoes & green peppers with onions & cheese
svinjska pečenka f	sveen'·ska pe·chen·ka	roast pork
škampi na žaru m	shkam·pee na zha·roo	grilled prawns
školjke f	shkol'·ke	clams
zelena solata f	ze·le·na so·la·ta	lettuce salad
zelenjavna juha f	ze·len·yav·na yoo·ha	vegetable soup

emergencies

basics

Help!	*Na pomoč!*	na po·*moch*
Stop!	*Ustavite (se)!*	oos·*ta*·vee·te (se)
Go away!	*Pojdite stran!*	poy·*dee*·te stran
Thief!	*Tat!*	tat
Fire!	*Požar!*	po·*zhar*
Watch out!	*Pazite!*	pa·*zee*·te
Call ...!	*Pokličite ...!*	pok·*lee*·chee·te ...
a doctor	*zdravnika*	zdrav·*nee*·ka
an ambulance	*rešilca*	re·*sheel*·tsa
the police	*policijo*	po·lee·*tsee*·yo

It's an emergency.
Nujno je. — *nooy*·no ye

Could you help me, please?
Pomagajte mi, prosim. — po·*ma*·gai·te mee *pro*·seem

I have to use the telephone.
Poklicati moram. — pok·*lee*·tsa·tee *mo*·ram

I'm lost.
Izgubil/Izgubila sem se. m/f — eez·*goo*·beew/eez·goo·*bee*·la sem se

Where are the toilets?
Kje je stranišče? — kye ye stra·*neesh*·che

police

Where's the police station?
Kje je policijska postaja? — kye ye po·lee·*tseey*·ska pos·*ta*·ya

I want to report an offence.
Želim prijaviti prestopek. — zhe·*leem* pree·*ya*·vee·tee pres·*to*·pek

I have insurance.
Zavarovan/Zavarovana sem. m/f — za·va·ro·*van*/za·va·ro·*va*·na sem

I've been ...	... *so me.*	... so me
assaulted	*Napadli*	na·*pad*·lee
raped	*Posilili*	po·*see*·lee·lee
robbed	*Oropali*	o·*ro*·pa·lee

I've lost my ...	Izgubil/Izgubila sem ... m/f	eez-goo-beew/eez-goo-bee-la sem ...
My ... was/were stolen.	Ukradli so mi ...	ook-rad-lee so mee ...
backpack	nahrbtnik	na-huhrbt-neek
bags	torbe	tor-be
credit card	kreditno kartico	kre-deet-no kar-tee-tso
handbag	ročno torbico	roch-no tor-bee-tso
jewellery	nakit	na-keet
money	denar	de-nar
passport	potni list	pot-nee leest
travellers cheques	potovalne čeke	po-to-val-ne che-ke
wallet	denarnico	de-nar-nee-tso

I want to contact my ...	Želim poklicati ... svoj/svojo ... m/f	zhe-leem pok-lee-tsa-tee ... svoy/svo-yo ...
consulate	konzulat m	kon-zoo-lat
embassy	ambasado f	am-ba-sa-do

health

medical needs

Where's the nearest ...?	Kje je najbližji/ najbližja ... ? m/f	kye ye nai-bleezh-yee/ nai-bleezh-ya ...
dentist	zobozdravnik m	zo-bo-zdrav-neek
doctor	zdravnik m	zdrav-neek
hospital	bolnišnica f	bol-neesh-nee-tsa
(night) pharmacist	(nočna) lekarna f	(noch-na) le-kar-na

I need a doctor (who speaks English).
Potrebujem zdravnika   pot-re-boo-yem zdrav-nee-ka
(ki govori angleško).   (kee go-vo-ree ang-lesh-ko)

Could I see a female doctor?
Bi me lahko pregledala   bee me lah-ko preg-le-da-la
zdravnica?   zdrav-nee-tsa

I've run out of my medication.
Zmanjkalo mi je zdravil.   zman'-ka-lo mee ye zdra-veel

symptoms, conditions & allergies

I'm sick.	*Bolan/Bolna sem.* m/f	bo-*lan*/*boh*-na sem
It hurts here.	*Tu me boli.*	too me bo-*lee*
I have (a) ...	*Imam ...*	ee-*mam* ...
asthma	*astmo*	*ast*-mo
bronchitis	*bronhitis*	bron-*hee*-tees
constipation	*zapeko*	za-*pe*-ko
diarrhoea	*drisko*	*drees*-ko
fever	*vročino*	vro-*chee*-no
headache	*glavobol*	gla-vo-*bol*
heart condition	*srčno bolezen*	*suhr*-chno bo-*le*-zen
toothache	*zobobol*	zo-bo-*bol*
pain	*bolečine*	bo-le-*chee*-ne
I'm nauseous.	*Slabo mi je.*	sla-*bo* mee ye
I'm coughing.	*Kašljam.*	*kash*-lyam
I have a sore throat.	*Boli me grlo.*	bo-*lee* me *guhr*-lo
I'm allergic to ...	*Alergičen/Alergična*	a-*ler*-gee-chen/a-*ler*-geech-na
	sem na ... m/f	sem na ...
antibiotics	*antibiotike*	an-tee-bee-*o*-tee-ke
anti-inflammatories	*protivnetna*	pro-teev-*net*-na
	zdravila	zdra-*vee*-la
aspirin	*aspirin*	as-pee-*reen*
bees	*čebelji pik*	che-*bel*-yee peek
codeine	*kodein*	ko-de-*een*
penicillin	*penicilin*	pe-nee-tsee-*leen*
antiseptic	*razkužilo* n	raz-koo-*zhee*-lo
bandage	*obveza* f	ob-*ve*-za
condoms	*kondomi* m pl	kon-*do*-mee
contraceptives	*kontracepcija* f	kon-tra-*tsep*-tsee-ya
diarrhoea medicine	*zdravilo za drisko* n	zdra-*vee*-lo za *drees*-ko
insect repellent	*sredstvo proti*	*sreds*-tvo *pro*-tee
	mrčesu n	muhr-*che*-soo
laxatives	*odvajala* n pl	od-va-*ya*-la
painkillers	*analgetiki* m pl	a-nal-*ge*-tee-kee
rehydration salts	*sol za rehidracijo* f	sol za re-heed-*ra*-tsee-yo
sleeping tablets	*uspavalne tablete* f pl	oos-pa-*val*-ne tab-*le*-te

english–slovene dictionary

Slovene nouns in this dictionary have their gender indicated by ⓜ (masculine), ⓕ (feminine) or ⓝ (neuter). If it's a plural noun, you'll also see pl. Adjectives are given in the masculine form only. Words are also marked as a (adjective), v (verb), sg (singular), pl (plural), inf (informal) or pol (polite) where necessary.

A

A

accident *nesreča* ⓕ nes-*re*-cha
accommodation *nastanitev* ⓕ na-sta-*nee*-tev
adaptor *adapter* ⓜ a-*dap*-ter
address *naslov* ⓜ nas-*loh*
after *po* po
air-conditioned *klimatiziran* klee-ma-tee-*zee*-ran
airplane *letalo* ⓝ le-*ta*-lo
airport *letališče* ⓝ le-ta-*leesh*-che
alcohol *alkohol* ⓜ al-ko-*hol*
all *vse* vse
allergy *alergija* ⓕ a-ler-*gee*-ya
ambulance *rešilni avto* re-*sheel*-nee *av*-to
and *in* een
ankle *gleženj* ⓜ *gle*-zhen'
arm *roka* ⓕ *ro*-ka
ashtray *pepelnik* ⓜ pe-*pel*-neek
ATM *bankomat* ⓜ ban-ko-*mat*

B

baby *dojenček* ⓜ do-*yen*-chek
back (body) *hrbet* ⓜ *huhr*-bet
backpack *nahrbtnik* ⓜ na-*huhrbt*-neek
bad *slab* slab
bag *torba* ⓕ *tor*-ba
baggage *prtljaga* ⓕ puhrt-*lya*-ga
baggage claim *prevzem prtljage* ⓕ
   prev-zem puhrt-*lya*-ge
bank *banka* ⓕ *ban*-ka
bar *bar* ⓜ bar
bathroom *kopalnica* ⓕ ko-*pal*-nee-tsa
battery *baterija* ⓕ ba-te-*ree*-ya
beautiful *lep* lep
bed *postelja* ⓕ *pos*-tel-ya
beer *pivo* ⓝ *pee*-vo
before *prej* prey
behind *zadaj* za-dai
bicycle *bicikel* ⓜ bee-*tsee*-kel
big *velik* ve-leek
bill *račun* ⓜ ra-*choon*
black *črn* chuhrn

blanket *odeja* ⓕ o-*de*-ya
blood group *krvna skupina* ⓕ kuhrv-na skoo-*pee*-na
blue *moder* mo-der
boat (ship) *ladja* ⓕ *lad*-ya
boat (small) *čoln* ⓜ chohn
book (make a reservation) v *rezervirati*
   re-zer-vee-ra-tee
bottle *steklenica* ⓕ stek-le-*nee*-tsa
bottle opener *odpirač* ⓜ od-pee-*rach*
boy *fant* ⓜ fant
brakes (car) *zavore* ⓕ pl za-*vo*-re
breakfast *zajtrk* ⓜ *zai*-tuhrk
broken (faulty) *pokvarjen* pok-*var*-yen
bus *avtobus* ⓜ av-to-*boos*
business *posel* ⓜ po-se-oo
buy *kupiti* koo-*pee*-tee

C

café *kavarna* ⓕ ka-*var*-na
camera *fotoaparat* ⓜ fo-to-a-pa-*rat*
camera shop *trgovina s fotografsko opremo* ⓕ
   tr-go-vee-na s fo-to-graf-sko o-*pre*-mo
campsite *kamp* ⓜ kamp
cancel *preklicati* prek-lee-tsa-tee
can opener *odpirač za pločevinke* ⓜ
   od-pee-rach za plo-che-*veen*-ke
car *avtomobil* ⓜ av-to-mo-*beel*
cash *gotovina* ⓕ go-to-vee-na
cash (a cheque) v *unovčiti (ček)* oo-nov-chee-tee (chek)
cell phone *mobilni telefon* ⓜ mo-*beel*-nee te-le-*fon*
centre *center* ⓜ *tsen*-ter
change (money) v *menjati (denar)* men-ya-tee (de-nar)
cheap *poceni* po-tse-nee
check (bill) *račun* ⓜ ra-*choon*
check-in *prijava za let* ⓕ pree-*ya*-va za let
chest *prsni koš* ⓜ *puhr*-snee kosh
child *otrok* ⓜ ot-*rok*
cigarette *cigareta* ⓕ tsee-ga-*re*-ta
city *mesto* ⓝ *mes*-to
clean a *čist* cheest
closed *zaprt* za-*puhrt*
coffee *kava* ⓕ *ka*-va
coins *kovanci* ⓜ pl ko-*van*-tsee

cold a *hladen* hla-den
collect call *klic na stroške klicanega* ⓜ
   kleets na strosh-ke klee-tsa-ne-ga
come v *priti* pree-tee
computer *računalnik* ⓜ ra-choo-*nal*-neek
condom *kondom* ⓜ kon-*dom*
contact lenses *kontaktne leče* ⓕ pl kon-*takt*-ne *le*-che
cook v *kuhati* koo-ha-tee
cost *strošek* ⓜ *stro*-shek
credit card *kreditna kartica* ⓕ kre-*deet*-na *kar*-tee-tsa
cup *skodelica* ⓕ sko-*de*-lee-tsa
currency exchange *menjava* ⓕ men-*ya*-va
customs (immigration) *carina* ⓕ tsa-*ree*-na

D

dangerous *nevaren* ne-va-*ren*
date (time) *datum* ⓜ *da*-toom
day *dan* ⓜ dan
delay *zamuda* ⓕ za-*moo*-da
dentist *zobozdravnik* ⓜ zo-boz-*drav*-neek
depart *oditi* o-dee-tee
diaper *plenica* ⓕ *ple*-nee-tsa
dictionary *slovar* ⓜ slo-*var*
dinner *večerja* ⓕ ve-*cher*-ya
direct *direkten* dee-rek-ten
dirty *umazan* oo-ma-zan
disabled (person) *invaliden* een-va-lee-den
discount *popust* ⓜ po-poost
doctor *zdravnik* ⓜ zdrav-neek
double bed *dvojna postelja* ⓕ *dvoy*-na *pos*-tel-ya
double room *dvoposteljna soba* ⓕ
   dvo-*pos*-tel'-na *so*-ba
drink *pijača* ⓕ pee-ya-cha
drive v *voziti* vo-zee-tee
drivers licence *vozniško dovoljenje* ⓝ
   voz-neesh-ko do-vol-yen-ye
drug (illicit) *mamilo* ⓝ ma-mee-lo
dummy (pacifier) *duda* ⓕ *doo*-da

E

ear *uho* ⓝ oo-ho
east *vzhod* ⓜ vzhod
eat *jesti* yes-tee
economy class *turistični razred* ⓜ
   too-rees-teech-nee raz-red
electricity *elektrika* ⓕ e-lek-tree-ka
elevator *dvigalo* ⓝ dvee-ga-lo
email *elektronska pošta* ⓕ e-lek-tron-ska posh-ta
embassy *ambasada* ⓕ am-ba-sa-da
emergency *nujen primer* ⓜ noo-yen pree-mer
English (language) *angleščina* ⓕ ang-lesh-chee-na

entrance *vhod* ⓜ vhod
evening *večer* ⓜ ve-cher
exchange rate *menjalni tečaj* ⓜ men-*yal*-nee te-chai
exit *izhod* ⓜ eez-hod
expensive *drag* drag
express mail *hitra pošta* ⓕ heet-ra posh-ta
eye *oko* ⓝ o-ko

F

far *daleč* da-lech
fast *hitro* heet-ro
father *oče* ⓜ o-che
film (camera) *film* ⓜ feelm
finger *prst* ⓜ puhrst
first-aid kit *komplet za prvo pomoč* ⓜ
   kom-plet za puhr-vo po-moch
first class *prvi razred* ⓜ puhr-vee raz-red
fish *riba* ⓕ ree-ba
food *hrana* ⓕ hra-na
foot *stopalo* ⓝ sto-pa-lo
fork *vilice* ⓕ pl vee-lee-tse
free (of charge) *brezplačen* brez-pla-chen
friend *prijatelj/prijateljica* ⓜ/ⓕ
   pree-ya-tel/pree-ya-tel-yee-tsa
fruit *sadje* ⓝ pl sad-ye
full *poln* poln
funny *smešen* sme-shen

G

gift *darilo* ⓝ da-ree-lo
girl *dekle* ⓝ dek-le
glass (drinking) *kozarec* ⓜ ko-za-rets
glasses *očala* ⓝ pl o-cha-la
go *iti* ee-tee
good *dober* do-ber
green *zelen* ze-len
guide *vodnik* ⓜ vod-neek

H

half *pol* poh
hand *roka* ⓕ ro-ka
handbag *ročna torbica* ⓕ roch-na tor-bee-tsa
happy *srečen* sre-chen
have *imeti* ee-me-tee
he *on* ⓜ on
head *glava* ⓕ gla-va
heart *srce* ⓝ suhr-tse
heat *vročina* ⓕ vro-chee-na
heavy *težek* te-zhek

help v *pomagati* po-*ma*-ga-tee
here *tukaj* too-kai
highway *visok* vee-*sok*
highway *hitra cesta* ① *heet*-ra *tses*-ta
(go on a) hike v *iti na pohod* ee-tee na po-*hod*
holidays *počitnice* ① pl po-*cheet*-nee-tse
homosexual *homoseksualec* ⑪ ho-mo-sek-soo-*a*-lets
hospital *bolnišnica* ① bol-*neesh*-nee-tsa
hot *vroč* vroch
hotel *hotel* ⑪ ho-*tel*
hungry *lačen* la-chen
husband *mož* ⑪ mozh

I

I *jaz* yaz
identification (card) *osebna izkaznica* ①
o-*seb*-na eez-*kaz*-nee-tsa
ill *bolan* bo-*lan*
important *pomemben* po-*mem*-ben
included *vključen* vklyoo-chen
injury *poškodba* ① posh-*kod*-ba
insurance *zavarovanje* ① za-va-ro-*van*-ye
Internet *internet* ⑪ een-ter-net
interpreter *tolmač* ① tol-*mach*

J

jewellery *nakit* ⑪ na-*keet*
job *služba* ① *sloozh*-ba

K

key *ključ* ⑪ klyooch
kilogram *kilogram* ① kee-lo-*gram*
kitchen *kuhinja* ① koo-heen-ya
knife *nož* ⑪ nozh

L

laundry (place) *pralnica* ① *pral*-nee-tsa
lawyer *odvetnik* ⑪ od-*vet*-neek
left (direction) *levo* le-vo
left-luggage office *garderoba* ① gar-de-ro-ba
leg *noga* ① *no*-ga
lesbian *lezbijka* ① *lez*-beey-ka
less *manj* man'
letter (mail) *pismo* ① pees-mo
lift (elevator) *dvigalo* ① dvee-*ga*-lo
light *svetloba* ① svet-*lo*-ba
like v *všeč biti* vshech bee-tee

lock *ključavnica* ① klyoo-*chav*-nee-tsa
long *dolg* *dolg*
lost *izgubljen* eez-goob-*lyen*
lost property office *urad za izgubljene predmete* ⑪
oo-*rad* za eez-goob-*lye*-ne pred-*me*-te
love v *ljubiti* lyoo-bee-tee
luggage *prtljaga* ① puhrt-*lya*-ga
lunch *kosilo* ① ko-*see*-lo

M

mail *pošta* ① *posh*-ta
man *moški* ⑪ *mosh*-kee
map *zemljevid* ⑪ zem-lye-*veed*
market *tržnica* ① *tuhrzh*-nee-tsa
matches *vžigalice* ① pl vzhee-*ga*-lee-tse
meat *meso* ⑪ me-*so*
medicine *zdravilo* ⑪ zdra-*vee*-lo
menu *jedilni list* ⑪ ye-*deel*-nee leest
message *sporočilo* ⑪ spo-ro-*chee*-lo
milk *mleko* ⑪ *mle*-ko
minute *minuta* ① mee-*noo*-ta
mobile phone *mobilni telefon* ⑪ mo-*beel*-nee te-le-*fon*
money *denar* ⑪ de-*nar*
month *mesec* ⑪ *me*-sets
morning *dopoldne* ① do-*pol*-dne
mother *mama* ① *ma*-ma
motorcycle *motorno kolo* ⑪ mo-*tor*-no ko-*lo*
motorway *motorna cesta* ① mo-*tor*-na *tses*-ta
mouth *usta* ① *oos*-ta
music *glasba* ① *glaz*-ba

N

name *ime* ⑪ ee-*me*
napkin *prtiček* ⑪ puhr-*tee*-chek
nappy *plenica* ① ple-*nee*-tsa
near *blizu* blee-zoo
neck *vrat* ⑪ vrat
new *nov* noh
news *novice* ① pl no-*vee*-tse
newspaper *časopis* ⑪ cha-so-*pees*
night *noč* ① noch
no *ne* ne
noisy *hrupen* hroo-pen
nonsmoking *nekadilski* ne-ka-*deel*-skee
north *sever* ⑪ *se*-ver
nose *nos* ⑪ nos
now *zdaj* zdai
number *število* ⑪ shte-*vee*-lo

O

oil (engine) *olje* ⓝ ol-ye
old *star* star
one-way ticket *enosmerna vozovnica* ⓕ
e-no-*smer*-na vo-zov-*nee*-tsa
open a *odprt* od-*puhrt*
outside *zunaj* zoo-nai

P

package *paket* ⓜ pa-ket
paper *papir* ⓜ pa-*peer*
park (car) v *parkirati* par-*kee*-ra-tee
passport *potni list* ⓜ *pot*-nee leest
pay *plačati* pla-cha-tee
pen *pisalo* ⓝ pee-sa-lo
petrol *bencin* ⓜ ben-*tseen*
pharmacy *lekarna* ⓕ le-*kar*-na
phonecard *telefonska kartica* ⓕ
te-le-*fon*-ska *kar*-tee-tsa
photo *fotografija* ⓕ fo-to-gra-*fee*-ya
picnic *piknik* ⓜ *peek*-neek
plate *krožnik* ⓜ *krozh*-neek
police *policija* ⓕ po-lee-*tsee*-ya
postcard *razglednica* ⓕ raz-*gled*-nee-tsa
post office *pošta* ⓕ *posh*-ta
pregnant *noseča* no-se-cha
price *cena* ⓕ *tse*-na

Q

quiet *tih* teeh

R

rain *dež* ⓜ dezh
razor *brivnik* ⓜ *breev*-neek
receipt *račun* ⓜ ra-*choon*
red *rdeč* rdech
refund *vračilo denarja* ⓝ vra-chee-lo de-*nar*-ya
registered mail *priporočena pošta* ⓕ
pree-po-ro-che-na *posh*-ta
rent v *najeti* na-ye-tee
repair v *popraviti* pop-*ra*-vee-tee
reservation *rezervacija* ⓕ re-zer-*va*-tsee-ya
restaurant *restavracija* ⓕ res-tav-*ra*-tsee-ya
return v *vrniti* vr-nee-tee

return ticket *povratna vozovnica* ⓕ
pov-*rat*-na vo-zov-*nee*-tsa
right (direction) *desno* des-no
road *cesta* ⓕ *tses*-ta
room *soba* ⓕ *so*-ba

S

safe a *varen* va-ren
sanitary napkins *damski vložki* ⓜ pl
dam-skee *vlozh*-kee
seat *sedež* ⓜ se-dezh
send *poslati* pos-*la*-tee
service station *servis* ⓜ *ser*-vees
sex *seks* ⓜ seks
shampoo *šampon* ⓜ sham-*pon*
share (a dorm) *deliti (sobo)* de-lee-tee (so-bo)
shaving cream *krema za britje* ⓕ *kre*-ma za *breet*-ye
she *ona* ⓕ o-na
sheet (bed) *rjuha* ⓕ *ryoo*-ha
shirt *srajca* ⓕ *srai*-tsa
shoes *čevlji* ⓜ pl *chev*-lyee
shop *trgovina* ⓕ tuhr-go-*vee*-na
short *kratek* kra-tek
shower *prha* ⓕ *puhr*-ha
single room *enoposteljna soba* ⓕ
e-no-*pos*-tel'-na so-ba
skin *koža* ⓕ *ko*-zha
skirt *krilo* ⓝ *kree*-lo
sleep v *spati* spa-tee
Slovenia *Slovenija* ⓕ slo-ve-nee-ya
Slovene (language) *slovenščina* ⓕ slo-*vensh*-chee-na
Slovene a *slovenski* slo-*ven*-skee
slowly *počasi* po-cha-see
small *majhen* mai-hen
smoke (cigarettes) v *kaditi* ka-*dee*-tee
soap *milo* ⓝ *mee*-lo
some *nekaj* ne-kai
soon *kmalu* kma-loo
south *jug* ⓜ yoog
souvenir shop *trgovina s spominki* ⓕ
tuhr-go-*vee*-na s spo-*meen*-kee
speak *govoriti* go-vo-ree-tee
spoon *žlica* ⓕ *zhlee*-tsa
stamp *znamka* ⓕ *znam*-ka
stand-by ticket *stand-by vozovnica* ⓕ
stend-bai vo-zov-*nee*-tsa
station (train) *postaja* ⓕ *pos*-*ta*-ya
stomach *želodec* ⓜ zhe-*lo*-dets

stop v *ustaviti* oos·ta·vee·tee
stop (bus) *postajališče* ⋒ pos·ta·ya·leech·che
street *ulica* ⋓ oo·lee·tsa
student *študent/študentka* ⋒/⋓ shtoo·dent/shtoo·dent·ka
sun *sonce* ⋒ son·tse
sunscreen *krema za sončenje* ⋓ kre·ma za son·chen·ye
swim v *plavati* pla·va·tee

T

tampons *tamponi* ⋒ pl tam·po·nee
taxi *taksi* ⋒ tak·see
teaspoon *čajna žlička* ⋓ chai·na zhleech·ka
teeth *zobje* ⋒ zob·ye
telephone *telefon* ⋒ te·le·fon
television *televizija* ⋓ te·le·vee·zee·ya
temperature (weather) *temperatura* ⋓ tem·pe·ra·too·ra
tent *šotor* ⋒ sho·tor
that (one) *tisti* tees·tee
they *oni/one* ⋒/⋓ o·nee/o·ne
thirsty *žejen* zhe·yen
this (one) *ta* ta
throat *grlo* ⋒ guhr·lo
ticket (entrance) *vstopnica* ⋓ vstop·nee·tsa
ticket (travel) *vozovnica* ⋓ vo·zov·nee·tsa
time *čas* ⋒ chas
tired *utrujen* oo·troo·yen
tissues *robčki* ⋒ pl rob·chkee
today *danes* da·nes
toilet *stranišče* ⋒ stra·neesh·che
tomorrow *jutri* yoot·ree
tonight *nocoj* no·tsoy
toothbrush *zobna ščetka* ⋓ zob·na shchet·ka
toothpaste *zobna pasta* ⋓ zob·na pas·ta
torch (flashlight) *baterija* ⋓ ba·te·ree·ya
tour *izlet* ⋒ eez·let
tourist office *turistični urad* ⋒ too·rees·teech·nee oo·rad
towel *brisača* ⋓ bree·sa·cha
train *vlak* ⋒ vlak
translate *prevesti* pre·ves·tee
travel agency *potovalna agencija* ⋓ po·to·val·na a·gen·tsee·ya
travellers cheque *potovalni ček* ⋒ po·to·val·nee chek
trousers *hlače* ⋓ pl hla·che
twin beds *ločeni postelji* ⋓ pl lo·che·nee pos·tel·yee
tyre *guma* ⋓ goo·ma

U

underwear *spodnje perilo* ⋒ spod·nye pe·ree·lo
urgent *nujen* noo·yen

V

vacant *prost* prost
vacation *počitnice* ⋓ pl po·cheet·nee·tse
vegetable *zelenjava* ⋓ ze·len·ya·va
vegetarian a *vegetarijanski* ve·ge·ta·ree·yan·skee
visa *viza* ⋓ vee·za

W

waiter *natakar* ⋒ na·ta·kar
walk v *hoditi* ho·dee·tee
wallet *denarnica* ⋓ de·nar·nee·tsa
warm a *topel* to·pe·oo
wash (something) *prati* pra·tee
watch *zapestna ura* ⋓ za·pest·na oo·ra
water *voda* ⋓ vo·da
we *mi* mee
weekend *vikend* ⋒ vee·kend
west *zahod* ⋒ za·hod
wheelchair *invalidski voziček* ⋒ een·va·leed·skee vo·zee·chek
when *kdaj* kdai
where *kje* kye
white *bel* be·oo
who *kdo* kdo
why *zakaj* za·kai
wife *žena* ⋓ zhe·na
window *okno* ⋒ ok·no
wine *vino* ⋒ vee·no
with *z/s* z/s
without *brez* brez
woman *ženska* ⋓ zhen·ska
write *pisati* pee·sa·tee

Y

yellow *rumen* roo·men
yes *da* da
yesterday *včeraj* vche·rai
you sg inf/pol *ti/vi* tee/vee
you pl *vi* vee

INDEX

251

INDEX

253